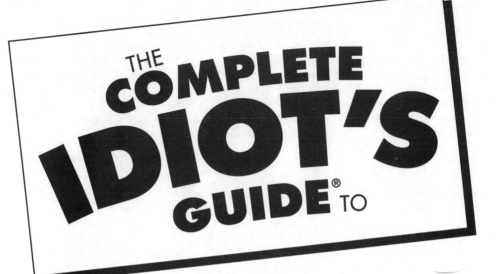

THE COMPLETE IDIOT'S GUIDE® TO

The Life of Christ

by Pastor William R. Grimbol

alpha
books

A member of Penguin Group (USA) Inc.

Publisher
Marie Butler-Knight

Product Manager
Phil Kitchel

Managing Editor
Cari Luna

Acquisitions Editor
Amy Zavatto

Development Editor
Tom Stevens

Senior Production Editor
Christy Wagner

Copy Editor
Heather Stith

Illustrator
Jody Schaeffer

Cover Designers
Mike Freeland
Kevin Spear

Book Designers
Scott Cook and Amy Adams of DesignLab

Indexer
Tonya Heard

Layout/Proofreading
Angela Calvert
John Etchison
Natashia Rardin

Contents at a Glance

Contents

Appendixes

Foreword

How I wish I had had a copy of this book by Bill Grimbol when I started out try-ing to be serious about the life of faith. It is the ideal book to put into the hands of an eager, enquiring, and perhaps earnest young person, or any other person who has begun to think that there is more to life than amassing more and more material possessions; or being famous and popular, that it cannot all be so super-ficial, seemingly without much meaning; that life can not surely be exhausted by an obsession with Number 1; that it is not illusory, the fleeting moments of an unspeakable joy, deep peace, and satisfaction that flood the soul when we have been altruistic, when we have sought to place the needs of others and their con-cerns before our own; that we have experienced, albeit fleetingly, a deep yearning for the good, the beautiful, and the true; that deep down we know that we are made for the transcendent, that we are made by and for God.

For those who are genuine seekers, this is the book to help them encounter the story of a remarkable young man whose public ministry lasted only a short three years, but whose impact has continued to modern times. Grimbol has tried to present a portrait of this young man, Jesus of Nazareth, so that it could speak for itself as unadorned as possible by later interpretations so that the enquirer might meet the so-called historical Jesus. I am not sure that such a portrait is possible, for even to say "Jesus is the Messiah" is to make considerable theological claims for him and to require accepting that we cannot access the original Jesus apart from what the sources of his story say about him. We cannot get behind the oral traditions, the sources. But Grimbol's effort is a most worthwhile one, not ram-ming points of view down the enquirer's throat.

He has distilled very substantial information into a manageable compass, with an attractive light touch, starting from the Old Testament antecedents of the story, right down to the presentation of the different genres that make up the Gospel accounts about this Jesus. Although he is telling us the "old, old story," I found his insights refreshing and indeed often inspirational and challenging.

Yes, I said I wish I had had this book at the beginning of my career. I am glad to have it now toward the end of my life. I am so deeply thankful to Grimbol for challenging me out of my comfort zone, my rut of complacency. I pray that many who are seeking will find a splendid guide in this delightful offering from one who loves Jesus deeply, who has sought to respond to his gift of grace by reflecting the compassion of Jesus and his concern for all, especially those pushed to the edges of society, that these enquirers will be set on the road to becoming fully human and, so, open to the possibility of becoming divine.

Desmond Mpilo Tutu

The Nobel Peace Prize Laureate in 1984 for his work against apartheid, Archbishop Desmond Mpilo Tutu is the former Archbishop (1986) and Archbishop Emeritus (1996) of Cape Town, South Africa, and the former Secretary General, South African Council of Churches (S.A.C.C.).

Introduction

So much is said and debated about the life of Jesus Christ but so little is understood. The story of his life is quite simple. Although we are offered four versions, the essence of the tale remains constant. It is a story of a man in history who had little or no immediate impact on the world he lived in. It was only much later that his influence was felt and his significant mark made.

The story itself is composed of equal parts tragedy, comedy, and fairytale. It is a story of both historical fact and often-vehement voices of faith. It claims to be a true story but readily admits to capturing a different kind of truth—the gospel truth, a truth that tells a story too good not to be true.

The story is about an ordinary man who, for the most part, leads a fairly plain and simple life. He is not wealthy. He is somewhat educated. He has no position or rank worthy of note. He becomes a carpenter. He is a devout Jew. He is devoted to his family, friends, and hometown. He is what my grandmother would have called "just a real good boy."

The story is also about the extraordinary compassion, conviction, and courage of this most ordinary man. The narrative tells of a man passionate in his pursuit of equality and justice for all people. It speaks of a champion of the outcast and defender of the vulnerable. It relates an account of a man willing to give up his own life on behalf of people seemingly unworthy of his love or devotion.

It is also the sad story of ridicule, persecution, abandonment, denial, and the ultimate slaughtering of this man named Jesus. It is not an easy read. He does not set an easy example to follow. For many, it seems yet another idle tale of a foolish idealist, a dreamer who thought he could save the world. For others, it points to the possibility that he in fact did save the world, or at the very least, gave us a shining example of how to try.

The story of Jesus is also the record of a man who functioned both as a rabbi and healer. He preached and taught. He performed what many called miracles—healings of the mind, body, and spirit. He is thought to have walked on water, turned water into wine, and fed 5,000 with a few fish and a couple loaves of bread. So it is fair to say that the story also contains some aspects that many claim as fantastic, while still others scoff and brand as pure fantasy.

This book is not evangelical in tone or purpose. It is not my goal to convert anyone. I simply wish to offer this enchanting and haunting story in all of its barebone majesty. I hope that I can provide a simple, direct encounter with a man named Jesus, who claimed, and was acclaimed, to be the Christ, the Messiah.

This book does not speak from the perspective of faith in the resurrection or from the standpoint that one must believe in Jesus Christ to be saved. This book tells the tale of a human life led with remarkable integrity, dignity, and maturity. It contains no confessional stands or creedal pronouncements.

Albert Schweitzer's effort to capture this basic narrative accounting was dubbed the quest of the historical Jesus. I don't consider my work here to be anything remotely resembling a quest, but it will be done in the same Schweitzer spirit that sought to free the original story from layers of dogma, doctrine, and creed. It was Schweitzer's belief, and my own, that the plain and simple saga of a man called Jesus would shine far brighter once the religious and evangelical varnish were removed.

A Sacred Story

Make no mistake, however, that I do consider this story to be a sacred story. A sacred story cannot be derived solely from facts. Facts simply cannot contain the message of the story, and a sacred story does claim to share a message. If we were to share only the historically documented facts of Christ's life, we could do so in a few brief and rather bland pages. It is the sacredness of the story that demands that we share what he is reported to have said and done, even when those reports seem to conflict or to be heavily and purposefully edited.

A sacred story aims to speak to the heart, not the head. It strives to impact our whole being, often giving us a lump in the throat, bloated with the truth of the story's message. A sacred story might momentarily take our breath away, and in that "mini-death" we may indeed feel reborn. A sacred story often leaves us speechless, and it is at such times that we are most clearly able to hear our own souls or God. It is when we are left dumbstruck that the wisdom of a sacred story can be imparted.

A Political Story

Don't talk about politics! Don't talk about religion! How many of us have been given or issued this familiar warning when meeting someone for the first time? The belief is that these two topics are too hot to handle, too potentially explosive, and too prone to upset and argument.

Well, the story of the life of Christ is both. It is definitely a potentially explosive tale. It is overtly political, economic, and social. It is adamantly against the spiritual abuses of the religious establishment. Those who call Jesus Christ a revolutionary do so with good reason. Those who feel that the Sermon on the Mount is a pretty radical document are only being rigorously honest. Those who point to the fact that Jesus did not appear to believe in private property of any kind are only accurately documenting the historical facts as we know them.

I want to be up front when I say that the story of the life of Jesus Christ is a controversial story, especially for those of us who live within the present American culture. Although this book does not advocate any political or economic perspective, just as it avoids any religious confessional language or appeal, I must acknowledge the following as critical to my own vantage point in relating the story:

➤ Jesus Christ is not an American, and America is not the new promised land.

➤ Jesus Christ was neither a Republican nor a Democrat.

➤ Jesus Christ was not a blond, blue-eyed Scandinavian. He was a dark-skinned Jew.

➤ Jesus Christ was not Catholic, Presbyterian, Methodist, Quaker, or Lutheran.

➤ When Jesus Christ spoke of an abundant life, he did not mean owning more and more stuff.

➤ Jesus' parable of the Good Samaritan creates a character who could be the poster child for what we in America call "a bleeding-heart liberal."

➤ Jesus claimed to speak to all people everywhere and for all time. His message and ministry was never exclusive, nor did he consciously or conscientiously leave anyone out.

➤ Jesus deeply appreciated diversity and demonstrated that in choosing 12 disciples who, by their very nature and tradition, could not agree on a thing.

➤ Jesus never gave up on love's capacity to break down walls or to build bridges.

Celebrating Humanness

As I look back on my work in first writing the outline for this book, I was struck by one common thread. Jesus Christ lived and taught us that it was the will of God for humans to be human and that we sadly spend a lifetime trying to be anything but human. Jesus celebrates being human. He laughs and weeps; he gets so furious he tips over tables; he grieves his losses and doubts his callings; he goes through the trials and triumphs of relationships, from denial and betrayal to devotion and love; he lives and he dies. In every way, Jesus lives his life to the fullest, and in the fullest sense, he celebrates the divine gift of his humanity.

If this book enables you to grasp this core truth of his life, I will have done what I have set out to do. If you come to see that being just human, is just fine—even more than fine, spectacular—I believe our time together, shared on the pages of this book, will have been time well spent.

About the Information Boxes

Jesus often called himself "the Way." He did so because he clearly presented us with a different path, a roadmap to a new way of living, a new direction in which to head. With that in mind, I have chosen to use references to that path and roadmap in the information boxes that will be scattered and splattered across the pages of this book.

Detours

How the story has been forced to go off its own path, and how we ourselves make it go our own way is noted in these boxes.

Major Highways

These boxes contain references taken directly from one of the four Gospels: Matthew, Mark, Luke, or John—the four "official" versions of the life of Christ.

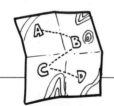

Map Key

These boxes define terms that the reader may not be familiar with.

Points of Interest

These boxes will highlight important data, ideas, or themes from the life of Jesus Christ.

Scenic Overlooks

These boxes are helpful insights and comments from a vast array of writers and thinkers, quotes carefully selected for their ability to further illuminate the basic story of Jesus' life.

A Note on the Scripture Passages

The scripture passages given throughout the book are from the *Revised Standard Version, Holy Bible,* New York City, Thomas Nelson, Inc., 1972.

A Note on Capitalization

To assure consistency and readability, capitalization conventions follow those of *The Chicago Manual of Style, 14th Edition.*

One Final Request

I know this won't be easy, but since I had to ask myself to do it in the writing of this book, I feel comfortable asking you to do the same. To the best of your ability, clean the slate. Remove all that you have been told or taught about Jesus of Nazareth. Try to read this book as if you have never heard of him at all, as if he were someone you were hearing about for the very first time.

Try to cleanse your mind of any religious teachings or parental or pastoral admonitions as to what you must believe. Try to hear the story not from the frame of reference of what your parents or family think, what some church or minister has to say, or even what you might have heard a TV evangelist say one night when you were channel surfing. Attempt to hear the story with "fresh ears."

I'm not asking you to disown what you know or to reject what you believe. I am saying that to hear the story with fresh ears will free you to meet an historical figure whose power to transform our lives and world is truly impressive, if not downright miraculous. Hearing the story with fresh ears will enable you to experience the story not as something to prove or defend but only and simply as a tale vital to hear.

Listen up!

Dedication

To the good folks of Shelter Island, New York, who have enabled (forced) me to walk the walk, practice what I preach, and locate a livable faith. We are a miracle of a community. On a daily basis we give the good Lord a good laugh and a good cry. In the midst of crisis, we are at our very best. Even our ever-present gossip is grounded in grace. More than anywhere, or at any time, it is on this small patch of soil where I have grown accustomed to seeing the sweet smile of Jesus Christ.

To Robert H. Shober, the kindest and sweetest man I have ever known. You were, without knowing it, my first conscious contact with the grace of God. In most everything you said and did, you quietly witnessed the power of love to offer healing and hope. I remain in your debt for giving me the gift of knowing that a real man can indeed be gracious and gentle. As a young man, most of my conceptions of Jesus were tightly tied to thoughts of you. That connection is clear again in your passing.

To my late beloved and deeply missed wife, Christine. I will never forget your reaction when you heard that I would sign a contract to write a book on the life of Jesus. You calmly screamed, "How wonderful, Bill. Now, how much do we get?" And then you danced and sang a lovely rendition of "Pennies from Heaven." Oh how I miss that raucous laughter. I can only imagine the joy Jesus now knows in your company. I am sure he finds you to be a splendid treat! I sure did!

Special Thanks to the Technical Reviewer

The Complete Idiot's Guide to the Life of Christ was reviewed by an expert who double-checked the accuracy of what you'll learn here, to help us ensure that this book gives you everything you need to know about Christ. Special thanks are extended to Forrest Church.

Trademarks

All terms mentioned in this book that are known to be or are suspected of being trademarks or service marks have been appropriately capitalized. Alpha Books and Penguin Group (USA) Inc. cannot attest to the accuracy of this information. Use of a term in this book should not be regarded as affecting the validity of any trademark or service mark.

Part 1

The Greatest Story Ever Told

I think of myself as a storyteller. Whenever I weave a tale, people invariably ask, "Where did that come from? Did you make that up? Did that really happen?" They want to know if it is the truth. They want to know who or what is the source of the story. They want to know if that came from inside me or from outside.

Most good stories come from the inside and *the outside. They are both historical and mythical. The life of Christ is such story. It is a story with many sources. It is an inspired and inspiring story. It is a story that is always transformed by the telling. We have all heard the story of Jesus referred to as "the greatest story ever told." Pretty bold commentary. To label something as "the greatest" is an editorial opinion. It is not something you seek to prove; it is something that you state with conviction. The proof is in the intensity and integrity with which you live the opinion.*

The story of Jesus Christ is a gathering of tales. It is the weaving together of a patchwork quilt of loving accounts and remembrances: sayings, parables, miracle stories, a major sermon, the thoughts of followers, and the events and experiences of faith and the faithful. It, too, is an effort to declare the man and his story as the greatest.

Chapter 1

The Standpoint of the Gospels

In This Chapter

➤ The oral tradition of the story of Christ

➤ Jesus serves! (according to the Gospel of Mark)

➤ Matthew and the Messiah

➤ Luke declares Jesus the champion of the poor and outcast

➤ John reveals the Son of God

Knowledge about the storyteller enhances the audience's understanding of a story. The storyteller ultimately weaves the tale, chooses the direction and flow of the story, conveys a certain tone, and becomes the lens through which you envision the story. Before we begin exploring the life of Jesus Christ, you must have a basic understanding of the sources of the story of his life. The main sources of this story are the biblical books of Matthew, Mark, Luke, and John, which are known as the Gospels. This chapter explains how the Gospels evolved from oral tradition and were arranged to present the life of Christ.

The Genesis of the Gospels

The English word *gospel* translates a Greek word meaning "good news." Initially, the gospel was transmitted orally. The oral tradition has deep spiritual roots in the times in which Jesus lived. Sharing stories was a common form of communication, entertainment, and worship. Storytelling was an art. Then, as now, people loved to hear a good story, especially a story that shared "good news."

Points of Interest

The oral tradition is alive today in wedding toasts, funeral tributes, and the swapping of family legends. Testimonials are still common in many forms of worship. Most AA meetings begin with someone telling his or her story. Other examples of stories based in oral tradition include Garrison Keillor's stories from Lake Wobegon (a fictional place where the gospel truth can often be heard) and Michael Lindvall's extraordinary collection of "gospel" stories, *The Good News from North Haven.*

I think of the story of Jesus Christ as a patchwork quilt. The quilt is composed of many different patches, and all of these patches come out of the oral tradition. The oral tradition provides the foundation for all subsequent written sources. In *Understanding the New Testament* by Howard Clark Kee, Franklin W. Young, and Karlfried Froehlich, these patches of oral tradition are categorized as …

➤ Pronouncement stories.
➤ Sayings.
➤ Miracle stories.
➤ Parables.
➤ Clusters of similes.
➤ Stories about Jesus.

Pronouncement Stories

Pronouncement stories share an encounter between Jesus and one or more persons. The setting of the story is insignificant, and only a few details are given. The key to these stories is a culminating pronouncement made by Jesus. The following is an example:

> "And they sent to him some of the Pharisees and some of the Herodians, to entrap him in his talk. And they came and said to him, 'Teacher, we know that you are true, and care for no man; for you do not regard the position of men, but truly teach the way of God. Is it lawful to pay taxes to Caesar, or not? Should we pay them, or should we not?' But knowing their hypocrisy, he said to them, 'Why put me to the test? Bring me a coin, and let me look at it.' And

they brought one. And he said to them, 'Whose likeness and inscription is this?' They said to him, 'Caesar's.' Jesus said to them, 'Render to Caesar the things that are Caesar's, and to God the things that are God's.'"

—Mark 12:13–17

Sayings

The oral tradition included a great many sayings attributed to Jesus. Often they were shared in clusters around a common theme. Consider the following:

"And he called to him the multitude with his disciples, and said to them, 'If any man would come after me, let him deny himself and take up his cross and follow me. For whoever would save his life will lose it; and whoever loses his life for my sake and the gospel's will save it. For what does it profit a man to gain the whole world and forfeit his life? For what can a man give in return for his life? For whoever is ashamed of me and my words in this adulterous and sinful generation, of him will the Son of man also be ashamed, when he comes in the glory of his Father with the holy angels.' And he said to them, 'Truly, I say to you, there are some standing here who will not taste death before they see that the kingdom of God has come with power.'"

—Mark 8:34–9:1

Miracle Stories

Miracle stories are the narrative accounts of the miraculous acts of Jesus. The following passage illustrates such a story:

"And a *leper* came to him beseeching him, and kneeling said to him, 'If you will, you can make me clean.' Moved with pity, he stretched out his hand and touched him, and said to him, 'I will; be clean.' And immediately the leprosy left him, and he was made clean. And he sternly charged him, and sent him away at once, and said to him, 'See that you say nothing to anyone; but go, show yourself to the priest, and offer for your cleansing what Moses commanded, for a proof to the people.' But he went out and began to talk freely about it, and to spread the news, so that Jesus could no longer openly enter a town, but was out in the country; and people came to him from every quarter."

—Mark 1:40–45

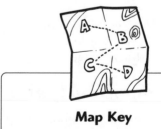

Map Key

A **leper** is an individual afflicted with the disease of leprosy, which results in rotting flesh.

Parables

A parable is a small story with a big point. Parables describe a commonplace incident or experience that reveals a most uncommon truth. These stories have two levels of meaning: the story itself and the truth that runs parallel to it.

The following passage contains a parable:

> "'Listen! A sower went out to sow. And as he sowed, some seed fell along the path, and the birds came and devoured it. Other seed fell on rocky ground, where it had not much soil, and immediately it sprang up, since it had no depth of soil; and when the sun rose it was scorched, and since it had no root it withered away. Other seed fell among thorns and the thorns grew up and choked it, and it yielded no grain. And other seeds fell into good soil and brought forth grain, growing up and increasing and yielding thirtyfold and sixtyfold and a hundredfold.'"
>
> —Mark 4:3–8

The sower is clearly God, and the soil symbolizes the soul. Just as soil must be fertile if the seed is to grow, a soul is made fertile by taking time to be with God.

Clusters of Similes

A cluster of similes functions exactly like a parable does, but without the story. The following illustrates a cluster of similes that convey a deeper meaning:

> "'No one sews a piece of unshrunk cloth on an old garment; if he does, the patch tears away from it, the new from the old, and a worse tear is made. And no one puts new wine into old wineskins; if he does, the wine will burst the skins, and the wine is lost, and so are the skins; but new wine is for fresh skins.'"
>
> —Mark 2:21–22

Here Jesus is pointing out that at times it is impossible to blend the old and the new. The new, as in the case of the message of Jesus, may be incompatible with the old, as in the message of the law.

Stories About Jesus

These stories, unlike the pronouncement stories, have no defining feature. They cannot be categorized and cover a wide range of subject matter. The birth stories (Matthew 1:18–25; Luke 2:1–20), the temptation of Jesus (Matthew 4:1–11; Luke 4:1–13), and the calling of the disciples (Mark 1:16–20) all fall under this loose classification, as does the following example:

"And they came to Jerusalem. And he entered the temple and began to drive out those who sold and those who bought in the temple, and he overturned the tables of the money-changers and the seats of those who sold pigeons; and he would not allow any one to carry anything through the temple. And he taught, and said to them, 'Is it not written, "My house shall be called a house of prayer for all the nations"? But you have made it a den of robbers.'"

—Mark 11:15–17

The Gospel Writers as Editors

Although the primary sources for the story of Jesus are the Gospels, the Gospels are not firsthand accounts. The writers of these books were not reporters. The Gospels were recorded several decades after the events of the life of Christ. They were written from the perspective of looking back upon Christ's life and forward in anticipation of his return. The Gospels are not your average modern history books.

The gospel writers gathered many patches of oral tradition concerning the life of Jesus. Each gospel writer received several of the same patches, some that were slightly different, and a few that were unique. Each gospel writer then weaved these patches together with the thread of his personal faith standpoint.

The gospel writers were editors. The job of a good editor is ...

➤ To gather as much material on the subject as possible.

➤ To assess the accuracy and credibility of that material.

➤ To organize the material.

➤ To give the material a sense of purpose and flow.

➤ To present the material in a readable fashion.

➤ To offer input and perspective to the material whenever necessary.

Some folks have a problem with the notion of the gospel writers as editors. It implies that these men may have manipulated the material and presented their own version of the story. That is exactly what they did, but they did so because they believed themselves called to do so. Just as they believed the stories and sayings they gathered to be divinely inspired, they also saw their role as editors similarly charged.

Points of Interest

Scholars have long debated whether Matthew, Mark, Luke, or John actually penned the Gospels. Because John and Matthew were thought to be original disciples and Mark and Luke were companions of Paul, their names may have been used to add credibility to the account. Many scholars argue that the gospel writers were disciples of disciples or members of communities who were influenced by Paul or the disciples.

At the core of each gospel is the radical contention of the resurrection. The focal point of each gospel is that Jesus Christ is a living Lord. This idea had profound implications for the gospel writers as authors and editors:

➤ The gospel writers were not overly concerned about events from the past because Jesus was alive and well within their faith community.

➤ They expected Jesus to return shortly.

➤ The future took on much greater importance than reflecting upon the past.

➤ The first Christians were not at all interested in gathering biographical detail; biographies did not exist in those times.

➤ The community of believers saw the resurrection as proof positive that Jesus was the Messiah.

➤ The community was not as interested in the facts of Jesus' life as it was in the impact of his presence and person.

➤ The Gospels are not meant to be biographies; they are proclamations of the good news and statements of faith.

The story of the life of Jesus Christ is a human story with divine implications. The four authors of the story of Jesus Christ, the gospel writers, were also human, yet they felt entrusted with a sacred responsibility. All four gospels carry the imprint of a uniquely human hand, heart, mind, and soul. The belief that these were moved by God is a matter of faith.

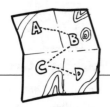

Map Key

Synoptic Gospels are the Gospels of Matthew and Luke, which contain what is called the Marcan outline, which is Mark's synopsis of the life of Jesus Christ. Because these three books each share this synopsis, they are referred to as the synoptic Gospels. All but 31 verses of Mark are quoted in the other two Gospels.

Mark's Standpoint

The Gospel of Mark is thought to be written by John Mark, who accompanied Paul on his first missionary journey (Acts 13:13). This gospel was written somewhere just before or after the fall of Jerusalem to the Roman army in A.D. 70 and was probably the first gospel written. It is the oldest surviving sequential account of the career of Jesus and is the foundation for the *synoptic Gospels*. The language of Mark was Greek, but the context of discussion throughout the gospel is definitely Jewish.

Mark's Main Ideas

Mark's general aim was to give Jesus a three-way function in the life of the church:

1. Jesus was to become the subject of preaching.

2. Jesus was to provide all authority for its teaching.

3. Jesus was to be the mediator of its worship to God. Mark wanted to bolster the church after the death of Jesus' original followers.

By making Jesus the centerpiece of his gospel, Mark hoped to give the church a strong and vibrant core. Mark clearly believed the continued existence of the church was in doubt and that the need for regrouping was urgent. In the first chapter alone, he uses the word *immediately* eight different times. Mark felt that the work of unifying and strengthening the church must happen now. This sense of urgency may also have been the result of his belief in the nearness of Jesus' return.

The Gospel of Mark has these central themes:

➤ Jesus Christ alone is the Son of God.

➤ Jesus demonstrates his divinity by driving out demons and healing those with disease.

➤ As the Messiah, Jesus fulfills the Old Testament prophecies.

➤ The world was waiting for a powerful king, but Jesus comes as a servant.

➤ God's will is seldom what the world expects or wants.

➤ Greatness in God's kingdom is shown by service and sacrifice.

➤ God frowns upon those who are overly ambitious or seek worldly wealth and power.

➤ Jesus turns the values of the world upside down. The mighty are brought low. The last are made first. The rich are sent away empty.

➤ Jesus' miracles prove that he is God. (Mark records more miracles than any other Gospel and records more miracles than sermons.)

➤ His miracles are centered in forgiveness, which can transform the human heart, mind, and body.

➤ His miracles are available to anyone. The past is not a determining factor.

➤ If you trust in God, you can be healed and made whole.

Jesus the Servant

The Gospel of Mark presents a seemingly paradoxical portrait of Jesus. On the one hand, Jesus is able to raise people from the dead. He quiets stormy seas. He restores deformed bodies. He gives sight to the blind. He drives out demons. On the other hand, he comes to this world as a servant, and the conception of Jesus as a servant is the distinguishing feature of Mark.

In Mark, we hear the gospel message that the power of God is not like the world's power. The power of God is willing to kneel, suffer, and serve. The power of God will sacrifice anything, even God's own Son, to save the world from sin.

Jesus as a servant is a potent image. Servants in the time of Jesus, and in our own, are thought of as having no identity, power, or worth. The image of Jesus as a servant declares the opposite. Those who serve are identified as disciples. Their power is divine and is found in weakness. Their worth is measured by its eternal value. Following Jesus is not about claiming rank or privilege; it is about serving others.

A good deal of the gospel message is about a radical reversal of values. What Jesus sees as priorities are not priorities to most of the world. What Jesus sees as significant is often ignored by the world. What Jesus thinks is of ultimate value is often viewed as worthless by the world. This reversal of values sets the stage for a crucified Messiah.

Points of Interest

I am often asked why we do not see more adolescents in the church. I think it is because most adolescents have difficulty embracing the idea of servitude. The church asks them to become servants, to wash people's feet, to make sacrifices, and to surrender their spirits to God. The message of the Gospels is a radical departure from the pursuit of the American good life, which ironically has nothing to do with goodness.

Matthew's Standpoint

The Gospel of Matthew is not only the first in the New Testament, but it is also probably the most frequently read piece of Christian scripture. The words of this gospel are among the most familiar. The Gospel of Matthew contains the coming of the wise men, the Sermon on the Mount, the familiar form of the Lord's Prayer, the coin in the fish's mouth, and the parable of the sheep and the goats. All of these stories are found only in Matthew. Also, only in Matthew is Peter addressed as the rock upon which the church will be built.

Matthew was dependent upon Mark in the composing of his gospel. Matthew clearly had the synopsis of Mark before him as he wrote. He also must have used what is called the *Q Source,* which is a collection of the sayings of Jesus. Like a good editor, Matthew reworked his material. He supplemented certain stories and abridged others.

The Gospel of Matthew was originally written in Greek. The dominant view among biblical scholars is that the gospel was written near Antioch. Matthew probably lived in a Greek-speaking community, strongly influenced by Jewish aspirations and viewpoints. Because the fall of Jerusalem, which occurred in A.D. 70, is mentioned in this gospel (Matthew 22:7), the gospel was probably written somewhere around A.D. 80 to 85.

It has long been assumed that the Gospel of Matthew was written by the disciple Matthew Levi, a Jewish tax collector. However, the late date of its composition and the reliance on Mark's outline would seem to suggest otherwise. Whatever the case, I will continue to use the name Matthew, because I am comfortable with the gospel being spiritually linked to the disciple.

Matthew's Method

The Gospel of Matthew is a manual for church instruction and administration. Clearly its author wanted to bring order to the church. This gospel is highly structured. In the main body of this gospel, the ministry of the Messiah, the material is divided into five clear sections:

1. Preparation and Program of the Ministry (Chapters 3–7)

2. The Authority of Jesus (Chapters 8–10)

3. The Kingdom and Its Coming (Chapters 11–13)

4. Life of the New Community (Chapters 14–18)

5. The Consummation of the Age (Chapters 19–25)

Preceding this first section is the story of the birth and infancy of Jesus, and following the fifth and final section is the account of the Passion and the Resurrection. Matthew has done an extraordinary job of editing and putting the story together as a working whole.

These major themes appear in the Gospel of Matthew:

➤ Jesus did not come to abolish the law of Moses, but to fulfill it (Matthew 5:17).

➤ Jesus was sent by God to save us.

➤ Jesus cannot be equated with any human.

➤ Jesus' power is that of a king; he is the king of our lives.

➤ Jesus came to begin his kingdom.

➤ Faith gains you entrance into Jesus' kingdom.

➤ We must actively build Jesus' kingdom now to prepare for his imminent return.

Jesus the Messiah

Though Matthew is an orderly account, it is not a chronological one. The whole purpose of this gospel is to provide clear and compelling evidence, especially to the Jews, that Jesus is the Messiah, the Savior. The gospel is filled with Messianic language. The phrase "Son of David" is used throughout the gospel, and the use of Jewish scripture is extensive: 53 quotes and 76 other references.

The people of Israel were waiting for the Messiah. The Messiah was to be their king and would return them to the glory that was known during the reign of King David. Matthew begins his book by claiming that Jesus was a descendant of David, but he seeks to portray Jesus not as an earthly king, but as one of heavenly powers and position.

At Jesus' birth, many thought of him as a king, and the gospel tells of the visitation of three kings. Herod was disturbed by the arrival of these three astrologers, and their question about a newborn king. Herod was thought to be afraid of Jesus' kingship because Herod was not the rightful heir to the throne of David. If Jesus truly was an heir, there could be trouble. Herod did not want the Jews uniting around a religious figure. However, the Jews rejected Jesus as a king. He was accused, arrested, and crucified.

Matthew explains that Jesus' kingdom is not anything like the kingdoms of the earth; it is full of mercy, justice, equality, wisdom, love, and hope. Only the Messiah could create a kingdom of this kind. The Messiah is the Prince of Peace. He is not a brave warrior who rides in a stallion to claim his prize. He is the merciful savior who comes in on the back of a donkey and claims the human heart.

Luke's Standpoint

Mark wrote a gospel in which the end would come after a period of *Gentile* evangelism. Matthew moved beyond Mark and declared that the church was the New Israel, because historic Israel had forfeited that right by rejecting Jesus. Matthew was careful in clearly defining a role for the church, as well as sketching out the basis for church discipline. Luke took on the task of developing a role for the church in God's overall plan. Simply put, it was Luke who had to figure out what the mission of the church was, if the end was coming later than sooner.

It is thought that Luke was a doctor, a Gentile, and a Greek. The belief that he was a doctor (Colossians 4:14) is supported by his many references to illnesses and diagnoses. He is the only Gentile author in Christian scriptures. He was thought to have been

Points of Interest

The Bible tells us not to make God in our own image. Yet if you listen to many of today's TV evangelists, you would swear that Jesus was white, American, Southern, Protestant, and Republican. You would also be convinced that his kingdom sounds a good deal like Dollywood.

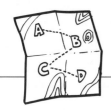

Map Key

A **Gentile** is anyone who is not a Jew.

a close friend of Paul, but that is difficult to verify. He was also the author of Acts, and the two books should be thought of as a single unit.

The Language of Luke

Luke is a comprehensive and beautifully written gospel. The language is elegant and picturesque. The many details make the reader feel that it is historically accurate and reliable, and the vocabulary and diction of this gospel indicate that the author was highly educated. The Gospel of Luke is focused on the Gentile, but it speaks in a language accessible to all. Luke's gospel is written for all people everywhere and for all time.

Luke places special emphasis on these topics:

➤ The role of prayer

➤ The positive and prominent role of women

➤ The role of angels

➤ Miracles and hymns of praise

➤ The role of the Holy Spirit, which is present at Jesus' birth, baptism, ministry, and resurrection

Luke's gospel stresses the following themes:

➤ Jesus was deeply interested in people and human relationships.

➤ Jesus had greatest sympathy for the poor, the despised, the hurt, and the sinners.

➤ Jesus rejected no one; no one was ignored. Jesus embraced all people with the same grace.

➤ Jesus is more than a teacher; Jesus loves and respects you and cares deeply about your well-being.

➤ Jesus is the model of wholeness, which is a life in perfect balance.

➤ Jesus asks us to be dependent on the Holy Spirit.

➤ The love and forgiveness of Jesus Christ are available to all.

Jesus the Champion of the Poor and Outcast

Consider the birth story that is found only in Luke. A young couple travels miles to be enrolled in a census. They are poor and as yet unwed. There is no room for them inside the inn, but they are allowed to stay out back. Jesus is born in a barn, wrapped in cloths, and laid in a manger, which is a hay trough for the animals. The barn stinks and is cluttered with animals. It is cold, damp, and uncomfortable. The first visitors are shepherds. Shepherds were thought of as unclean, unkempt, and unholy.

This king is not born in a palace, and his court is full of local scoundrels, not princes and princesses.

Points of Interest

From Luke's perspective, if Jesus were to come to earth today, he would head straight for the streets of our urban centers. There he would minister to the homeless and hungry, the mentally ill, the addicted, those with AIDS and other illnesses, and those who are spiritually lost. I would hate to think what Luke's Jesus would have to say to those of us who just walk on by those same folks.

From beginning to end, the Gospel of Luke presents a Jesus who is the champion of the poor and outcast. Jesus brings together not the rich and powerful, but the weak, the sick, the despised, and the rejected. This Jesus invites the wretched of the earth to his banquet table. This Jesus incessantly reminds folks that there is no such thing as private property and that everything belongs to God. Luke's Jesus blasts the rich with a message that elevates the poor and lowly and sends those with a lot of stuff far, far away.

The Gospel of Luke expresses a theme of liberation. It is a social, political, and economic gospel. This gospel declares God's kingdom to be built from bricks of justice. From Luke's perspective, justice is a radical celebration of the equality of all people. Luke's Jesus embraces the planet and its people with *grace,* and grace is an equal opportunity employer.

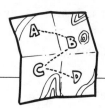

Map Key

Grace is the unconditional and undeserved love of God. Jesus can be thought of as an instrument of this grace. For the believer, he is the very event of grace.

John's Standpoint

The Gospel of John is attributed to John the Apostle, but that seems unlikely because the writing was done in A.D. 90 to 100. However, I am comfortable with linking this gospel with the apostle, just as an artist in the Rembrandt school was inextricably bonded to the style and spirit of the famed artist.

The Gospel of John differs from the synoptic Gospels in form and content. The similes and sayings of the synoptic Gospels are glaringly absent. John's gospel does not contain a genealogy or any record of the birth of Jesus. We do not hear of his childhood, the temptation or transfiguration, the appointment of the disciples, nor any accounting of the great parables. John prefers symbolic language and often gives words and events a double meaning. The themes of the synoptic Gospels were righteousness, forgiveness, and the coming of God's kingdom. John takes on new themes: eternal life, light and darkness, blindness and sight, truth and glory. In John's gospel, the ministry of Jesus lasts about three years, whereas in the synoptic Gospels, it takes place in one. John locates Jesus' ministry mainly in Jerusalem and Judea; the synoptic Gospels focus on Galilee.

The Gospel of John is the best case for the vital role of editor in the Gospels. Clearly, the Gospel of John is written from a unique spiritual perspective. John's editing of the life of Jesus is so thorough that at times one might feel compelled to check whether it's the same story. The vast majority of John's version of the life of Christ is unique to this gospel.

Many Miracles

Of the eight miracles recorded in the Gospels, six of them are unique to the Gospel of John. All of these miracles reveal the gracious nature of Jesus:

➤ Turning water into wine (2:1–11)

➤ Healing the official's son (4:46–54)

➤ Healing the lame man at the Pool of Bethesda (5:1–9)

➤ Feeding the 5,000 with just a few loaves and fish (6:1–14)

➤ Walking on water (6:15–21)

➤ Restoring sight to the blind man (9:1–41)

➤ Raising Lazarus from the dead (11:1–44)

➤ Showing his disciples how to make an amazing catch of fish (21:1–14)

The Gospel of John doesn't have a standpoint as much as a flight record. It is a truly spiritual work, with a heavy dominance of eternal themes:

➤ Jesus is unique and God's special Son.

➤ Jesus was with us before we were born.

➤ Jesus is at our side all of our life.

➤ Jesus will reign forever.

➤ Jesus offers us the promise of eternal life.

➤ Jesus invites us to share an intimate and eternal relationship with him.

➤ The Holy Spirit will serve as our guide and counselor.

➤ The Holy Spirit expresses the will and way of Jesus.

➤ The Holy Spirit conveys the eternal nature of grace.

John describes the power of Jesus as unlimited, eternal, and available to all people. This power is pure in its love and forgiveness and calls us to faith.

Jesus Is the Son of God

John dispels any notion that Jesus is just a good man or merely a moral teacher. He declares him to be the Son of God. The image of Jesus as the Son of God is powerful and intimate. It establishes a link between Jesus and God that is soaked in love. Because Jesus is God's Son, you can trust him. You can be certain that his ministry is of and about the truth. Only God's Son could offer a gift as magnificent as eternal life. Also, because Jesus is the Son of God, you should pay strict attention to his message, seek to follow the path of his ministry, and receive the good news of his grace.

Intimacy and eternity are the twin focal points of this gospel and of the concept of the Son of God. You are called by this gospel to embrace a close personal relationship with Jesus, just as Jesus is on intimate terms with God. You are also challenged to believe that this relationship spans eternity.

Points of Interest

The Gospel of John is fond of using titles to reveal the true identity of Jesus. Phrases beginning with "I am" are used to declare that Jesus is divine and eternal:

➤ I am the bread of life (6:35).

➤ I am the light of the world (8:12).

➤ I am the gate (10:7).

➤ I am the good shepherd (10:11).

➤ I am the resurrection and the life (11:25).

➤ I am the way, the truth, and the life (14:6).

➤ I am the true vine (15:1).

The Least You Need to Know

➤ The original source of the gospel story was oral tradition.

➤ The writing of the Gospels involved editing, the assembling and creative altering of the material.

➤ The Gospel of Mark was the first gospel and formed the outline used by Matthew and Luke. In his gospel, Mark portrayed Jesus as a servant.

➤ Matthew's gospel declared that Jesus was the Messiah and gave the church a clear mission statement, as well as a basic guide to discipline.

➤ Luke's gospel presented Jesus as the radical champion of those who are disenfranchised in society.

➤ John's gospel took on an eternal vantage point. In this gospel, Jesus was the granter of eternal life.

Chapter 2

The Standpoint of Paul

In This Chapter

➤ Why Paul is important

➤ How a Jewish student became a Christian missionary

➤ What Paul had to say about Jesus

I have often heard people speak the words of Paul as if they were the words of Jesus. This mistake is not a terrible transgression. Paul's life, pastoral ministry, and missionary journeys were so vital to the development of the early Christian church that it is not surprising that folks at times freely exchange Paul's words with those of Christ. He was more than just a follower of Jesus; he was in many respects *the* follower.

The Importance of Paul

In my congregation on Shelter Island, New York, I work with two children whose mother died after a brief bout with cancer. I did not know the mother well, but the more time I spend with her kids, the closer I feel to her. Her daughter and son bear the powerful spiritual imprint of her soul. I can easily imagine how she might react to a given situation, even what she might say, simply by observing her kids and listening to their stories about her.

In a similar fashion, Paul helped his followers and readers get to know Christ. Paul's conversion was so dramatic, the spiritual impact so transforming, that his soul was indelibly marked by Christ. Though Paul did not experience Christ firsthand, his conversion experience and subsequent faith were filled with the presence and power of

Christ. Reading Paul's words of faith brings Jesus Christ to life. Through Paul, we feel better able to grasp the man Jesus, his message, and the meaning of the entire Christian ministry. Paul is a valid medium of understanding the life of Jesus Christ.

Detours

The defining role of Paul in the formation of Christian faith can't be overestimated. However, keep in mind that Paul is a follower of Jesus, not an equal of him. Paul is not a lord or a savior; he is an apostle. He is a model for ministry and was the first true Christian missionary. He was not, however, the Son of the Messiah.

An understanding of Paul is vital to an understanding of the life of Jesus for the following reasons:

➤ Paul was converted to Christianity as the result of a direct encounter with the risen Christ. This conversion was crucial in the formation of the early church and is acknowledged three times in the book of Acts (Acts 9:3–19; 22:6–16; 26:9–23).

➤ Paul's letters account for over half (14 of the 27) of the books of Christian scripture.

➤ Paul's ministry and message shaped the faith of much of the early church.

➤ Paul's missionary efforts are central to the establishment of several new churches and the maintaining of several others.

➤ The early church had a dramatic impact on our contemporary understanding of the life of Jesus Christ.

Who Paul Was

An apostle was thought to be a bearer of divine truth. Paul was a newcomer to an existing group of Jewish-Christian apostles, as is clearly stated in Galatians 1:17. Paul was certain that God had chosen him to bring the good news of Jesus Christ to the Gentile nations. The fact the he was a Jew reared in a Gentile city, Tarsus, and was bilingual, knowing the scriptures in both the original Semitic as well as Greek, made him well-equipped to do so.

Paul was a Jew born at Tarsus in the Roman province of Cilicia, which was a university town and a center for trade and government. The Greek culture of Tarsus had a strong impact on Paul, and he became familiar with a Gentile perspective. He was also particularly fortunate to be born into a family on which Roman citizenship had been conferred, a privilege of which he was especially proud. His upbringing, however, was thoroughly Jewish in every way.

Paul was an extraordinary student of *the Torah,* and his earnings as a tentmaker allowed him to pursue his studies, which took him to Jerusalem, the heart of Judaism. There he was educated at the school of the famous teacher Gamaliel, the grandson and successor of the great Rabbi Hillel, according to the strictest interpretation of the

Jewish law as laid down by the Pharisees. He was so zealous for the traditions of his people that his religious faith soon advanced far beyond most of his contemporaries. He could even claim to be almost faultless in his obedience to the Jewish law. Education was important to Paul, and the uneducated followers of Jesus repulsed him.

Paul was a *Pharisee*. Pharisees believed that history had a goal and purpose; they also believed in a future life (heaven), angels, and demons. As a Pharisee, Paul became a persecutor of the followers of Jesus Christ, who were a community called "The Way." Paul thought Jesus was another false Messiah. When Stephen, a follower of Jesus, claimed that the days of the temple and the Jewish faith were numbered, Paul decided that Christianity posed a genuine threat and became proactive in his persecution.

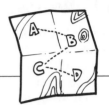

Map Key

The Torah is a work of Jewish law composed of Genesis, Exodus, Leviticus, Numbers, and Deuteronomy, which are the first five books of Jewish scripture and the Bible.

On the road to Damascus, an extraordinary event occurred. Paul claimed to have met the risen Christ. After this event, Paul became an active defender of the Christian faith. His missionary travels took him to Jerusalem, Damascus, Arabia, Caesarea, Tarsus, Cilicia, Syria, and Antioch. Paul's missionary work proved quite successful, especially in Ephesus, a hotbed for pagan worship, magicians, and sorcerers.

During this time, Paul became convinced that Gentiles should be admitted to the Christian fellowship without having to be circumcised or observant of the Jewish law. Paul became hated in Judea, where he was seen as a traitor to the Jewish faith. He no longer saw the Jewish scripture as either a means of salvation or as a source of moral inspiration.

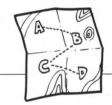

Map Key

The **Pharisees** were a Jewish religious group which zealously followed the laws of the Hebrew scripture.

Paul and his companions Silas and Timothy wound up in prison. In Acts, they are described as men who have turned the whole world upside down. Paul was sent before the Sanhedrin, the Jewish version of the Supreme Court. Here he declared himself to still be a good Pharisee who believed in resurrection from the dead.

Paul was tried before Felix and Festus, who were both Roman procurators (agents of the emperor). Felix thought Paul was innocent, but delayed his decision in order to avoid further conflict. Festus granted Paul's wish to be sent for trial in Rome. Paul traveled in a prison ship with his companions Luke and Aristarchus. The fact that he was allowed to travel with companions indicates that he was given special treatment and that both procurators believed him to be innocent. Nevertheless, Paul met a martyr's death in Rome during the Christian persecution ordered by Nero in A.D. 64.

Paul's Writings

Paul is most famous for his letters to the various Christian churches. In his letters, Paul claimed the authority of being an apostle. These letters were primarily efforts to respond to questions raised about doctrinal teachings, as well as calls for moral and ethical conduct. The letters became a means of instruction on how to follow Jesus and how to lead an exemplary Christian life. Paul's letters to the churches in Rome and Corinth became the centerpiece of his writing.

Paul's letters are at times called epistles, but don't let the fancy name fool you. They are in every way letters written in exact accordance with the standard form of ancient letters:

1. They begin with a greeting.
2. They include a prayer for the health and well-being of the recipients.
3. They give thanksgiving to God.
4. The main body of the letters contains the purpose of the communication.
5. The letters end with salutations and personal greetings.

Paul's letters are not theological treatises. They are not academic exercises. They are letters written down by Paul's secretaries as he poured out his heart and soul.

At times, Paul is tough to understand. His sentences begin, but don't finish. The grammar can be atrocious. Plus, reading a letter is like hearing one side of a phone conversation. The other side, which is just as important, is something you can only deduce. Trying to figure out what prompted Paul's words is no easy task.

Through these letters, Paul has composed another kind of gospel. Paul's gospel is not a record of the life of Jesus Christ, but it is an accounting of the transforming impact of Jesus Christ on Paul's life and faith. In a sense, Paul's gospel is more practical than the other Gospels. It is a testimonial as to what it means to be a follower of Jesus. The other Gospels seek to bring you to Jesus, but Paul is out to tell you what to do and be once you have arrived. Paul was the catalyst for the formation of the church, and Paul's faith standpoint has had a profound influence on the way many contemporary Christians understand the story of the life of Jesus Christ. Paul's gospel may not say much about the faith journey of Jesus, but it has a tremendous amount to say about where Jesus intends to take you.

Paul's Gospel: All Have Sinned

Before his encounter with the risen Christ, Paul was a religious fanatic. His faith had become compulsive. The Torah was his obsession, and his goal was spiritual perfection.

After his conversion, Paul came to see that all people are sinners and that no human being is perfect. Everyone has flaws and failings. Paul gave up his notion that sin and sinners could be ranked and that the Pharisees were somehow more pure than other people. He came to believe that the very law he worshipped was the source of his greatest sin: a judgmental and self-righteous spirit. Paul came to realize that although he knew the law by heart, his own heart was bitter, and he loved nobody.

Paul's gospel proclaims a Jesus who loves people who sin and who, with his grace, washes away sin. That grace frees people from the futility of trying to be perfect and instead encourages them to pursue excellence. The pursuit of excellence is always inspiring and exciting; whereas, the pursuit of perfection is always exhausting and maddening.

Paul's Gospel: Justified by Faith

Do you ever feel that you are not ready to come to God because you aren't good enough yet? Do you ever think you have to prove to God that you are worthy of his love? Do you think of God as a ruthless judge, who has nothing to offer you but a giant wagging finger? Is faith for you nothing but a journey into shame and guilt? Do you measure your faith by how often you worship, pray, or act religious?

Paul states clearly that Christ's love for you has nothing to do with you proving something to him. Paul's gospel is taking a bold stand here: Christ's love is yours for free. It is the original free lunch. The love of Jesus is his choice to give, and you were chosen at birth, the day you became his child. Jesus is not looking for you to be sin-free, nor is he looking for you to put your faith flamboyantly on display. All Jesus wants from you is to believe in him, and he will do the rest.

Major Highways

"[S]ince all have sinned and fall short of the glory of God, they are justified by his grace as a gift, through the redemption which is in Christ Jesus ..."

—Romans 3:23–24

Major Highways

"Then what becomes of our boasting? It is excluded. On what principle? On the principle of works? No, but on the principle of faith. For we hold that a man is justified by faith apart from works of law."

—Romans 3:27–28

Do not fall in the trap of thinking that this unconditional love means you can do whatever you please and that by claiming to believe in Jesus you're eternally fine. What Paul is saying is that if you love your God with your whole heart, which is the essence of faith, you will also love your neighbor as yourself. In the spirit of putting the cart back behind the horse, Paul is calling upon the followers of Jesus to simply choose to follow Christ on a daily basis and trust that Christ will lead the way.

Paul's Gospel: We Are in Christ

Paul believed that God was in Jesus Christ and that the life of Jesus illustrated the workings of the heart and mind of God. The presence of God in Jesus was for Paul the distinguishing feature of Christ's life and his own faith. Jesus was a human who encased the divine will, a man who enveloped and was enveloped by the divine.

Major Highways

The following passage contains the message that Jesus brings people home to God—to the original relationship humanity had with God:

"All this [newness of life] is from God, who through Christ reconciled us to himself and gave us the ministry of reconciliation; that is, in Christ. God was reconciling the world to himself, not counting their trespasses against them, and entrusting through us the message of reconciliation. So we are ambassadors for Christ, God making his appeal through us. We beseech you on behalf of Christ, be reconciled to God."

—2 Corinthians 5:18–20

Paul also came to believe that those who believe in Jesus Christ were now living in him. They had entered a new state and were a new creation. They could wear Christ like a cloak. If you did not feel capable of forgiving someone, Christ could accomplish this significant spiritual task for you; your job was to surrender the matter. You must let go of the grudge or wound or pain.

For Paul, the following ideas were true:

➤ Living in Christ means living in obedience.

➤ Obedience is living out the will of God.

➤ Living in obedience to the will of God is being human.

➤ Being human is the one thing we have trouble accepting on a daily basis. Just being human is not the sin. Failing to accept our humanity is the source of most of our sinning.

Paul's gospel is preaching against perfectionism and playing God. It tells you that you are free to be human and to celebrate the gift of your humanness. Paul encourages the followers of Jesus Christ to be wise. Wisdom, from Paul's unique faith perspective, comes when you finally surrender to the fact that you are not in control. You are not in charge. You are finally free to be fully alive. Once you no longer have to play God, you can enjoy the blessedness of being loved by God.

Living in Christ is to live in a state of peace, safety, security, and incredible strength. Paul did not see Jesus Christ as a hiding place, but as the sanctuary in which you can find the rest you need, the courage you must possess, and the faith you must muster if you are to be able to conduct a ministry of hope and joy. Living in Christ is to be immersed in a passionate and compassionate love, a love whose heat could melt a thousand suns.

Paul's Gospel: One in Baptism

Baptism is a Christian sacrament. A *sacrament* is what I would call a sacred moment, a moment guaranteed to be filled with the presence of God. Baptism and communion are two sacraments that are called for in Christian scripture. *Baptism* is a spiritual washing, a sprinkling or a dunking of an infant or an adult. All those who have been baptized have experienced the event of grace, Jesus the Christ. Though the spiritual experiences vary widely, the reception of grace remains the symbolic thrust of baptism.

Paul's gospel declares that all who have received the gift of grace through baptism share equally in Christ. Although many diverse functions exist within the church, there is no hierarchy of function. Just as all body parts are of equal value, all people within the church are equally important. Because the church had long been riddled with spiritual strife over matters of hierarchy, this was a piercing point.

It may be human nature to believe that some people are more holy than others or that some are more sinful or that some roles within the church are of greater significance than others. But that is not the nature of Jesus Christ. Paul asserts that Jesus was a champion of diversity and a celebrator of equality. Christ did not have favorites. Christ did not design a hierarchy for his own disciples and was furious with them when they started competing over who would hold the top positions in heaven.

Major Highways

"For just as the body is one and has many members, and all the members of the body, though many, are one body, so it is with Christ. For by one Spirit we were all baptized into one body—Jews or Greeks, slaves or free—and all were made to drink of one Spirit."

—1 Corinthians 12:12–13

Paul's Gospel: We Are All Transformed

Paul's gospel speaks of spiritual transformation. To know Jesus and to believe in Jesus is to be transformed. The transformation of which Paul speaks is a total reordering of values. It is seeing the world through new eyes and listening with new ears. It is being in touch with a new dimension, that of your soul. Paul called this transformation living in the spirit, and he contrasted it with living in the flesh. Paul was not speaking of flesh only in sexual terms, but rather as a description of a life without faith or hope. Life in the spirit was full of hope and grounded in faith.

Major Highways

In the following passage, Paul tells the congregants of the church in Corinth that those of faith will know eternal life:

"Lo! I tell you a mystery. We shall not all sleep [die], but we shall all be changed ...."

—1 Corinthians 15:51

To Paul, life in the flesh was life in the traditional Jewish law. It was trying to be perfect and keep everyone happy. It was playing God and feeling superior. It was being compulsive about proving the depth of your faith. Paul taught that Jesus completed the law by freeing people of the need to rigidly adhere to it.

Jesus brought the gift of forgiveness, which loosened the grip of guilt and shame. Jesus chose not to celebrate those who thought they were pure, but those who were stained with sin and knew it. Jesus did not become the champion for those who climbed the ranks of some religious hierarchy, but for those who were on the bottom rung yet knew their need of God.

Jesus made all things new. He was the granter of eternal life, the completion of the transformation. His presence turned human hearts inside out and the world upside down.

Paul's Gospel: Wisdom Is for Adults Only

On the surface, it sounds as though Paul was not a very strong or effective preacher (some say he may have had a stutter) and was defending himself against criticism from the church in Corinth. He was obviously critiqued for offering a sermon that was too simple, which must have left nobody feeling particularly inspired—a common fate for many preachers.

His defense, however, is interesting and makes a sharp point. Paul says that he cannot deal with weighty subjects and spiritual matters with those who are infantile in their faith. He makes it clear that he is saving his "good stuff" for those who are far more spiritually mature. My first reaction is that this too is a pretty sad defense. But, upon further reflection, I can see Paul's point. It would take a mature faith to handle hearing the message of a crucified Messiah.

Major Highways

"When I came to you, brethren, I did not come proclaiming to you the testimony of God in lofty words or wisdom. For I decided to know nothing among you except Jesus Christ and him crucified. And I was with you in weakness and in much fear and trembling; and my speech and my message were [very plain] ....

"Yet among the mature [Christians] we do impart wisdom, although it is not a wisdom of this age or of the rulers of this age, who are doomed to pass away."

—1 Corinthians 2:1–6

The idea of a crucified Messiah was at odds with all worldly wisdom. A Messiah was to come and reign in peace. A Messiah was to wipe away all illness and hunger and human pain. How could such a Messiah come to such a brutal finish? Paul is reprimanding the church in Corinth for not recognizing that they had not yet accepted this basic tenet of faith.

The faithful folks in the Corinthian church may not have been prepared to hear the message of Jesus as the Christ. It took great maturity to hear a message that asked them to serve, sacrifice, and suffer; to accept that the first was to be last and the last first; to welcome the outcast, feed the hungry, clothe the naked, and visit the imprisoned and the sick. It takes maturity to hear a message that goes against most of what the world teaches is important. It is hard to choose to be a spiritual adult when to do so demands a good deal of spiritual discipline.

Paul tells us a lot about Jesus in his message in this letter. He speaks of a Jesus who lived and preached a message the world was prone to reject. Jesus taught his followers to view success and happiness in a whole new light. Most of all, Paul makes it clear that Jesus did not come to please the world or to be popular, but to transform the world. Jesus wanted to build a kingdom, and this kingdom would look nothing like the world as it was or is. The kingdom will be a place of peace, justice, equality, diversity, compassion, mercy and extravagant love, even love of one's enemies.

The Least You Need to Know

➤ Paul had a tremendous influence on the formation of the early Christian church and the shaping of modern faith. Because 14 of the 27 books of the Christian scriptures were letters attributed to Paul, much of how we now understand and experience Jesus Christ is the result of Paul's perspective.

➤ Paul was a zealous Jew who experienced a dramatic conversion on the road to Damascus, where he witnessed the risen Christ, and became an equally zealous Christian.

➤ Paul's gospel preached that Christ was crucified for our sins, that all people have sinned, and that there was no ranking of either sin or sinners.

➤ Paul's gospel was grounded in a message of grace. Faith in Jesus Christ transformed lives and freed people from the slavery of sin.

➤ Paul no longer believed it important to follow a religious law that strove for spiritual perfection. He believed that Jesus loved all people, flaws and all.

➤ Paul recognized that it takes a mature faith to be wise enough to believe in Jesus as the Christ and to daily be willing to choose to follow him.

Part 2

Jesus the Jew

Roots. I believe we all recognize today how important it is to understand where we came from. Our ancestry as a place and a people is vital to knowing who and why we are what we are.

The same can be said of Jesus. Jesus was a Jew—a devout Jew. His faith was that of a Jew. He was a member of a Jewish people. You cannot possibly understand his life or ministry or message without having a grasp of his background. The Jews have a distinctive sense of history. I think it is fair to say that being Jewish indelibly marks the soul with an historical trail of tears—tears of grief, sadness, happiness, and joy.

There is no way to capture the whole scope and depth of the Jewish experience, but in this part you get a sense of the integrity and dignity of these magnificent roots.

Jewish Roots: Part One

When you look at the history of the Jewish faith and people, you are convinced they are worthy of the spiritual label of God's chosen people. The sacred history of Israel begins with a promise between God and the patriarchs: Abraham, Isaac, and Jacob. Up until this point, history had set forth a humanity that was estranged from God. Before the promise, folks were scattered over the earth in confusion, war, and strife. Yet God's promise did not mean an easy life for the Jews; they had to endure many hardships before they became a nation.

Beginning with Abraham

The story of Abraham shows a new kind of history, sacred history, which records the activity of God in the lives of a people. Abraham's call comes right after the story of the Tower of Babel, a tale of God's harsh judgment on humanity, and thus offers a new vision of hope.

God chose Abraham to receive the promise. The divine promise was threefold:

➤ To possess a new land

➤ To become a great nation

➤ To be a blessing to the peoples of the earth

In accepting this promise, Abraham was summoned to leave his country for a new homeland and became the father of the Jewish people.

Major Highways

"And I will make you a great nation, and I will bless you, and make your name great, so that you will be a blessing. I will bless those who bless you, and him who curses you I will curse; and by you all the families of the earth shall bless themselves."

—Genesis 12:2–3

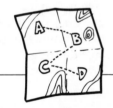

Map Key

A **covenant** is a spiritual relationship bound by faith. In this case is refers to the relationship between God and the Jews.

Yahweh is the most commonly used Jewish name for God.

The promise is a huge spiritual event. Abraham is entrusted with sharing the message of this *covenant,* and he must explain to his people that they are now in a most intimate relationship with God. This God, *Yahweh,* loves this special people like a parent. He cherishes and embraces them with respect. He sets boundaries and borders on their conduct and has expectations, hopes, and dreams for them. The Jews become God's children.

The birth of Isaac, the son of Abraham and his wife Sarah, is seen as a dramatic affirmation from God. Abraham and Sarah are quite old, and they did not expect to be able to conceive a child. (The name Isaac means "laughter." I am sure that Sarah, finding herself pregnant in her 80s, felt as though God were playing a joke on her and her husband.) Jewish scripture describes Isaac as a spiritual replica of Abraham.

Rebekah, Isaac's wife, was also barren, but divine intervention leads to the birth of two sons: Esau, the father of the Edomites, and Jacob, the ancestor of Israel. The Jewish scriptures tell us that these two were struggling in the womb, just as Edom and Israel would in history. Esau was born first, so he was destined to inherit his father's role and rights. However, Jacob shrewdly tricked him out of his birthright and father's final blessing (Genesis 25–27). In Jewish history, a blessing is a reality. Jacob's blessing, no matter how it was attained, would yield the promised results: Israel and Jacob would gain preeminence over Esau and Edom.

Jacob came into great wealth. He had two wives, Rachel and Leah; two concubines; eleven sons; all kinds of servants; and a huge flock of sheep. With this wealth, he would try to win back Esau's love with a lavish display of gifts. Jacob's favorite son, Joseph, becomes the center of a cycle of stories recorded in Genesis chapters 37 to 50. These fascinating stories ultimately tell of Joseph's rise to power in Egypt and how Joseph was able to save the land from famine. Joseph's role in Egypt's attainment of prosperity and security is seen as yet another confirmation of the original promise made to Abraham.

Scenic Overlooks

"Joseph's brothers tried to murder him by throwing him into a pit, but if they had ever been brought to trial, they wouldn't have needed Clarence Darrow to get them an acquittal in any court in the land. Not only did Joseph have offensive dreams in which he was Mr. Big and they were all groveling at his feet, but he also recounted them in sickening detail at the breakfast table the next morning. He was also his father's pet, and they seethed at the sight of the many-colored coat he flaunted while they were running around in T-shirts and dirty jeans."

—Frederick Buechner (from *Peculiar Treasures*)

Moses and the Exodus

After the death of Joseph, Jacob's family loses favor in Egypt. There had been a change in administration; a new king now presided over the land. During the sixteenth through thirteenth centuries before the birth of Christ, Egypt went through a remarkable revival. The *pharaohs* were in need of cheap labor in order to construct many ambitious projects. The Jews became state slaves and were put to work creating the cities of Rameses and Pithom in the Delta. The oppression of the Jews was devastating.

The Jewish faith is often a fearless faith. Where most modern religion and spirituality seeks to remove pain and eliminate struggle, the faith of Israel embraces the suffering experienced during this time of slavery. One would think that the Jewish faith would strive to forget a period of the seeming absence of their God, but the opposite is

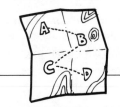

Map Key

Pharaoh was the name given to the leader of Egypt.

true. The Jews choose to recall this time as filled with the presence of God. God alone got them through this ordeal and eventually led them out of their bondage. The deliverance of the Jewish people from their slavery in Egypt, known as the Exodus, is the defining moment of Jewish faith. Jews see this historic event as a clear expression of their favored and chosen status. Only Yahweh could have managed the extraordinary events that led them to freedom.

The spiritual leader of the Exodus was Moses. Moses was not only the historical leader of Exodus, but he also became the spiritual mediator of the relationship between God and the Jewish people. Moses was born a Jew, but his mother, fearing for his safety, sent him in a basket of bulrushes down the river (Exodus 2:1–10). After he was found by an Egyptian princess, Moses was raised in the pharaoh's court, but he retained a profound sense of being a Jew.

As a young man, Moses was so appalled by a guard's beating of a Jewish slave that he murdered the guard. He then fled to the land of Midian to avoid retribution. While in Midian, Moses married the daughter of Jethro, the Midian priest. God spoke to Moses through a burning bush (another way of saying that Moses saw the light) and called him to lead the Jews out of Egypt and to deliver them from the tragedy of being state slaves.

Moses asked the pharaoh to give freedom to his people, but the pharaoh refused. God punished the pharaoh by sending plagues to Egypt: water turned to blood; frogs, gnats, and flies invaded the land; cattle became ill; the Egyptians were covered with boils; and hail, locusts, and darkness (probably a sandstorm) arrived. In the last plague, the Egyptian firstborn die, but the Jewish children are passed over. Passover is the celebration of this sign from God that he was indeed on their side. (These events are recorded in Exodus chapters 7 to 11.)

Major Highways

"... Sing to the Lord, for he has triumphed gloriously; the horse and his rider he has thrown into the sea!"

—Exodus 15:21

The pharaoh finally let the Jews leave, but after they left, he decided to pursue them to where they were camped near the Red Sea. The Jews' crossing of the Red Sea, probably at the eastern shore of Lake Timsah, occurred when the eastern wind drove the waters back. Even today, there are times when the waters recede sufficiently to allow passage in this shallow area. To the Jews, the timing of that eastern wind that allowed them to pass was no coincidence; it was the action of a loving God. The Jews walked across this soggy bottom, but the pursuing Egyptian soldiers on horseback and chariots became hopelessly mired in the mud.

The Wandering in the Wilderness

The Jews turned their backs on the land of Egypt and journeyed into the wilderness of the Sinai. The journey was incredibly tough, and food and water were scarce. They were under attack from hostile desert tribes, primarily the Amalekites. They felt physically and spiritually lost. Where was their God? The people were growing increasingly upset with Moses and questioned his ability to lead.

Finally, Moses managed to guide the staggering band into the oasis at Sinai. Here they were able to rest and gain spiritual renewal. They had time to look back upon the extraordinary events that had led them to this place. They could not deny the crucial nature of Moses' leadership, nor the active presence of God. It was in Sinai that they entered into a new covenant with God. With Moses as the chosen interpreter, the new covenant was conceived in the following experiences and events (as described in Exodus chapters 19 to 24):

Major Highways

"... Thus says the Lord God: On the day when I chose Israel, I swore to the seed of the house of Jacob, making myself known to them in the land of Egypt, I swore to them, saying, I am the Lord your God. On that day I swore to them that I would bring them out of the land of Egypt into a land that I had searched out for them, a land flowing with milk and honey, the most glorious of all lands."

—Ezekiel 20:5–6

➤ Yahweh called the people of Israel to be his private possession.

➤ Yahweh called the Jewish people to be a community separated from the world.

➤ Yahweh commissioned the Jews to be a nation of priests.

➤ A meal was celebrated on the mountain's summit. The participants were all leaders, including Moses, Aaron and his two sons, and 70 elders. During this meal, the presence of God became vivid and tangible.

➤ At the base of the mountain, Moses built an altar for another ceremony. Twelve pillars were erected to represent the 12 tribes of Israel. Moses then sprinkled some of the blood saved from animal sacrifices on the people as a sign of the new covenant.

➤ The Jewish people received the law, which included conditional law that goes case by case and absolute law that has no conditions at all. The Ten Commandments are an example of absolute law. The law was seen as a means of expressing the covenantal bond and was accepted by the Jews in gratitude for all that God had already done.

Points of Interest

The Ten Commandments, known as the Decalogue, are as follows:

1. You shall have no other gods before me.

2. You shall not make for me any graven images or any likeness.

3. You shall not invoke the Name of Yahweh your God in vain.

4. Remember the Sabbath day to keep it holy.

5. Honor your father and your mother.

6. You shall not commit murder.

7. You shall not commit adultery.

8. You shall not steal.

9. You shall not bear false witness against your neighbor.

10. You shall not covet your neighbor's house.

The Promised Land

The Jews spent 40 years wandering in the wilderness south of Beer-sheba. (Forty years was a common expression for a full generation or for simply describing a very long time.) During this period of wandering, Moses was again under attack. Dissension had broken out in his own tribe, the tribe of Levi, and his brother Aaron and Aaron's wife Miriam led a revolt. Several factors led to this period of strife:

➤ Lack of food and water

➤ Tribal rivalries

➤ Power struggles for leadership

➤ The human difficulty in maintaining a strong faith

➤ Exhaustion and boredom

➤ Questioning whether they were better off than before

Major Highways

"And you shall remember all the ways which your Lord your God has led you these forty years in the wilderness, that he might humble you, testing you to know what was in your heart, whether you would keep his commandments or not. And he humbled you and let you hunger and fed you with manna, which you did not know, nor did your fathers know; that he might make you know that man does not live by bread alone, but that man lives by everything that proceeds out of the mouth of the Lord."

—Deuteronomy 8:2–3

During this time of wandering and grave doubts, two sacred objects helped to hold the Jews together:

➤ **The Tent of Meeting.** Moses would pitch this tent in order to hold his encounters with God. It marked a place of sacred sanctuary.

➤ **The Ark of the Covenant.** A portable throne, upon which Yahweh was thought to sit.

The Jews' belief in the active involvement and presence of God, symbolically represented by the Ark of the Covenant and Tent of Meeting, gave them the faith and courage to move forward to Canaan, the Promised Land.

The Jews who originally fled Egypt, including Moses, did not survive to enter Canaan. Joshua lead a whole new generation of Jews to conquer Canaan. Though it was believed to be primarily the result of faithful obedience, Joshua's success in leading this invasion can also be attributed to the lay of the land and the historical situation in the Fertile Crescent. The warlike Jews, spearheaded by the tribes of Benjamin and Joseph, were able to conquer a good chunk of the central hill country from the Canaanites.

The Jews overcame extraordinary difficulties and issues to succeed in gaining access to the Promised Land. The experience of suffering and sacrifice was a true testing of faith. During this time, many Jews questioned whether God was present or absent and wondered whether the Jews were blessed or cursed? Many of these same themes crop up in the life story of Jesus.

The Tribal Confederacy

Joshua was well aware of the challenge the Canaanite culture presented to the Jewish people and faith, so he gathered all the tribes of Israel together at Shechem. Here Joshua reviewed with his people the sacred history of the Exodus, the reception of the law at Sinai, the divine guidance during the lengthy period of wandering, and the successful conquering of the Promised Land. Joshua skillfully confronted his people with their responsibility to renew the covenant first made at Sinai. Israel was the name of the covenant community.

The 12 tribes of Israel were thus loosely formed into a tribal confederacy. Their faith bound the tribes together. The confederacy also brought some degree of uniformity of language, customs, and political interests. It was also assumed that if there were a military emergency, the tribes would be united in facing a common foe.

The tribal confederacy was informally governed by judges, who were much more than what we think of as a judge. These judges claimed and held a unique spiritual role in the community. They were not a dynasty. Each judge was selected for one or more of the following reasons:

➤ Possessing great spiritual power and charisma (Gideon)

➤ Reflecting Yahweh's spirit (Gideon)

➤ Success in battle (Deborah)

➤ Physical prowess (Samson)

➤ Wisdom in interpreting the religious law (Samuel)

Judges ruled the confederacy from 1200 to 1020 B.C.

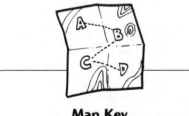

Map Key

Prophets were messengers of God, whose words sought to keep God's people in line.

Israel Becomes Like a Nation

Samuel was the last great judge of the tribal confederacy, and though he was not a charismatic leader, he was a prophetic one. The role of the *prophet* thereafter played a dominant role in the life of Israel. Under Samuel's powerful spiritual influence and guidance, Israel was able to move from governance by a tribal confederacy to governance by monarchy.

This change was necessary because the tribal confederacy was simply not stable enough. The confederacy had always encouraged tribal independence, but because of threats from outside political forces, namely the Philistines, it became apparent that a more stable form of government was necessary.

King Saul

Initially, Samuel clung to his leadership role. He warned the Jews of the tyranny that might come with the selection of a king, and he opposed the idea of one person at the top. Though a judge had power, the people granted this power. A king, on the other hand, could claim powers not given by his constituents and thus went against the sacred notion of God's chosen people. The people insisted, however, and Samuel finally relented. In I Samuel 12, Samuel gives his valedictory speech as the last judge of Israel, and Saul is acclaimed king at the city of Mizpah. Saul was proclaimed a deliverer, and once again the hand of God was invoked. Saul was God's response to the cries of his people.

Israel was constantly under the threat of Philistine aggression. The Philistines had come to Canaan at the beginning of the Iron Age and were successful in mastering the use of this new metal. They made weaponry and farming tools and implements. The Israelites had no such weaponry or equipment, and the Philistines were in the position to dominate the Israelites both economically and politically. Under Saul's reign, however, the Jews gained mastery of the use of iron and successfully defeated the Philistines. Later, the Philistines defeated Saul at Mount Gilboa. However, the Philistines chose not to wipe out all pockets of resistance, and David soon led a regrouping of Jewish forces. David successfully defeated the Philistine armies and went on to establish a dynasty that lasted nearly 400 years.

Major Highways

"Then all the elders of Israel gathered together and came to Samuel at Ramah, and said to him, 'Behold you are old and your sons do not walk in your ways; now appoint for us a king to govern us like all the nations.'"

—1 Samuel 8:4–5

King David

David's life and reign was the stuff of legend:

➤ He was an obscure shepherd who wound up playing harp at King Saul's court.

➤ He slayed the giant Goliath with a slingshot. (Shepherds could kill wild animals at great distances with a slingshot, so this was not an extraordinary event.)

➤ He lead a band of outlaws and became a Robin Hood figure in the minds of his people.

➤ He married Michal, Saul's daughter, and later liquidated Saul's male heirs.

➤ At age 37, he was the unchallenged ruler of Israel. He declared Jerusalem, the City of David, as the capital and brought the Ark of the Covenant to Jerusalem.

➤ He established a special class of men called "servants to the king" and made it known that God would now communicate to his people through David. A census was taken to remind everyone that their allegiance was to David, not to the tribal unit.

➤ David's leadership was threatened by his own sons; Absalom lead a revolt in Judah.

Ultimately, David was extolled as Israel's great king. He centralized power and established Israel as a great nation.

Scenic Overlooks

"He had feet of clay like the rest of us if not more so—self-serving and deceitful, lustful and vain—but on the basis of that dance alone, you can see why it was David more than anybody else that Israel lost her heart to and why, when Jesus of Nazareth came riding into Jerusalem on his flea-bitten mule a thousand years later, it was as the Son of David that they hailed him."

—Frederick Buechner (from *Peculiar Treasures*)

King Solomon

With Egypt in decline and Assyria yet to be a true power, the time was ripe for Israel to declare itself a mighty empire. No other king, not even David, ever reigned in greater material splendor than Solomon, and his name came to represent worldly wealth. The age of Solomon was dominated by the conflict between culture and faith.

Solomon's 20-year long building campaign utilized forced labor and resulted in the following achievements:

➤ A magnificent temple

➤ A massive palace complex

➤ The building of "chariot cities" outside Jerusalem for defense

➤ A fleet of ships at Ezion-geber on the Gulf of Aqabah, Israel's first seaport

In addition to building things, Solomon maintained a huge harem and was known as a great lover of women. He also was open-minded to the religious practices of his foreign wives.

The Least You Need to Know

➤ The patriarchs—Abraham, Isaac, and Jacob—received the divine promise that the Jews were God's chosen people.

➤ Moses was called by God to lead the Jews out of bondage in Egypt.

➤ At Sinai, the Jews received the law, which served to bind them together and to God.

➤ After 40 years of the Jews wandering in the wilderness, Joshua led a whole new generation of Jews into the Promised Land, Canaan.

➤ As a result of the threat of foreign forces, a loose confederacy of 12 tribes was formed. The tribal confederacy was ruled by judges, who were charismatic spiritual leaders and successful warriors.

➤ King David centralized Israel's power in himself and was revered as Israel's greatest king. His son, Solomon, led a 20-year building campaign and achieved great material wealth.

Jewish Roots: Part Two

The tribal confederacy was never able to heal the numerous rifts between the tribes of Israel, and even David's centralizing reign managed only a superficial healing of the split. The northern tribes were never comfortable with the faith and customs of the southern tribes, so the kingdom divided upon the death of Solomon in 922 B.C. The southern tribes of Judah maintained allegiance to the Davidic dynasty and were first ruled by Rehoboam, son of Solomon. Israel was ruled by Jeroboam, who was eventually denounced as the man who led Israel into sin. Jeroboam sought to reform the faith of the northern tribes of Israel.

The history of the divided kingdom is vast and complex, and I cannot possibly do it justice in the confines of this book. The important thing to keep in mind is that the entire period was one of religious and political upheaval and was filled with a ceaseless turnover of leadership and power, the trauma of military defeat, and political exile. The Jewish people and faith were split into two camps. The influences of foreign religions and cultures were rampant. During this time of instability, prophets and prophecy took root within the Jewish faith.

The Prophets

Prophets were messengers sent by God. Their authority was not in themselves but in the one who sent them. Their message, delivered in a time of great religious confusion, was one of returning to a purity of faith. Prophets told the truth and felt called and compelled by God to tell their people not what they wanted to hear, but what they needed to hear. Prophets were fearless in their faith and unflinching in their devotion to their God. Prophecy was intimately connected to politics, economics, and societal values and ethics. The prophets felt inspired by God (a state often referred to as ecstatic) to call their people to a renewal of faith.

The following themes are common to the prophets and their messages and calling:

➤ The prophets believed God had something to say and chose them to deliver this message.

➤ The messages were not easy to hear, and the prophets were not popular.

➤ Prophets called their people to task for their sins, especially the neglect of the poor, the widowed, and the imprisoned.

➤ Prophets railed against injustice and oppression.

➤ Prophets despised the worship of money and things.

➤ Prophets called their people back to focusing on God and showing themselves to be his people.

➤ Prophets sought to bring a unity of faith.

➤ Prophets sometimes saw military defeat or captivity as the result of faithlessness.

➤ Prophets saw trust in God's will to be the most critical matter of faith.

➤ Prophets sought to have their people focus their love on God and their neighbor.

➤ Prophets were intolerant of the influence of foreign religions or any other spiritual distractions.

➤ Prophets celebrated the equality of all believers.

Major Highways

This passage records Samuel's declaration that Saul shall be king:

"... and there, as you come to the city, you will meet a band of prophets coming down from the high place with harp, tambourine, flute, and lyre before them, prophesying. Then the spirit of the Lord will come mightily upon you, and you shall prophesy with them and be turned into another man."

—1 Samuel 10:5–6

The following is a brief review of the major biblical prophets and their messages.

Micaiah

Micaiah mocked the paid professional prophets Ahab, leader of Israel, and Jehoshaphat, leader of Judah. He was a prophet of doom and predicted that Syria would defeat Israel. His prophecy proved correct, and the 400 professional prophets were proven wrong.

Elijah

Elijah was the greatest ninth-century B.C. prophet during the later reign of Ahab. Jezebel, Ahab's wife, tried to destroy Israel's covenantal faith and imported the Baal religion from Phoenicia. Elijah predicted a drought and directly challenged the prophets of Baal, the god of fertility, on Mt. Carmel. Ahab eventually repented to Elijah for his wife having conspired to kill Naboth, owner of a vineyard he had coveted.

Amos

Amos was active in Israel during the reign of Jeroboam II. Amos was a native of Judah and sought to remind the northern tribes of Israel that they were united in faith with the southern tribes. Amos also predicted doom: Israel would fall. Amos told Israel that her punishment would be severe because she knew God. He was merciless in his attacks on Israel's faithlessness. He chastised public leaders for reveling in luxury and being corrupted by indulgence. He called his people to repent.

Hosea

Hosea's prophetic career took place during the last years of Jeroboam II and the period of instability that followed his death. Like Amos, Hosea predicted doom for Israel, but he also offered the hope of restoration and renewal.

Isaiah

Isaiah had deep affection for Jerusalem and was committed to the Davidic dynasty and lineage. He

Major Highways

Here the prophet Amos tells his audience, the people of Israel, of coming judgment. Their faith fails to be grounded in acts of mercy and justice, and God is displeased:

"Take away from me the noise of your songs; to the melody of your harps I will not listen. But let justice roll down like waters, and righteousness like an ever-flowing stream."

—Amos 5:23–24

Major Highways

Hosea's wife Gomer had been unfaithful to him, but Hosea forgave her and restored her as his wife. In this quote, he compares the unfaithfulness of the people of Israel to that of a fickle woman:

"For the spirit of harlotry is within them, and they know not the Lord."

—Hosea 5:4

was called in the Temple of Solomon, where he had a vision of God being lifted up on a heavenly throne. Isaiah reaffirmed that the greatest resource in times of trouble was faith. He advocated total trust in God.

Major Highways

Isaiah's earliest message was that the Day of Yahweh would be dark and that God would send forth judgment on human pride and self-sufficiency:

"And the haughtiness of man shall be humbled, and the pride of men shall be brought low; and the Lord alone will be exalted in that day."

—Isaiah 2:17

During Isaiah's time, Syria and Israel formed an alliance against Judah, and Isaiah predicted both the downfall of this alliance as well as disaster for Judah. He went on to predict the coming of a child Messiah from the House of David. This child would first endure the ravages of the Assyrian invasion but would eventually lead Judah back to a time of peace and prosperity. This prophecy is fulfilled when Joseph and Mary, both descendants of David, have a son named Jesus.

Ahaz, the Judean ruler, paid homage to the Assyrian king, Tiglath-pileser. This homage was final evidence of Judah's complete lack of faith. Isaiah withdrew into a small, prophetic circle of a faithful few. In his later years, Isaiah saw Assyria as the rod of God's anger. However, he made a sudden and unexplained change and counseled against capitulating to the Assyrians. Isaiah envisioned the building of a New Jerusalem by the remaining faithful.

Micah

Micah may have been a disciple of Isaiah. He saw the city as the source of spiritual destruction. He was a rural prophet who was appalled by the disparity of the actions of Yahweh and those of his people. One of Micah's prophecies is that the Messiah would be born in Bethlehem (Micah 5:2), the eventual birthplace of Jesus.

Zephaniah

Zephaniah saw the judgment of God taking place in the affairs of history. His central thrust was that the Day of Yahweh was near. He saw Judah as a shameful land, loaded with paganism and spiritually rebellious. He sought a group of repentant people.

Major Highways

"... [W]hat does the Lord require of you but to do justice, and to love kindness, and to walk humbly with your God?"

—Micah 6:8

Jeremiah

Jeremiah was the most personal and human of all the prophets. He freely admitted his loneliness and pain, his shame and guilt, as well as his abundant fear. Jeremiah spent time in prison and also did frequent battle with court prophets, but he saw crisis and catastrophe as cathartic. He declared a new covenant (Jeremiah 31:31–34) and asserted the following:

➤ All initiative was God's.

➤ All authority was God's.

➤ The Torah would be written upon the human heart.

➤ The new covenant would create a new people.

➤ This new covenant would rest upon divine forgiveness.

➤ A New Age was coming.

➤ The Messiah will soon arrive—the coming of Jesus Christ is predicted.

Jeremiah pictured God as a potter and Judah as a shattered vessel. God would create a new vessel made from better clay.

Major Highways

Jeremiah announced that the Day of Yahweh would be a dark day of bitter defeat. God was angry over Judah's pagan practices and called the temple a den of robbers. Jeremiah said that God's wrath would be sent in the form of an invasion by Babylon:

"Your ways and your doings have brought this upon you. This is your doom, and it is bitter; it has reached your very heart."

—Jeremiah 4:18

Ezekiel

Ezekiel was a prophet to those in exile in Babylonia. Like Isaiah, Ezekiel was called by a vision of God seated in majesty on a transcendent throne. He believed that the fall of Jerusalem to Nebuchadnezzar was divinely ordained and that exile in Babylonia was to be accepted as God's will. He made it clear that he experienced Israel as a sinful nation that was forever breaking its covenant with God. Ezekiel stated that each individual had to be responsible for his own destiny.

Ezekiel was not a rugged individualist anymore than Jeremiah was, but he also managed to personalize his message. After the fall of Jerusalem, Ezekiel preached a message of hope. He offered the vision of a good shepherd who would lead his flock to safety. The good shepherd was Yahweh, who would pay special attention to those sheep who were lost or lame.

Major Highways

Ezekiel encourages Israel to become more compassionate, and grounded in mercy:

"A new heart I will give you, and a new spirit I will put within you; and I will take out of your flesh the heart of stone and give you a heart of flesh."

—Ezekiel 36:26

Major Highways

"Turn to me and be saved, all the ends of the earth! For I am God, and there is no other."

—Isaiah 45:22

Second Isaiah

Second Isaiah was a prophet of the Babylonian exile who wrote almost 150 years after the Isaiah of Jerusalem. Unlike first Isaiah, whose message was one of harsh warning, second Isaiah offered a message of pardon and grace.

A central message of second Isaiah was that of a new exodus. This new exodus would lead to a new creation and the completion of redemption. Israel was to become a light to all the nations. Through Israel, God would achieve world salvation.

Second Isaiah introduces the idea of "the servant of the Lord." The concept meant both an individual as the servant as well as Israel as the servant. This servant would attain victory through suffering, would wear the garb of humiliation, and would be a man of sorrows. He would be offered as a vicarious sacrifice for all people and would ultimately be exalted.

Christianity came to understand the entire mission and ministry of Jesus Christ in the light of these servant poems from second Isaiah. Christians feel certain that Jesus was the servant, and they see Jesus as the fulfillment of Israel's history. According to Christian tradition, Jesus opened his ministry in Nazareth by reading from the scroll of Isaiah and saying, "this scripture is now fulfilled in your hearing (Luke 4:16)." The passage that he read was:

"The Spirit of the Lord God is upon me, because the Lord has anointed me to bring good tidings to the afflicted; he has sent me to bind up the brokenhearted, to proclaim liberty to the captives, and the opening of the prison to those who are bound; to proclaim the year of the Lord's favor, and the day of vengeance of our God; to comfort all who mourn ..."

—Isaiah 61:1–2

This passage becomes the actual call Jesus Christ claims as the definition of his ministry. The linkage here between the ministry and message of the prophets and those of John the Baptist and Jesus Christ is unmistakable.

Under Foreign Domination

In the early sixth century B.C., the Babylonians demolished Jerusalem and Temple of Solomon, laid waste to much of the land of Judah, and led the political and religious leadership, as well as thousands of their countrymen, into captivity. The time of Babylonian captivity became another defining moment in the life of the Jews, a traumatic yet sacred event they chose never to forget.

The *Persians* overthrew the Babylonians and allowed the Jewish exiles to return home. The Persians were quite tolerant of the Jewish faith. Though the Jews had no political power, they were able to freely develop their own religious life and thought. By the end of the fifth century B.C., Jerusalem was again the center of Jewish religious and social life.

When Alexander of Greece conquered Persia, the Jews met him as a great liberator. After Alexander's death, the Jews were subjected first to the Ptolemies and then the Seleucids, but they basically were treated with the same religious tolerance. During the reign of Antiochus IV, however, the Jewish faith would meet its greatest threat since the Babylonian captivity.

Antiochus IV had state financial worries due to vast holdings in the east, so he chose to raise the taxes on the Jews. He also offered the job of high priest to the highest bidder, and the Jewish high priest Onias was replaced by Jason, a major supporter of Antiochus IV. Antiochus IV saw himself as a connoisseur of Greek culture and sought to impose this worldview on all his subjects. Young Jewish men were forced to exercise in the nude at gymnasiums constructed by Jason, and the marks of circumcision were surgically removed on some Jews.

The Hasidim, or pious ones, was formed to fight off all efforts to adopt Greek ways, and Antiochus made a decision to destroy the Jewish faith. Under penalty of death, Jews were forbidden to …

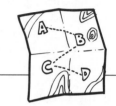

Map Key

Persians were the people of the Persian Empire, which was dominated by the worship of idols. The Jewish faith was threatened by association with the many cultic practices of the Persian Empire.

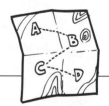

Map Key

The **Greek Empire** was dominated by worship of a great many gods. The Jewish belief in one God was threatening to the Greeks, and vice versa.

➤ Circumcise.

➤ Celebrate religious festivals.

➤ Observe the Sabbath.

➤ Own or read a copy of the Torah.

To further humiliate the Jews, Antiochus set up an altar to Zeus in Jerusalem, upon which swine were sacrificed. To enforce his edicts, he stationed troops throughout Israel.

The Jews revolted under the leadership of Mattathias. Mattathias killed a Jew he witnessed making a sacrifice at a pagan altar and fled with his five sons to the hill country that surrounded Jerusalem. There he gathered a band of followers who were ready to fight off Antiochus' oppression. The Maccabean Revolt ensued, and the Jews were led by Judas Maccabeus, the son of Mattathias. The revolt was basically guerilla warfare, because the Jews were outnumbered and had only the crudest of weapons. After a courageous effort, Judas and his men managed to win a peace treaty from Antiochus' general, Lysias. The Jews were now able to conduct traditional Jewish worship in the Temple at Jerusalem. This great victory is celebrated in the Festival of Hanukkah, the Festival of Lights.

In 63 B.C., Pompey arrived in Jerusalem, and the territory would now come under Roman rule. The political independence of the Jews was once again removed. In 40 B.C., Rome named Herod as ruler of both Judea and Samaria. Herod paid homage to Augustus Caesar, the Roman emperor, and built temples to honor him throughout Palestine and Asia Minor. Like Antiochus IV, Herod was a devout advocate of Greek culture and sought to build gymnasiums, theaters, and stadiums to encourage the Greek way of life. Herod was also ruling at the time of Jesus' birth.

From A.D. 6 to 66, 14 procurators (Roman officials) were sent to Judea. These procurators were consistently cruel in their dealings with the Jews, showing not only a lack of compassion, but a lack of wisdom as well. The tension between Rome and the Jewish people continued to mount. As time went by, an increasing number of Jews came to favor armed rebellion. During the rule of Felix (A.D. 51–60), the *Zealots* rebelled. This rebellion was lost before it began. The Roman generals Vespasian and Titus subjected the Jews to an annihilating defeat, including the destruction of the Temple of Jerusalem.

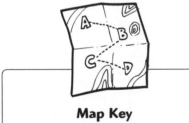

Map Key

The **Zealots** were those Jews fanatically opposed to Roman occupation and influence.

Beyond Exile

The Babylonian captivity yielded a true renewal of faith. The prophets Amos, Hosea, Isaiah, and Jeremiah had repeatedly warned the Jews about their disobedience to God and predicted the destruction that was to come. As a result, the returning exiles were determined to never repeat these spiritual mistakes. They would never again turn to foreign gods, nor would they have their faith contaminated by foreign influence or practices. They would uphold the law that God had given them. They would prove to the world that they were indeed his people, a chosen race.

The books of Ezra and Nehemiah went to great lengths to establish the Jews as a people set apart. Jews are asked not to marry foreigners, and those who had were asked to put them aside. The Jews were convinced that great efforts had to be made to avoid a recurrence of the mistakes made by their fathers, the mistakes that led to the Babylonian captivity. These efforts included the following:

➤ The Torah was made central to Jewish faith and took on a role of total authority in Jewish life. The Torah also required a multitude of sacrifices.

➤ The Sanhedrin was established as a religious court to deal with infractions against the Torah. The high priest headed the Sanhedrin.

➤ The synagogue become the vibrant center of Jewish spiritual life.

➤ Sacrificial offerings were viewed as essential to the Jewish faith. Priests were selected to oversee these ritualized offerings, and the Torah was used to ensure all priests were spiritually pure.

➤ All priests and Levites were supported by the offerings of the people.

➤ Only the high priest was allowed to enter The Holy Of Holies, the central chamber of the Temple of Jerusalem where it was believed God dwelled.

Though the Jews remained united by Torah and temple, several significant disputes arose over different interpretations of the Torah. These divergent views resulted in the formation of three distinctive sectarian groups:

➤ **The Sadducees.** The Sadducees' central guide to faith was the law of Moses, the first five books of the Old Testament. Their primary concern was the legitimate succession of the priestly office. They held dominant roles in the Temple of Jerusalem and the Sanhedrin. They were drawn from the wealthy, aristocratic, and priestly families and followed a path of peaceful coexistence with Rome. They did not want to rock the boat because they had very good seats on the boat.

➤ **The Pharisees.** Members of a lay movement who were spiritually linked to the Hasidim. The Pharisees were separatists. They paid great attention to the writings of the prophets, and they also validated the oral Torah. The piety of the Sadducees was focused on the Temple of Jerusalem, but the piety of the Pharisees was focused on Torah. The Pharisees were rigid in their absolute adherence to the law.

➤ **The Essenes.** Also spiritually descended from the Hasidim. They practiced a radical withdrawal from normal religious and social associations. The Essenes established a community in Qumran, the site of the Dead Sea Scrolls. This community believed they were living in the end time. They read the prophets as if their words were speaking directly to their present life and saw themselves as the divine remnant. They took vows of poverty and lived in expectation of two messiahs. The Messiah of Aaron was to fulfill the priestly lines, and the Messiah of Israel was to fulfill the royal line. When these messiahs came, the Essenes believed that a new temple and a new Jerusalem would be established.

The Least You Need to Know

➤ After the state of Israel divided into Israel in the north and Judah in the south, the role of the prophets intensified.

➤ Prophets were messengers sent by God to deliver a difficult and often troubling message. John the Baptist and Jesus were both prophets.

➤ The Jewish people had to live under Persian, Greek, and Roman rule and were constantly confronted by foreign influence and domination.

➤ The Jews decided that their disobedience to God was the catalyst for the Babylonian exile, and to ensure that never happened again, they strove for a purity of faith.

➤ The Temple of Jerusalem and the Torah became the unifying forces of Jewish life and faith. The Sadducees, Pharisees, and Essenes were Jewish sectarian groups formed as the result of divergent perspectives on the Torah and worship.

Part 3

Jesus the Babe, the Boy, and the Man

Have you ever walked on a swinging bridge? It is an eerie, and for some a nauseating, experience. I think of the world into which Christ was born as spiritually akin to a swinging bridge. Nothing was stable. Nothing felt grounded. The people felt rootless. Anxiety reigned. The universe was hostile. With the world in a state of flux, people began to desire the next world. In a sense, the end became the hope.

The people who lived at the time of Christ's birth were at a complete loss to comprehend the universe. Nothing seemed to make sense. Leadership was changing constantly, often overnight. Hunger and disease ravaged the land. The faithful acted faithless. The presence of pagan gods and influences was everywhere. The threat to survival was incessant. Hope appeared to have evaporated. Joy became nothing but a memory recalled at religious festivals. Hate seemed to be winning the battle with love. The people of Christ's time were indeed a people who dwelled in great darkness. In this part, you learn just what life was like during Christ's lifetime both for the people in his world and for him.

Chapter 5

The Babe and the Boy

In This Chapter

➤ The first miracle birth: Elizabeth and Zechariah have a son

➤ Mary gives birth in a Bethlehem stable

➤ Jesus is given a good Jewish upbringing

The story of Jesus' birth is recorded in the Gospel of Luke. It is a haunting, charming, and highly controversial story. This story is clearly meant to challenge traditional conceptions of the birth of a Messiah-king.

The Birth of the Baptist

Jesus' extraordinary birth story is foreshadowed in the first chapter of Luke, which tells the story of the birth of a son to Zechariah and Elizabeth. Zechariah came from the line of Aaron and was thus automatically a priest. He was considered a righteous man. He married a woman also of lineage to Aaron, named Elizabeth. The couple was childless, a state so significant within Jewish faith that it was grounds for divorce.

Zechariah was overjoyed to be serving his designated week as priest at the temple, but he was still deeply troubled by not being a father. During this time of sacred service at the temple, he had a vision. The angel Gabriel told him that he and Elizabeth would have a son. He could not believe that he would be a father because he and Elizabeth were fairly old. He was left dumbstruck; he could not utter a sound. He returned home to his beloved wife, and it was then revealed to her that she would bear a child. This child would become John the Baptist.

The angel Gabriel next visited Mary and told her that she would soon become pregnant and have a son named Jesus. To illustrate God's power to work miracles, Gabriel tells Mary that Elizabeth, who was old and thought to be infertile, is pregnant. Mary, who is a relative of Elizabeth's, visits her.

Luke made a strong case for a direct spiritual link between John the Baptist and Jesus Christ. John the Baptist was the spiritual prophet who was described as a voice crying in the wilderness and went out into the desert to call the faithful to repent and to experience a spiritual revolution.

Also in this opening chapter, Mary documents three such revolutions ordained by God:

➤ God will scatter the proud in the plans of their hearts.

➤ God will cast down the mighty, and exalt the humble.

➤ God will fill the hungry, and send the rich empty away.

Luke also set a dramatic stage for a revolutionary birth, a birth of a Messiah who would radically reverse the morals, values, and ethics of the world. This birth will turn the world upside down.

Major Highways

While visiting Elizabeth, Mary makes the following speech, known as the Magnificat:

"... 'My soul magnifies the Lord, and my spirit rejoices in God my Savior, for he has regarded the low estate of his handmaiden. For behold, henceforth all generations will call me blessed; for he who is mighty has done great things for me, and holy is his name. And his mercy is on those who fear him from generation to generation. He has shown strength with his arm, he has scattered the proud in the imagination of their hearts, he has put down the mighty from their thrones, and exalted those of low degree; he has filled the hungry with good things, and the rich he has sent empty away. He has helped his servant Israel, in remembrance of his mercy, as he spoke to our fathers, to Abraham and to his posterity forever."

—Luke 1:46–55

Mary and Joseph

Mary was young, poor, and female. At this time in history, and in this place, these three categories would have declared her useless to God. God was supposed to revere age as the context of wisdom, wealth as a sign of blessing, and maleness as the private domain of faith. Choosing Mary as the vehicle for delivering the Christ child was nothing less than scandalous. Through his description of God's choice of Mary, Luke declared that God's choices were not subject to human boundaries or borders.

Major Highways

"In those days, a decree went out from Caesar Augustus that all the world should be enrolled. This was the first enrollment, when Quirinius was governor of Syria. And all went to be enrolled, each to his own city. And Joseph also went up from Galilee from the city of Nazareth, to Judea, to the city of David, which is called Bethlehem, because he was of the house of lineage of David, to be enrolled with Mary his betrothed, who was with child. And while they were there, the time came for her to be delivered. And she gave birth to her first-born son and wrapped him in swaddling cloths, and laid him in a manger, because there was no place for them in the inn."

—Luke 2:1–7

Mary was betrothed to Joseph. Betrothal lasted for a year and was thought of as every bit as binding as marriage. If you were betrothed and the man you were betrothed to died, you were thought of as a widow. Mary became pregnant, and this point in the story is at the center of one of the great debates of the Church. Was Mary a virgin? There are reasons that you can accept that she was:

➤ You can take the literal meaning of Matthew 1:18–25.

➤ You can take the leap of faith and simply believe it to be the case.

➤ You can contend that the Messiah would not be born in any ordinary manner.

Or you can find reasons to say that she was not a virgin:

➤ The genealogies of both Luke and Matthew trace the lineage of Jesus back through Joseph.

Detours

The world continues to judge you by external appearances: how you look, what you wear, where you live, who you know, what you drive, your skin color, your religion (or lack thereof), your size and weight. Jesus was concerned solely with what is on the inside: What is the state of your soul? How tender is your heart? How open is your mind? How have you made a difference in this world?

➤ Jesus is repeatedly referred to as Joseph's son (Matthew 13:55).

➤ When Mary is looking for Jesus at the temple, where he had remained for more dialogue, she says, "Your father and I have been looking for you anxiously (Luke 2:48)."

➤ The remainder of the New Testament never mentions the virgin birth.

A young unwed mother spelled disaster. If the father of the unborn child did not agree to marry her, she would have to remain unmarried for life. Often she would be rejected by her own family and forced into begging or prostitution. By claiming to be pregnant by the Holy Spirit, Mary not only risked the wrath of Joseph, but she also risked the scorn and ridicule of her friends and neighbors. She might have been thought to be crazy.

Whether or not you believe in a virgin birth, the emphasis of the story is on Mary being a lowly woman who is fully receptive to the will of God. She is a woman of great faith. The last place on earth God should expect to find great faith is exactly where God finds it.

O Little Town of Bethlehem

The journey from Nazareth to Bethlehem was approximately 80 miles. Mary and Joseph made the long journey with Mary on the verge of delivery. As the story goes, no rooms were available for the weary travelers because the town was jammed with folks arriving for the *census*.

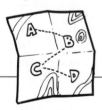

Map Key

A Roman **census** was taken every 14 years to determine the population for military conscription and taxes. Jews were not allowed to serve in the Roman army, but they were required to pay taxes.

The fact that there was no room for Mary and Joseph, parents of the Messiah, is symbolic of how often there is no room in our own lives for God. Luke contends that God is often an afterthought, or a bottom-rung priority. Humanity tends to leave God out back.

Mary was forced to give birth in a stable. Stables of this time were often caves with feeding troughs, called mangers, carved right into the walls. This setting was no Christmas card. Stables were dark, dank, and dirty. The stench would have been awful, and sleeping on a bed of hay would have been no treat. Most kings are born in palaces, but the setting for the birth of the king of the Jews, Jesus, was one more fitted to the birth of an animal or a human of the lowest social status.

The Shepherds

The first announcement of the arrival of the Messiah is to the shepherds. Shepherds were despised by the wealthy religious elite of that time. Shepherds were uneducated and were filthy much of the time. Their lack of cleanliness kept them from observing many of the ritual laws, especially those concerning washings and cleanliness. Their flocks also occupied most of their time, so they could devote little time to the Torah or the temple. These were not the sort of people you would expect to receive a holy message. Again, Luke asserts, God chooses what the world rejected.

These shepherds were probably those who raised the lambs that were sacrificed at the temple. The same shepherds who looked after the temple lambs were the first to hear of the arrival of the lamb of God, who was said to be sacrificed for the sins of the world.

Major Highways

"And in that region there were shepherds out in the field, keeping watch over their flock by night. And an angel of the Lord appeared to them, and the glory of the Lord shone around them, and they were filled with fear. And the angel said to them, 'Be not afraid; for behold, I bring you good news of a great joy which will come to all the people; for to you is born this day in the city of David a Savior, who is Christ the Lord. And this will be a sign for you: you will find a babe wrapped in swaddling cloths and lying in a manger.' And suddenly there was with the angel a multitude of the heavenly host praising God and saying, 'Glory to God in the highest and on earth peace among men with whom he is pleased!'"

"When the angels went away from them into heaven, the shepherds said to one another, 'Let us go over to Bethlehem and see this thing that has happened, which the Lord has made known to us.'"

—Luke 2:8–15

The Wise Men

The wise men are not mentioned in the Gospel of Luke but are found in the Gospel of Matthew. Matthew tells of travelers from the east following a huge star to Bethlehem. The star may have been the conjunction of Jupiter, Saturn, and Mars in

6 B.C. or even Halley's comet. These wise men were *Magi*. Magi were Persian holy men who were known for great wisdom and were skilled in the arenas of medicine, natural science, and philosophy. Magi were also known to be skilled interpreters of dreams, as well as astrologers.

Major Highways

"Now when Jesus was born in Bethlehem of Judea in the days of Herod the king, behold, wise men from the East came to Jerusalem, saying, 'Where is he who has been born king of the Jews? For we have seen his star in the East, and have come to worship him.' When Herod the king heard this, he was troubled, and all Jerusalem with him; and assembling all the chief priests and scribes of the people, he inquired of them where the Christ was to be born. They told him, 'In Bethlehem of Judea; for so it is written by the prophet: "And you, O Bethlehem, in the land of Judah, are by no means least among the rulers of Judah; for from you shall come a ruler who will govern my people Israel."'"

—Matthew 2:1–6

Matthew paints a portrait of Magi who have long hoped for the arrival of this child. The men from the east are wise enough to seek that alone which can fill the emptiness in their lives. In the story, the Magi follow the star to the stable where Jesus, Joseph, and Mary are. The Magi worship Jesus and bring him three gifts:

➤ **Gold.** The gift given to kings.

➤ **Frankincense.** The gift given to priests. This sweet perfume was used in temple services.

➤ **Myrrh.** A gift given to someone who will die. Myrrh was used in embalming.

These gifts foreshadow the life of the child to whom they were given.

Herod

In the account of the birth of Jesus, Herod the Great is portrayed as a suspicious and ruthless ruler who was crazily wary of being overthrown. Herod was only half-Jewish and was not the rightful heir to the throne of David. Many Jews held him in contempt and despised him as an interloper. Herod definitely did not want the Jews to unite around a religious figure.

Herod was a murderer. When he came to the throne, he wiped out most of the Sanhedrin (a religious court headed by the high priest). He had his own wife, Marianne, put to death, as well as her mother, Alexandra, and three of his sons, Antipater, Alexander, and Aristbulus.

Herod responded to news of the birth of the Messiah with bitterness and fear. He was not about to accept the birth of a child who might rally the Jews against him, so he gave the order to slaughter all children under the age of two in Bethlehem. (Bethlehem being a small town, there were probably about 20 to 30 children of that age.) Fortunately, as the story goes, Joseph was warned of this possibility in a dream and fled with Mary and Jesus into Egypt.

In due time, Herod died. The land over which he reigned was divided between his three remaining sons:

➤ Judea went to Archelaus.

➤ Galilee went to Herod Antipas.

➤ The region beyond Jordan and to the northeast went to Philip.

Joseph was guided to Galilee, because it was commonly believed that Herod Antipas was a far better king than Archelaus, who continued his father's murderous ways in Judea. Joseph settled in the hills south of Galilee. By climbing those hills, a boy could see the serene beauty of the Mediterranean as well as the magnificent highway from Damascus to Egypt. Jesus had been brought to Nazareth, a gateway to the world.

The Ancient Ceremonies

Every Jewish boy was circumcised on the eighth day after his birth. This ceremony was so sacred that it was one of few that could be performed on the Sabbath. At this time, the child would also be named. In accordance with their Jewish faith, Joseph and Mary had their son circumcised when he was eight days old and named him Jesus—a name given to him by the angel Gabriel, according to Luke.

In Jewish tradition, if a woman gave birth to a boy, she was considered unclean for 40 days. If she gave birth to a girl, she was not considered clean for 80 days. She was not allowed back to temple until this period of time was complete. After this time, the mother would bring an offering to the temple. Mary came with an offering of two pigeons, the offering of the poor, to mark the purification after childbirth. Wealthier women often would bring lambs instead of pigeons to mark the occasion.

Another ceremony surrounding birth was called the Redemption of the First-born. For the sum of five shekels, the parents could buy back their child from God. This sum was paid to the priests and could not be paid sooner than 31 days after the birth of the child. This ceremony was a reminder that a child was a gracious gift from God. All three ceremonies made it clear that Jesus was a Jew, that he was a child of God, that he was a gift from God.

Major Highways

"And at the end of eight days, when he was circumcised, he was called Jesus, the name given by the angel before he was conceived in the womb."

"And when the time came for their purification according to the law of Moses, they brought him up to Jerusalem to present him to the Lord (as it is written in the law of the Lord, 'Every male that opens the womb shall be called holy to the Lord') and to offer a sacrifice according to what is said in the law of the Lord, 'a pair of turtledoves, or two young pigeons.'"

—Luke 2:21–24

Jesus the Boy

What we know of the first 30 years of the life of Jesus Christ we could put in a thimble. We can, however, make some excellent deductions, some pretty trustworthy assumptions, and a few strong speculations. Donald Spoto, in his extraordinary work *The Hidden Jesus,* points out that during the times in which Jesus lived and ministered there was no such literary form as the modern biography. Like it or not, we must do some interpretation. We have to gather together anecdotes, impressions, historical references, scholarly and faith-filled perspectives, as well as our own personal "take."

Here is my take on those mysterious 30 years of the life of Jesus Christ:

➤ Jesus was the first-born son of Mary and Joseph.

➤ Joseph and Mary had five sons and an undetermined number of daughters.

➤ Joseph was a carpenter or woodworker, and Jesus as the first-born son would follow in his father's footsteps.

➤ Jesus' family was middle-class.

➤ Jesus was raised in a home that was comfortable with prayer.

➤ Jesus' family was devoutly Jewish; the family observed all Jewish ceremonies and holy days.

➤ Jesus was fluent in Hebrew and was well-read in Jewish scriptures. He would have had much of his religious education at the local synagogue in Nazareth.

➤ Jesus attended his first Passover in Jerusalem at age 12. He stayed behind at the temple to carry on further discourse with the teachers. He was recognized for his acute religious and spiritual wisdom (Luke 2:41–50). By this time he realized that he had a special relationship with God.

➤ Jesus must have lived in a home that showed unusual respect for women. His comfort with women was revolutionary for his time. To at least some degree, he must have been taught this.

➤ Jesus must have lived in a home that was deeply compassionate toward the needy and the outcast. His willingness to dine with outcasts would have been unheard of within the Jewish community. This too was learned behavior.

➤ He remained celibate. This may have been the influence of the Essenes, who felt that the end of the world was near and, therefore, that there was no need or reason to marry.

➤ Joseph died before Jesus began his ministry. Mary was at the Wedding at Cana, but no mention was made of Joseph.

➤ Up through his 20s, Jesus continued to discern his own calling. He remained an ordinary, hard-working young man with a deep faith. He somehow learned to live his faith. He did not just talk the talk like the Pharisees and scribes. He walked the walk.

➤ The Pharisees must have profoundly affected Jesus. He was well versed in the literature of the prophets, as were they, and his subsequent condemnation could only have been the result of having first passionately loved them.

Scenic Overlooks

"The entire life of Jesus up to the time of his ministry has always been called, in popular piety, the hidden life—and on it the New Testament is quite succinct: 'They went back to Galilee, to their own town of Nazareth,' writes Luke about the family after his birth, 'and Jesus increased in wisdom, in stature, and in favor with God and with people.' And that is the digest of more than thirty years. Still, it is possible to say something about the contours of life at the time and to have at least some general idea of the kind of man Jesus was becoming during this long hidden period."

—Donald Spoto (from *The Hidden Jesus*)

The Least You Need to Know

➤ The birth of Jesus Christ was not in any way what the world expected for the arrival of a Messiah-King. The young unwed mother, the stable, the shepherds, and the Magi from the east all broke the conventional mold.

➤ The Gospel of Luke offered a peaceful accounting of the birth of Christ. Luke's perspective established a close physical and spiritual bond between Jesus and the poor and the needy.

➤ The Gospel of Matthew offered a much more chaotic version of Jesus' birth, dominated by the insane suspicions of Herod the Great.

➤ Joseph and Mary observed all the appropriate Jewish ceremonies concerning the birth of a son and raised Jesus in a middle-class, devoutly Jewish home.

➤ Jesus was greatly influenced by the Pharisees and prophetic literature. Throughout his youth and young adulthood, his awareness of his own unique spiritual role slowly began to reveal itself to him.

Chapter 6

Jesus the Man

In This Chapter

➤ John the Baptist baptizes Jesus

➤ The devil tempts Jesus

➤ Twelve diverse disciples choose to follow Jesus

➤ Jesus is rejected, gets angry, grieves, makes friends, and dies—just like the rest of us

---

In the film *The Last Temptation of Christ* (based on the wonderful book by Nikos Kazanstakis), director Martin Scorcese, a deeply spiritual man who once trained for the priesthood, brilliantly portrays Christ's humanity. Jesus questions himself, exhibits a violent temper, withers with fear, and expresses sexuality (although he remains celibate). The film depicts a Jesus who was true to his calling to be a whole human being.

My faith in Jesus Christ is rooted in the reality that he completely understands who and what and why I am. His grace is grounded in loving the all of me. I cherish Christ's choice to celebrate all of life and being human. I treasure his celebration of diversity. I could not stand to have my faith focus only on what lies beyond while treating this life as some kind of endurance test that nobody passes. This chapter describes how Jesus embraced his humanity and all of ours.

The Baptism

John the Baptist was one wild and crazy guy. He was not the kind of young man a girl would bring home to meet the family. Except for the times when he preached and baptized people, he lived alone in the desert. He ate honey and locusts, wore a garment made of scratchy camel hair, and must have looked like a lunatic. His sermons gave new meaning to the idea of fire and brimstone, and his baptisms were full dunkings in the Jordan River. Those who came to be baptized saw him as a prophet.

Major Highways

"'I baptize you with water for repentance, but he who is coming after me is mightier than I, whose sandals I am not worthy to carry; he will baptize you with the Holy Spirit and with fire. His winnowing fork is in his hand, and he will clear his threshing floor and gather his wheat into the granary, but the chaff he will burn with unquenchable fire.'"

"... And when Jesus was baptized, he went up immediately from the water, and behold, the heavens were opened and he saw the Spirit of God descending like a dove, and alighting on him; and lo, a voice from heaven, saying, 'This is my beloved Son, with whom I am well pleased.'"

—Matthew 3:11–17

John the Baptist was a man of passionate faith, with a fiery message:

➤ He indirectly demanded that his people claim their sin and their need for a spiritual cleansing.

➤ He called his people to repent.

➤ He called his people to lead holy lives.

➤ He told these orthodox Jews not to rely on their ancestry to Abraham as a defense for their disobedience.

➤ He called the scribes and Pharisees a brood of vipers.

➤ He predicted that the Messiah would come with fire to purify their souls and warm their hearts.

➤ He offered a radical call to religious renewal.

One day, Jesus came to John to be baptized. At first, John was shocked to be asked by Jesus to conduct his baptism. He made it clear that he believed that Jesus should be doing the baptizing, but ultimately he relented and chose to be obedient.

Jesus had waited 30 years for this moment. He had carefully chosen this time and event as the symbolic beginning of his ministry. Why?

➤ Jesus saw in John the Baptist a prophetic and passionate faith.

➤ John the Baptist had created a spiritual path that Jesus wanted to follow. John had laid down a profound challenge to the religious establishment and was calling them to total transformation.

➤ Jews were not baptized. Baptism was for sinners and proselytes. Jesus' baptism was to be a powerful symbol of redemption.

➤ Jesus' baptism also symbolized a new beginning. In case anyone missed the symbolism, a voice from the heavens declared after the baptism, "This is my beloved Son, with whom I am well pleased." This quote made it clear that Jesus was the suffering servant that had been prophesied in Jewish scripture.

➤ Those who came to be baptized by John were searching for something more than they were receiving from traditional faith, and were open to the idea that Jesus was the longed-for Messiah.

➤ The baptism of Jesus linked him with humanity, a bond that would eventually move him toward the cross.

By using John the Baptist as the spiritual catalyst for his ministry, Jesus made it clear that he knew that he would meet much of the same ridicule and rejection that must have haunted John. I cannot think of a more dynamic way to embrace humanity and your own humanness than to willingly set upon a course destined to bring sorrow and pain to yourself. There was nothing about being human that Jesus would avoid or ignore and nothing he would not embrace with his grace.

The Temptation

Temptation is a reality for everyone. It is a major component of life, and it is also vital to faith. The temptation is to play God and not to obey God. The temptation is to follow our own will, and not the guidance of God. Temptation forces us to make choices, and faith is about making choices. Faith is about becoming a slave to God to be truly free—free to make the right choices. This is the paradox and the problem of human existence. To fully gain our human freedom, we must strive to conform our human will to the will of God. This is the primary test of faith.

Jesus was tempted in the desert and chose to be tempted. He went out to face his demons. Jews were not raised to run from grief, pain, or suffering. They were taught to make all of life welcome, including their human temptations.

The Bible says that Jesus spent a season in hell. He went out to a limestone quarry called the Devastation (where the heat must have been blistering) to grapple with the devil:

➤ The first temptation was to turn stone into bread. Jesus was being tempted to bribe people to follow him by doing magic tricks.

➤ The second temptation was fascinating and frightening. The devil offered all the riches and splendors of the world if Jesus followed him. Note that the devil is the one who owns the riches of the world to give them away. Jesus was tempted with power, popularity, and possessions, just as we are. Jesus was asked to choose his allegiance, which is the test of faith we face every single day.

➤ The third temptation was to be sensational, to do something stupendous. Jesus was asked to throw himself off the pinnacle of the Temple of Jerusalem and to let the angels catch him. Jesus was wise enough to know that what is spectacular never lasts. Service and sacrifice, on the other hand, are eternal. The choice of that which is of eternal value is made as the result of the satisfaction and joy it can produce.

Major Highways

"And Jesus ... was tempted by the devil. And he ate nothing in those days .... The devil said to him, 'If you are the Son of God, command this stone to become bread.' And Jesus answered him, 'It is written, "Man shall not live by bread alone."' And the devil took him up, and showed him all the kingdoms of the world in a moment of time, and said to him, 'To you I will give all this authority and their glory; for it has been delivered to me, and I give it to whom I will. If you, then, will worship me, it shall all be yours.'"

—Luke 4:1–8

The Rejection

Jesus chose to attend Sabbath services at the synagogue, as was his habit—another indication of his being raised in a devoutly Jewish home. Jesus then read scripture from the prophet Isaiah. The scripture he read concerned the suffering servant and dealt directly with the belief that the Messiah would come to bring a message of peace and joy to those who were poor, lost, outcast, or in prison. (The Jewish audience would also have understood this statement as paying a back-handed compliment to Gentiles.) He then did something that no one expected: He declared that he was the fulfillment of that scripture.

Imagine what it was like for the people of Nazareth to accept the notion the Jesus was the Messiah. These folks knew Jesus as a boy and as a teenager. They knew his family. They had probably witnessed him being rude, misbehaving, or making some silly mistake. He could not possibly have been the suffering servant. He could not have been the chosen one. He was not special enough. He wasn't unique. He was just one of them.

Major Highways

"And he began to say to them, 'Today this scripture has been fulfilled in your hearing.' And all spoke well of him, and wondered at the gracious words which proceeded out of his mouth; and they said, 'Is not this Joseph's son?' And he said to them, 'Doubtless you will quote to me this proverb, "Physician, heal yourself; what we have heard you did at Capernaum, do here also in your own country."' And he said, 'Truly, I say to you, no prophet is acceptable in his own country. But in truth, I tell you, there were many widows in Israel in the days of Elijah, when the heaven was shut up three years and six months, when there came a great famine over all the land; and Elijah was sent to none of them but only to Zarephath, in the land of Sidon, to a woman who was a widow. And there were many lepers in Israel in the time of the prophet Elisha; and none of them was cleansed, but only Naaman the Syrian.' When they heard this, all in the synagogue were filled with wrath. And they rose up and put him out of the city, and led him to the brow of the hill on which their city was built, that they might throw him down headlong. But passing through the midst of them he went away."

—Luke 4:21–30

Prophets are without honor in their own land. We fail to listen to those we know, because we assume they cannot know more than us. If we know their humanness, we seem unwilling to claim their divinity. God has no such problem. God is able to anoint humanness and divinity at the same time. In that humble good boy from Nazareth, God saw a man whose faith was sufficient to save the world. The world sees humanness as a sign of weakness, whereas God experiences it as the doorway to divinity. The people of Jesus' hometown said, "He cannot possibly be The One!" God alone knew that Jesus was the one and only.

Points of Interest

Scripture tells us that in our weakness God is glorified. What does this mean? It means that when we are on our knees long enough to know we are human, that we are not God, we are also then open to embracing an intimate relationship with God. To the world, human flaws and failings are thought to discredit one from serving the Lord. From God's perspective, those flaws are the required qualifications.

John the Baptist preached a message of doom. His preaching was an urgent call to shape up or ship out. Jesus came bearing much better news. He came telling us that the world would steadily improve if we swamped it with a wave of grace. His message was softer, kinder, and far more hopeful.

Major Highways

"The Passover of the Jews was at hand, and Jesus went up to Jerusalem. In the temple, he found those who were selling oxen and sheep and pigeons and the money-changers at their business. And making a whip of cords, he drove them all, with the sheep and oxen, out of the temple; and he poured out the coins of the money-changers and overturned their tables. And he told those who sold the pigeons, 'Take these things away; you shall not make my Father's house a house of trade.'"

—John 2:13–17

The Temper

The Passover celebration took place every year at the Temple of Jerusalem, and every Jewish male was expected to make the pilgrimage to this festival. Passover was only one day, but the rest of the week was the Feast of Unleavened Bread. The temple was an imposing sight, and thousands of travelers would have made their way to Jerusalem to attend services. The court of the Gentiles would have been quite crowded. Added to the chaos was the presence of merchants and money-changers. The temple tax had to be paid in local currency, and sacrifices had to be offered for atonement of sins. The religious leaders felt that the revenues from these booths would help with temple upkeep and provide convenience for out-of-town visitors. The truth is that these booths kept people from their true purpose: worship. This infuriated Jesus.

My minister for confirmation class was careful to say that Jesus was not truly angry in this situation but was showing righteous indignation. Wrong! Jesus was ticked off big time. I think using a whip to drive out the merchants and money-changers and turning over tables qualifies as rage. However, I don't think Jesus was out of control. I think just the opposite: He was in complete control of the situation. He was furious with the mockery being made of worship and the house of God, and he expressed it dramatically and without hesitation. He did so because he was comfortable with being human, and part of being human is being really angry at times.

Scenic Overlooks

"My home is here. I feel just at home overseas, but I think my roots are here and my language is here and my rage is here and my hope is here. You know where your home is because you've been there long enough. You know all the peculiarities of the people around you, because you are one of them."

—Pieter-Dirk Uys

Points of Interest

When the Passover travelers came to the Temple of Jerusalem, they were trapped. They had to pay the prices demanded by the merchants who were allowed to set up booths in the Court of the Gentiles. Jesus was livid at the greed and dishonesty of these merchants and money-changers. He was appalled at their complete lack of integrity, especially when it was present in the house of God.

The Grief

I recently received a call from my best friend to let me know that his father had just died. To be honest, I had been subconsciously furious with my friend for months, mainly because our busy lives had managed to keep us apart for almost four full years. As I heard my friend's sad, quiet voice on the phone, I once again felt deeply connected to him. I had learned more about grace and graciousness from my friend's father than any other man in my life, so his death was a traumatic event for me. When I hung up the phone, I wept. In my prayers that night, I thanked God for the chance to have known my friend's father, and for the first time in a very long time, I gave abundant thanks for the gift of my friendship to his son.

Grief is an experience that humanizes and bonds us together like no other. It is an excellent spiritual tutor. Grief ignites more love than any other human emotion. It is also the only accumulative emotion I know of. When you go through one loss, all your other losses suddenly flash before your eyes.

Major Highways

"When she had said this, she went and called her sister Mary, saying quietly, 'The Teacher is here and is calling for you.' And when she heard it, she rose quickly and went to him. Now Jesus had not yet come to the village, but was still in the place where Martha had met him. When the Jews who were with her in the house, consoling her, saw Mary rise quickly and go out, they followed her, supposing that she was going to the tomb to weep there. Then Mary, when she came where Jesus was and saw him, fell at his feet, saying to him, 'Lord, if you had been here, my brother would not have died.' When Jesus saw her weeping, and the Jews who came with her also weeping, he was deeply moved in spirit and troubled; and he said, 'Where have you laid him?' They said to him, 'Lord, come and see.' Jesus wept. So the Jews said, 'See how he loved him!' But some of them said, 'Could not he who opened the eyes of the blind man have kept this man from dying?'"

—John 11:28–37

Jesus also grieved. He grieved with his friends Mary and Martha over the death of Lazarus, Mary and Martha's brother and Jesus' good friend. As is typical for people in grief, Martha and Mary argued over what could have been done to have changed the outcome. How could Lazarus have been kept alive? Why hadn't Jesus arrived earlier?

Humans always want to be in control, even over death. When we lose someone, we are often initially convinced that had we done something differently the person would not have died. Had we only noticed a symptom earlier; taken him or her to the right doctor or hospital; saw to it that he or she had eaten better, exercised more, or quit drinking or smoking; or loved him or her more so that he or she might have taken better care of him- or herself. Grief is often bloated with guilt.

Both Martha and Mary were frustrated with Jesus' humanness. He failed to come. He failed to come on time. He didn't do what he should have and could have done. Jesus felt great compassion for these two women as he shared in their grief. He too wept over the loss of his friend. He too felt as though life had punched a hole into the center of his being.

Scenic Overlooks

"Friendships multiply joys and divide griefs."

—H. G. Bohn

In a later chapter, you will read how this deep sense of empathy led Jesus to miraculously raise Lazarus from the dead. Here I want to point out only that Jesus had good friends. He also knew the anguish of grief. There is not an aspect of being human that Jesus did not grasp and embrace.

Major Highways

"And he called to him his twelve disciples and gave them authority over unclean spirits, to cast them out, and to heal every disease and every infirmity. The names of the twelve apostles are these: first, Simon, who is called Peter, and Andrew his brother; James the son of Zebedee, and John his brother; Philip and Bartholomew; Thomas and Matthew the tax collector; James the son of Alphaeus and Thaddaeus; Simon the Cananaean; and Judas Iscariot, who betrayed him."

"These twelve Jesus sent out, charging them, 'Go nowhere among the Gentiles, and enter no town of the Samaritans, but go rather to the lost sheep of the house of Israel. And preach as you go, saying, "The kingdom of heaven is at hand."'"

—Matthew 10:1–7

The Disciples

Jesus called 12 disciples. He did not recruit them. He didn't ask for volunteers. These 12 men felt compelled to follow Christ. I think of the 12 disciples as good, solid, hard-working men with busy but empty lives. I sense that secretly they had always longed for something different—an adventure or journey perhaps, something that would make them feel more alive. Whatever the case, I think of them as having a deep yearning for a life that was richer and fuller. In Jesus they saw the chance for a better life.

Jesus called 12 disciples as an obvious linkage to the 12 tribes of Israel. Jesus never ceased to love his people or to cherish his religious roots. He chose ordinary men from a wide range of backgrounds. Some were rich, and some were poor. Some had an education, and others had never opened a book. Some caught fish for a living, and another collected taxes. We know very little about these disciples other than that they were Jesus' closest friends and that these 12 were called because they were so different from each other.

Detours

We tend to choose friends who are like us. We gather to socialize primarily with those with whom we agree. We are prone to have as friends only those people we find easy and relaxing to be around. We don't want much conflict. We don't want our opinions challenged often. We like feeling safe and secure in a friendship. We enjoy having friends who are for the most part spiritual clones.

Jesus chose the opposite. He chose people who could not possibly be more different from him or one another. He chose people who were political and religious zealots, individuals who easily offend. He chose folks who would argue much of the time and squabble the rest. He chose to spend his ministry with a band of 12 who could only beget spiritual chaos. Jesus knew that it was solely from chaos that genuine creativity could emerge. He also knew that such creativity was vital to maturity, and it was maturity he truly valued and needed.

Though what we know of these relationships is sparse to miniscule, it is evident that Jesus experienced all of the normal triumphs and tragedies of friendship. He ate meals and went to weddings and worshipped with these men. He shared stories and ideas, worries and fears, hopes and dreams. Together they received praise and were heaped with scorn and ridicule. The disciples were his buddies, as well as his spiritual comrades.

Jesus certainly had his fair share of frustration with these guys. Often when he needed them most they were nowhere to be found. When he was off in the Garden of Gethsemane wrestling with the disturbing revelation that he was going to be crucified, he returned to find them all sleeping soundly (Mark 14:32–42). Half of the time they didn't understand what he was trying to teach them, and the other half they were asking inane questions.

James and John once made the sad request for a place of honor in the coming kingdom. That showed they still had no idea what God's kingdom was to be like. They clung to the notion that the kingdom would be a return to the glory days of the reigns of David and Solomon. Even though everything that Jesus preached and taught and did was about building a kingdom from justice, mercy, and equality, these two continued to want the best seats in the house (Mark 10:35–45).

Great adversity brought the humanness of the disciples to light. When the going got tough, the disciples got going, but they were off and running in the wrong direction. I identify with the disciples in this case. Crucifixion had to be terrifying. I don't know that I would have had the strength of faith, let alone the physical will, to have stayed true to Jesus in the face of such horror.

Judas became furious with Jesus for letting a woman anoint his head with expensive perfume and completely missed that this event was symbolic of his impending death and preparation for the grave (Mark 14:3–9). Judas believed that Jesus had given up on their ministry to the poor, which was the core of their mission, and so Judas gave up on Jesus. Judas is often depicted as a greedy man who didn't really care about Jesus, but I think Judas' suicide is proof positive that he loved Jesus dearly and could not forgive himself for failing to comprehend Jesus' need to foreshadow his own death. Judas' only real sin in my book was failing to recognize that even he was worthy of being forgiven.

Major Highways

"Then Satan entered into Judas called Iscariot, who was of the number of the twelve; he went away and conferred with the chief priests and officers how he might betray him to them. And they were glad, and engaged to give him money. So he agreed, and sought an opportunity to betray him to them in the absence of the multitude."

—Luke 22:3–6

Major Highways

"'Simon, Simon, behold, Satan demanded to have you, that he might sift you like wheat, but I have prayed for you that your faith may not fail, and when you have turned again, strengthen your brethren.' And he said to him, 'Lord, I am ready to go with you to prison and to death.' He said, 'I tell you, Peter, the cock will not crow this day, until you three times deny that you know me.'"

—Luke 22:31–34

Peter was Christ's closest, dearest friend and confidant. Clearly, he was also the moderator and mediator to the other disciples. Jesus knew Peter so well that, as the crucifixion drew near, Jesus knew Peter would not be able to admit that he was a disciple. Peter was told that on three occasions he would deny he even knew Jesus, which is exactly what Peter did. It is tragic that Jesus could see so far into Peter's heart that he knew Peter would be unable to remain faithful to the end. It is also a true sign of Jesus' compassion that he predicted Peter's denial without the slightest hint of sarcasm. Jesus understood. He knew Peter and loved him, even in Peter's most glaring moment of spiritual frailty.

The disciples were Jesus' friends. They were also very human. Jesus embraced all this humanness with profound forgiveness. He chose to love these 12 through thick and thin, and from my take on the story, the thin patches were frequent.

The Questionable Women

Jesus was a Jew. He functioned often as a prophet and as a rabbi, both of which were roles defined within Jewish tradition. Women had a limited role in this tradition; they were given less value than the family ox. Women were not encouraged to grow spiritually. A woman would never be allowed to discuss issues with a rabbi or to read or know scripture. Women did not attend services at temple, and they had no role in any celebrations or rites. They were physical and spiritual servants to men.

Major Highways

"Soon afterward he went on through cities and villages, preaching and bringing the good news of the kingdom of God. And the twelve were with him, and also some women who had been healed of evil spirits and infirmities: Mary, called Magdalene, from whom seven demons had gone out, and Joanna, the wife of Chuza, Herod's steward, and Susanna, and many others, who provided for them out of their means."

—Luke 8:1–3

In contrast, Jesus had women who called him friend and teacher. Martha and Mary had him over for supper and considered him a close enough friend to share their grief over the loss of their brother Lazarus. Jewish society and religious circles would have viewed this friendship as scandalous. These women supported Jesus with their own money, and some followed him on his travels. The tongues of the religious establishment must have been wagging away.

Not only that, but the women Jesus befriended were often of questionable moral standards. Mary Magdalene was reportedly a prostitute. I suspect many felt his relationship to her was far too close. The woman Jesus talks to at the well had five husbands (John 4:1–26). Keep in mind that even talking to a woman who was not your wife at that time would raise more than a few eyebrows. Repeatedly Jesus reached out to those whom the world had branded lost or bad. He did not seem to care one lick what the world thought. His tender mercies were shared with everyone.

Jesus also used women as models of faith. The poor old woman who could give only two pennies, because that was all she had, is offered as an example of genuine giving (Luke 21:1–4). Here again Jesus knowingly offended the rich men who could give so much more. But he made his point. Only the widow made a sacrifice. To lift up women as the stars of faith was outrageous, even unseemly, in the eyes of the religious establishment.

Major Highways

"And when the sixth hour had come, there was darkness over the whole land until the ninth hour. And at the ninth hour, Jesus cried with a loud voice, 'Eloi, Eloi, lama sabachthani?' which means, 'My God, my God, why hast thou forsaken me?' And some of the bystanders hearing it said, 'Behold, he is calling Elijah.' And one ran and, filling a sponge full of vinegar, put it on a reed and gave it to him to drink saying, 'Wait, let us see whether Elijah will come to take him down.' And Jesus uttered a loud cry, and breathed his last. ... And when the centurion, who stood facing him, saw that he thus breathed his last, he said, 'Truly this man was the son of God!'"

"There was also women looking on from afar, among whom were Mary Magdalene, and Mary ... [and] many other women who came up with him to Jerusalem."

—Mark 15:33–41

The Death

Why didn't Jesus live to a ripe old age and die peacefully in his sleep? Why the need for such a brutal finale? Why would anyone want to worship a God who was so tortured? Is it any wonder that he was mocked and beaten and that the whole world shouted at him, "If you really are the King of the Jews, then come on down!"

To believe in Jesus as the Christ is to know why Good Friday is called good. Christians believe in Christ because he didn't come down off the cross. He did not avoid the worst the world could dish out. In so doing, he gave credibility to his passionate desire to bring out the best in us. The crucifixion was not some spiritual necessity by which God proved his love for us. It was a predictable result of one man choosing in faith to be radically committed to both love and forgiveness. For a human being to lead a life of complete faith requires all of who that human is.

Jesus died an agonizing death. His last breath was a pained gasp. To the very last moment, he was true to his calling to be fully human.

It should come as no surprise that it was the women who were there to watch him die and the women who first heralded the resurrection. Jesus turned the world upside down, especially the world of the religious establishment. Jesus was truly the first genuine feminist.

The Least You Need to Know

➤ The baptism of Jesus by John the Baptist confirmed that Jesus would be calling his people to a radical transformation of the heart.

➤ Jesus grappled with human temptations, the ordeal of grief, and rejection by his family and friends. He even displayed a potent temper.

➤ Jesus called 12 disciples to share in his ministry. It was significant that Jesus chose not to go it alone. These 12 disciples were a paradigm for the celebration of spiritual diversity.

➤ Jesus developed close and meaningful relationships with women. He considered women to be the equal of men and treated them accordingly.

➤ Jesus was human in every way. He had a faith that cried, "Why hast thou forsaken me?" in an expression of radical doubt.

Part 4

Jesus the Kingdom Builder

Jesus spent the last years of his life conducting a ministry. It was not a traditional ministry. He did not conduct traditional worship or work within the walls of a church or synagogue. His preaching was infrequent and informal. His teaching was primarily the telling of a simple story. He was not a theologian. He held to no dogma or doctrine. He had no degrees.

His was a ministry on the move. He addressed many different gatherings and sought to spiritually move his audience. He was evidently a moving preacher and teacher. His ministry was fluid. It grew and matured. It changed and transformed almost daily and defied prediction. It did not conform to pattern. It clearly did not fit the mold of the religious establishment.

The one constant of his ministry, however, was his call to prepare for and build the kingdom of God. Jesus had a clear set of blueprints for this kingdom. He knew how he wanted it built, and by whom. He knew what spiritual materials needed to be used—he warned of their expensive spiritual, emotional, and even physical cost. He was even precise about when and where to build. These blueprints are the subject of the next four chapters, as Jesus instructs his followers on how to become master craftsmen/women of the kingdom.

Chapter 7

What to Do

In This Chapter

➤ Surrendering the spirit

➤ Taking the difficult path

➤ Serving, sacrificing, and suffering for faith

➤ Preaching good news to the poor

➤ Seeking those who are lost or rejected

As a child, I lived nine blocks from Lake Michigan. During the summer, my whole neighborhood moved to the beach—at least all the mothers and children. I loved the lake; my mother feared the lake. Each time I went in the water I was told that if I went past the buoys, which was where the water went over my head, I would drown.

I was 38 years old before my wife taught me how to swim in water over my head. She taught me not to fear the water. She reminded me of my natural tendency to float and that I did know how to swim—not well, but not all that badly either. Basically, she helped me overcome my terror of deep water by teaching me to trust myself, the water, and the body God gave me.

Jesus taught his followers to trust in God. He told them to stop worrying about all the stuff over which they had no control, which was just about everything. He reminded them that they were not in control. They were not in charge. He encouraged them to surrender their silly notions of personal power and pride. He asked them to give up on their efforts to be perfect or to make the world move according to their own plans.

Major Highways

"'But if God so clothes the grass of the field, which is today alive and tomorrow is thrown into the oven, will he not much more clothe you, O men of little faith? Therefore do not be anxious, saying, "What shall we eat?" or "What shall we drink?" or "What shall we wear?" For the Gentiles seek all these things; and your heavenly Father knows that you need them all. But seek first his kingdom and his righteousness, and all these things shall be yours as well.'"

"'Therefore do not be anxious about tomorrow, for tomorrow will be anxious for itself.'"

—Matthew 6:30–34

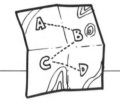

⸢ Map Key

The **kingdom** is the dwelling place of God and the faithful. It is a sacred spot governed solely by the will of God.

Let Go

Jesus constantly informed his flock that they needed to relax and receive and that God would provide. He stated that their supposed certainties were illusion. He scoffed at their wisdom. He found their efforts at immortality silly. He found their desire to build Towers of Babel, monuments to human pride and power, offensive.

Simply put, the *kingdom* of God can be built only by those who understand that God must supply all the building materials. God's blueprints must be meticulously followed, and all efforts must be aimed at building that which can last eternally.

Take the Road Less Traveled

Jesus was often remarkably bold. He did not mince words. He told his followers that the pathway offered by the world was not anything like the way to the kingdom. The path the world encourages us to take is swift and easy, but it heads straight to hell. The road to the kingdom is rocky, mountainous, and loaded with peril, but it moves in the direction of heaven. Jesus often pitted the wisdom and ways of the world against those of the kingdom. The world and the kingdom almost always moved in opposing spiritual directions.

Jesus instilled in his followers a tremendous respect for the difficulty and dangers of the journey of faith. Building the kingdom would require blood, sweat, and tears. Jesus had no desire to be popular, so he did not offer quick or easy solutions. He boldly outlined a lifestyle of service, sacrifice, and suffering. Faith, which results in the construction of the kingdom, would require a complete investment of heart and soul.

Pay the Price

The Jewish faith is built upon enormous respect for the family. The honoring of parents is a longstanding and well-known aspect of Jewish faith and moral tradition. Jesus told his potential followers that if they were to become his disciples, they would have to turn their backs on their families. They would not only be forced to uproot themselves from their homes, but they would also have to disown much of their religious heritage. Why was Jesus so blunt and so blatantly offensive? Can you imagine any minister or rabbi preaching such a message today?

Jesus had a deep and profound understanding of the spiritual path, as well as the qualifications required of those who chose to build the kingdom. Jesus knew …

> ➤ Parents want their children to be safe.

> ➤ Parents want their children to be secure.

> ➤ Parents want their children to be successful.

> ➤ Parents want their children to be well-liked.

> ➤ Parents want their children to lead healthy, happy and problem-free lives.

> ➤ Parents want only the best for their children.

Jesus also knew that a disciple committed to building the kingdom would …

> ➤ Be forced to take risks, often risking personal safety and assuredly worldly security.

> ➤ Know the suffering necessitated by the pursuit of justice.

> ➤ Know the many sacrifices of making peace.

Major Highways

"Enter by the narrow gate; for the gate is wide and the way is easy, that leads to destruction, and those who enter by it are many. For the gate is narrow and the way is hard, that leads to life, and those who find it are few."

—Matthew 7:13–14

Detours

Just as in many respects Jesus has been Americanized, so has the concept of God's kingdom. Often the kingdom is spoken of as if it were akin to Disney World, Camelot, or Oz. The kingdom of which Christ spoke was a spiritual and not a material conception.

➤ Be scorned and ridiculed by the world, which condemns and mocks idealists.

➤ Have to face the problems of the world, for it is in the midst of these problems that God can be found.

➤ Face personal crosses (conflicts or problems) and pick up those crosses and follow (Luke 9:23–26).

➤ Not avoid the burdens of others, but help to carry them (Matthew 11:28–30).

Major Highways

"'He who loves father or mother more than me is not worthy of me; and he who loves son or daughter more than me is not worthy of me; and he who does not take his cross and follow me is not worthy of me. He who finds his life will lose it, and he who loses his life for my sake will find it.'"

—Matthew 10:37–39

Scenic Overlooks

"All I have seen teaches me to trust the Creator for all I have not seen."

—Ralph Waldo Emerson

What parents and family want for their children is not what Jesus would expect of his "children." Jesus strove to inspire his followers to take a rugged path. The way to the kingdom is not a stroll down a country lane, but a pilgrimage up the side of a demanding and daunting mountain. The only way to arrive at the kingdom is to trust your faith to lead you.

Jesus did not try to win converts by painting a pretty picture of discipleship. He drew an almost ugly portrait of such a life. Still, he was telling his would-be followers the truth. A life spent building the kingdom would be difficult.

The Poor and the Lost

Jesus taught his followers that if they chose to be people of faith who were willing to build the kingdom, they would have to …

➤ Surrender to God.

➤ Choose the road less traveled.

➤ Leave home.

➤ Risk safety and security.

➤ Serve, sacrifice, and suffer.

➤ Carry crosses and bear burdens.

➤ Trust that the way of God would lead to the kingdom.

But what does it mean to build the kingdom? How do you do it? I am sure that question was on the minds of those who listened to Jesus preach and teach. It is probably on your mind as well.

Jesus again was clear; his message strong and firm. God's kingdom is built with two primary kinds of bricks:

➤ Preaching good news to the poor.

➤ Seeking those who are lost and rejected in this world.

Here, again, Jesus chose to be dramatically offensive to the establishment. He centered his ministry and his kingdom on those folks who had been left out by the world. Jesus was the champion of the poor and the needy, the sick and suffering, and the ridiculed and scorned. He did not focus his ministry on those of political or religious power and prestige. He did not offer words of comfort for those already comfortable. He did not seek to protect the status quo.

No, Jesus wanted to take care of those the world had neglected, abused, or denied. He wanted to bring those who were in the shadows into the light. (Imagine this message being preached in today's world!)

Jesus sought disciples. He looked for followers. He looked for folks to build the kingdom. He did not candy-coat the job description. He was clear that the hours were long, the work tough, and the rewards primarily spiritual. He advocated a different kind of good life, one that had a lot to do with goodness and treating others with kindness. Goodness knows that the kingdom of God is not anything like the kingdoms of the world.

> **Scenic Overlooks**
>
> "Although the world is full of suffering, it is also full of the overcoming of it."
>
> —Helen Keller

> **Major Highways**
>
> "And his disciples came and took the body and buried it; and they went and told Jesus."
>
> "Now when Jesus heard this, he withdrew from there in a boat to a lonely place apart. But when the crowds heard it, they followed him on foot from the towns. As he went ashore he saw a great throng; and he had compassion on them, and healed their sick."
>
> —Matthew 14:12–14

The Least You Need to Know

➤ God's kingdom would be built from and out of faith.

➤ Jesus understood that faith required people to do things that the world felt were foolish.

➤ Faith demanded that Jesus' followers leave home to become part of the family of humanity as a whole.

➤ Jesus understood faith as the courage to pick up crosses and the willingness to see burdens as blessings.

➤ Jesus wanted to build the kingdom for the poor and those the world rejects. In the kingdom, all people would be treated with respect and dignity.

Chapter 8

What Not to Do

In This Chapter

➤ The fear factor

➤ The right way to treat others

➤ The importance of forgiveness

➤ The danger of materialism

➤ The need for nonconformity

Jesus was unfailing in his devotion to a particular way of life and a clear set of values. His followers knew exactly where he stood and where they stood in relation to that message. Christ's message was pointed, short, and not so sweet. It was a message with a few themes that he repeated again and again. The message of Jesus was like a pulse: it beat with the blood of life's meaning and worth.

Jesus was clear about what it would take to build the kingdom. His followers knew what they were expected to do. He was, however, even more vehement about what not to do. The kingdom was not only the presence of certain attitudes, behaviors, and beliefs, but it also was the glaring absence of others. This chapter is devoted to exploring how Jesus taught his followers what not to do in the effort to build the kingdom.

Don't Be Afraid

Jesus saw fear as a major contaminant of faith. It was fear that led folks to take the easy route and kept them from building the kingdom. Fear robbed people of the courage required to live a faithful life and called people into hiding.

Fear forces people to face the world with clenched fists, doubt, and sweeping generalizations. Fear causes bigotry. Fear limits people to being more interested in things than people, successes than satisfaction, notoriety than respect. Fear causes people to run from both death and life. With fear, people cannot feel, believe, hope, or love.

Jesus believed that faith was the opposite of fear. Fear expects the worst, and faith expects the best. Faith approaches the world with open arms, mind, and heart. Faith is free to feel, hope, and love. Faith cannot hide, because it seeks open spaces. Faith tells the truth and lives it. Faith is real.

The kingdom must be built with faith. The kingdom has no room for fear. Fear threatens to dismantle the kingdom with prejudice and suspicion. The kingdom of God is a place of peace and calm, a sacred spot where fear is not welcome.

Over and over again, Jesus told his followers not to be afraid. He knew that if they chose to live in fear, the seedlings of faith he had planted would soon be trampled or swept away. He was incessant in his recognition of fear as the culprit that can spoil the soul.

Major Highways

"'You have heard that it was said to the men of old, "You shall not kill; and whoever kills shall be liable to judgment." But I say to you that every one who is angry with his brother shall be liable to judgment; whoever insults his brother shall be liable to the council, and whoever says, "You fool!," shall be liable to the hell of fire. So if you are offering your gift at the altar, and there remember that your brother has something against you, leave your gift there before the altar and go; first be reconciled to your brother, and then come and offer your gift. Make friends quickly with your accuser, while you are going with him to court, lest your accuser hand you over to the judge, and the judge to the guard, and you be put in prison; truly, I say to you, you will never get out till you have paid the last penny."

—Matthew 5:21–26

Don't Harm Anyone

Christ confronted the harshness of his times with a message grounded in gentleness and grace. He repeatedly called his followers to ...

➤ Speak to one another without anger and show respect.

➤ Refrain from using an insulting or mocking tone.

➤ Recognize the great harm that mere words can do.

➤ Never slander a person or seek to destroy his reputation.

➤ Work diligently and daily to resolve conflicts and quarrels.

➤ Know that to love is impossible when you still carry a grudge in your heart.

➤ Know that broken human relationships often keep us from being intimate in our relationship to God.

Jesus got angry fairly often. His anger, however, was never mean. He sought nobody harm. The point of his anger was transformation, not punishment. His anger was not selfish. It was not motivated by a desire to get revenge. Because he never seemed to keep score, he never tried to even the score. Jesus was a man who was slow to anger. He had a long, long temper. He chose to vent his anger only when to do so was productive.

Detours

Jesus was not speaking of removing anger. Nothing is more sickeningly sweet than a religious person who pretends to have never been burned by the fires of anger. To receive the smile of someone you know is furious with you is to feel your soul scraped raw. Jesus spoke of the dangers of anger that gets out of control. Like a wildfire that whips and leaps and scorches anything in its path, this kind of anger, rage, has no other function but to destroy.

Jesus believed that our attitudes toward one another reflect our attitude about God. It is impossible to feel close to God if our hearts are bloated with bitterness toward our neighbors. To be at peace with God, we must first be at peace with our friends and neighbors.

Jesus was a peacemaker in every sense of that word. He sought to preach, teach, and live a message of reconciliation. He sought to whittle away at differences, rather than build them up. He encouraged compromise. He invited folks to settle scores and to put down the burden of their grudges.

As you consider what Christ's life and lifestyle must have been like, reflect upon this basic tenet of his faith: He sought nobody harm. He used anger to his and God's advantage. He respected the awesome power of words, thoughts, and attitudes to do damage or good.

Major Highways

"'For if you forgive men their trespasses, your heavenly Father also will forgive you; but if you do not forgive men their trespasses, neither will your Father forgive your trespasses.'"

—Matthew 6:14–15

Scenic Overlooks

"Never does the human soul appear so strong and noble as when it forgoes revenge and dares to forgive an injury."

—E. H. Chapin

Don't Stop Forgiving

In many respects, this book is all about interpreting the life of Jesus by striving to understand his faith—no easy task, but not impossible either. Jesus lived his faith, which makes our task so much easier. His faith dictated his behaviors as well as his attitudes.

Jesus saw forgiveness as the fuel of faith. Without forgiveness, faith does not grow or deepen. It is not pleasing to God. Faith without forgiveness eventually stagnates and even rots; it is empty and powerless.

As Jesus continually instructed his followers, forgiveness is important and powerful because it …

➤ Clears the mind.

➤ Cleanses the heart.

➤ Cleans the slate of the soul.

➤ Best displays the heart of God.

➤ Best demonstrates the transforming power of faith.

My wife of 23 years died suddenly as I was writing this book. In many ways, this loss has made the writing very difficult physically. It has also made the writing seem so much more alive and powerful spiritually. This gaping personal loss has offered me uncanny spiritual clarity. The daily grappling with this tragedy has made me so much more reliant on my faith. Jesus seems so close, like a long shadow.

Many nights, just before bed, I let myself reflect upon my marriage. We had a marriage made on the outskirts of heaven and residing occasionally in the suburbs of hell. It was a good marriage. In retrospect, I have come to realize the frequency of our forgiveness of one another. I never noticed it while I was living it, but I sure do now.

We were both stubborn. We often wielded words like weapons and were quick to point out flaws or failings in each other. We often neglected each other or took each other for granted. Yet somehow we managed to forgive and forgive again. We built our loving upon the firm foundation of forgiveness.

Don't Worship Your Wallet

Money may not be the root of all evil, but Jesus felt that it was definitely part of evil. The pursuit of money keeps us from loving our neighbor and makes us unable to love God.

Preachers hate to preach about money, especially the need for it or the hope that we value it less. All over the world, but particularly in America, ministers and priests make every effort to soften the blow of Jesus' commentary about money. It never works because our spirits know the truth.

Jesus had a unique relationship to money:

➤ He never appeared to have any.

➤ He never bought or owned anything.

➤ He did not appear to believe in private property.

➤ He shared everything he had, and he asked his followers to do the same.

➤ His ministry asked for nothing but the barest necessities: food, shelter, and clothing.

➤ He sacrificed easily and often.

➤ He gave most to those whose need was dire.

➤ He was what my mother would have called a tramp, but in his times he must have been considered a nomad. There was nothing luxurious about his lifestyle.

➤ He lived off of the kindness (welfare) of strangers.

Jesus had little to no use for money. He often warned his followers about the addictive potential of money. Though he respected the power of

Major Highways

"'No one can serve two masters; for either he will hate the one and love the other, or he will be devoted to the one and despise the other. You cannot serve God and mammon [money].'"

—Matthew 6:24

Scenic Overlooks

"Dollars have never been known to produce character, and character will never be produced by money."

—W. K. Kellogg

money, he saw that power as almost exclusively negative. His lifestyle was that of a pre-modern communist. The community owned all, and what they owned was to be utilized solely for the benefit of the community. It is small wonder that American preachers often refrain from discussing the economic beliefs or actions of Jesus Christ.

Don't Conform

Jesus was a nonconformist. He did not conform to the standards or beliefs of his family, religion, society, or world. He saw conformity as …

- ➤ The desire to play it safe.
- ➤ The need to avoid conflict or controversy.
- ➤ The need to fit in at all costs.
- ➤ The mugger of the spirit.
- ➤ The corrupter of the soul.
- ➤ The failure of faith to uphold convictions.
- ➤ The road well traveled.
- ➤ The easy out.
- ➤ The quickest and surest way to hell.
- ➤ Pain-free and numbing.

Jesus recognized that those who would build the kingdom would have to be individuals unafraid to break rules, to be unpopular, to risk safety and security, to be mocked and humiliated, to be treated as outcasts or misfits, and to be viewed as failures or losers. Once again, Jesus reminded his followers that building a kingdom asks a heavy price of the builders.

Don't Give Up

Jesus made it abundantly clear to his followers that building the kingdom would be anything but easy. The way of faith is long and lonely and often is filled with pain. He stressed that the weak of heart, mind, and body need not apply. Building the kingdom is not a calling for those who desire the easy life, want their share of the pie, and think of the good life only in material terms.

Major Highways

"'Every tree that does not bear good fruit is cut down and thrown into the fire. Thus you will know them by their fruits."

"Not every one who says to me "Lord, Lord," shall enter the kingdom of heaven, but he who does the will of my Father who is in heaven.'"

—Matthew 7:19–21

Scenic Overlooks

"Conformity is the jailer of freedom and the enemy of growth."

—John F. Kennedy

"Conformity is the ape of harmony."

—Ralph Waldo Emerson (from *Emerson Journals*, 1840)

Major Highways

"And he said to them, 'Which of you who has a friend will go to him at midnight and say to him, "Friend, lend me three loaves; for a friend of mine has arrived on a journey, and I have nothing to set before him;" and he will answer from within, "Do not bother me; the door is now shut, and my children are with me in bed; I cannot get up and give you anything"? I tell you, though he will not get up and give him anything because he is his friend, yet because of his importunity he will rise and give him whatever he needs.'"

—Luke 11:5–8

Jesus warned that the path to the kingdom would be tough. Because it would be so difficult, he admitted that his followers would often be tempted to retreat or give up. Jesus asked his followers to be strong and persistent. He told them of the importance of going the extra mile. He acknowledged that the kingdom would be built brick by painful brick. He claimed that those who persevered would know the satisfaction.

We live in a culture that prizes the quick and the easy. We want what we want, and we want it now. We are always in a hurry. Fast is better. The easy way is always the best way to go. But Jesus was clear that the kingdom would not be built in a day, but an eternity. The kingdom would be built by those whose faith is patient and persistent. Jesus was clear that this spiritual project would require all we have for all the time we have.

Scenic Overlooks

"Fall seven times, stand up eight."

—Japanese proverb

"Go the extra mile. It's never crowded."

—*Executive Speechwriter Newsletter*

"The man who removes a mountain begins by carrying away small stones."

—Chinese proverb

The Least You Need to Know

➤ Jesus recognized that fear would destroy faith.

➤ Jesus lived in such a way that he sought nobody harm.

➤ Jesus felt it was critical to always treat people with respect and honesty.

➤ Jesus was convinced that people could not worship God and money at the same time.

➤ Jesus was a nonconformist. He saw conformity as that which enslaves the soul and shrivels courage.

➤ Jesus knew that the way of faith would require great patience and perseverance, as would the building of the kingdom.

What to Be

Jesus believed strongly that his followers would have to live as if they had been to the kingdom. He wanted his followers to look and act as if they knew the kingdom first-hand. He knew that the kingdom could be built only by people who held a vision of that kingdom within them.

Be Happy

The passage of scripture commonly called the Beatitudes offers a stark contrast between the values of the world and those of the kingdom. It is a direct challenge to the superficial faith of the Pharisees. The Pharisees saw faith as acting religious. Jesus saw faith as a way of life.

Faith is an attitude. It is a perspective on life and how to live it. Faith is not simply about doing good from time to time; it is about being good all the time. True faith comes from a pure heart and a soul that is saturated with the grace of God.

Major Highways

The following passage of scripture is commonly referred to as the Beatitudes:

"Seeing the crowds, he went up on the mountain, and when he sat down, his disciples came to him. And he opened his mouth and taught them, saying: 'Blessed are the poor in spirit, for theirs is in the kingdom of heaven. Blessed are those who mourn, for they shall be comforted. Blessed are the meek, for they shall inherit the earth. Blessed are those who hunger and thirst for righteousness, for they shall be satisfied. Blessed are the merciful, for they shall obtain mercy. Blessed are the pure in heart, for they shall see God. Blessed are the peacemakers, for they shall be called sons of God. Blessed are those who are persecuted for righteousness' sake, for theirs is the kingdom of heaven. Blessed are you when men revile you and persecute you and utter all kinds of evil against you falsely on my account.'"

—Matthew 5:1–11

Major Highways

"As he said this, a woman in the crowd raised her voice and said to him, 'Blessed is the womb that bore you, and the breasts that you sucked!' But he said, 'Blessed rather are those who hear the word of God and keep it!'"

—Luke 11:27–28

The Beatitudes offered the followers of Jesus a clear code of conduct, defined a uniquely challenging set of values, and established a radically new set of priorities. Jesus confronted his culture's false belief in blessings and curses. In the culture of Christ's time, and within the religious establishment, people were thought to be blessed if they …

➤ Were wealthy.

➤ Were well educated, especially in the Torah.

➤ Were male.

➤ Were healthy.

➤ Had no disabilities.

➤ Came from ancestry with good seats in the synagogue.

➤ Were considered physically attractive.

➤ Were thought of as successful and wise.

➤ Had a life relatively free of pain and tragedy.

➤ Were popular and powerful.

➤ Owned many beautiful and expensive things.

➤ Could eat and drink when and what they wanted.

➤ Appeared to be happy.

Sound familiar? It is amazing how closely our contemporary American culture unconsciously promotes a similar belief in blessings, with accompanying curses. Those who are blessed, then and now, are thought to be those who by all appearances are happy.

Jesus challenged this whole network of blessing and curses. He stated that what the world defines as happiness has little to do with what God believes can make us truly happy. Jesus turned the whole concept of blessings and curses upside down and assigned blessings and genuine happiness to those who …

➤ Are aware of their deep need for God.

➤ Are compassionate and genuinely merciful.

➤ Know the brutal pain of loss.

➤ Are willing to claim their grief.

➤ Value justice.

➤ Strive to defeat or harm nobody.

➤ Respect all of God's children.

➤ Have a heart that desires only the best for all people.

➤ Are peacemakers, not troublemakers.

➤ Are creators of community and celebrators of diversity.

➤ Are unwilling to sit in judgment.

➤ Are unwilling to see faith as a means of superiority.

Jesus presented his followers with a demanding, even disturbing, vision. God's blessings are not the result of having achieved a great deal by the standards of the world, but rather having achieved a great deal solely by God's standards. These standards define happiness in a far deeper way. Happiness is now intimately connected to service and sacrifice, compassion and mercy, conviction and courage. Happiness is not free of problems, pain, or tragedy. Just the opposite, true happiness necessitates the experience of true suffering.

The Beatitudes issue a call to a deeper faith. They offer a direct challenge to the superficiality of the culture. They attack the notion that the good life is limited to those who look good, sound good, or feel good. The Beatitudes speak of a deep faith that is rich in love and forgiveness, unafraid of pain or persecution, and willing to risk everything in the pursuit of peace and justice.

In a sense, Jesus was telling his followers that all blessings are mixed blessings. Every joy is born in sorrow. Even in the mud and gloom of winter, the buds and blossoms of spring are being born.

Be Loving

Jesus seldom made things easy. He did not simply ask his disciples to love. He asked them to love each other, to love the lost, to love those the world hated, and to love those they found repulsive. He went so far as to ask them to love their enemies. That is a long, long way to go. Loving one's enemies is true tough love. Many have labored long and hard defining just exactly who is their enemy. It has never taken me much time, at least not when I'm being honest.

Major Highways

"'You have heard that it was said, "You shall love your neighbor and hate your enemy." But I say to you, Love your enemies and pray for those who persecute you, so that you may be sons of your Father who is in heaven; for he makes his sun rise on the evil and the good and sends rain on the just and on the unjust. For if you love those who love you, what reward have you? Do not even the tax collectors do the same? And if you salute only your brethren, what more are you doing than others? Do not even the Gentiles do the same? You, therefore, must be perfect, as your heavenly Father is perfect.'"

—Matthew 5:43–48

What Jesus meant by being loving was not acting in a silly, sweet manner. Being loving is knowing that you are loving someone exactly as you believe God loves you. For Jesus, love was a divine compulsion, a spiritual drive. Jesus challenged his followers to love others, even enemies, in such a way that they would bring out the best in others, which in turn would bring out the best in his followers.

Jesus asked his followers to love extravagantly and without condition. He asked them to love the ones who are hard to love and to love most of all during the toughest of times. Jesus saw love as a verb, the action of faith, and the force that would build the kingdom of God.

Points of Interest

If you consider the basic story of Jesus' life, you are bound to be amazed at his capacity to love. Almost everything we know about him is thick with loving. His willingness to touch a leper, embrace a prostitute, and seek out a man who claimed to be infested with demons spoke volumes about the depth of his love. He never gave up on the power of love to transform the human heart, the landscape of our world, or our future.

Be Grateful

At first glance, the passage describing the chance meeting and cleansing of 10 lepers on Jesus' way to Jerusalem seems a pretty innocuous passage. It seems to highlight the importance of gratitude and how few people remember to be grateful. This message appears to be solid, but not particularly pointed. The opposite, however, is true.

Major Highways

"On the way to Jerusalem, he was passing along between Samaria and Galilee. And as he entered a village, he was met by ten lepers, who stood at a distance and lifted up their voices and said, 'Jesus, Master, have mercy on us.' When he saw them he said to them, 'Go and show yourselves to the priests.' And as they went they were cleansed. Then one of them, when he saw that he was healed, turned back, praising God with a loud voice; and he fell on his face at Jesus' feet, giving him thanks. Now he was a Samaritan. Then said Jesus, 'Were not ten cleansed? Where are the nine? Was no one found to return and give praise to God except this foreigner?' And he said to him, 'Rise and go your way; your faith has made you well.'"

—Luke 17:11–19

The one man who turns out to be grateful is both a leper and a *Samaritan*. Lepers were thought to be cursed by God. Their rotting, disfigured flesh was seen as a sure sign of God's anger and their sinfulness. Samaritans were despised by the Jews. They were thought to be half-breeds and a contaminated race. They were held in contempt by the religious establishment.

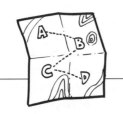

Map Key

The Assyrians had moved the Israelites out of Palestine and the surrounding foreigners in. While living outside of Palestine, the Israelites intermarried. This "mixed race" later resettled in Israel, and came to be known as the **Samaritans,** who were then despised by the Jews.

Jesus is not only acknowledging the importance of gratitude in this story, but he is also making a strong social and spiritual commentary. The folks you might believe to have the least reason to be grateful often are. Why does he drill home this point?

➤ Gratitude often comes when we are most aware of our need for God.

➤ Gratitude is frequently the result of having endured pain and suffering.

➤ Gratitude is an attitude born from being on one's knees.

➤ The exclusivity of the religious establishment is countered by the inclusiveness of God.

➤ The elitism of society is confronted by the kingdom's celebration of equality.

➤ The kingdom will be full of folks who neither the world nor the religious establishment expect to be there.

➤ The harder the world pushes a person away, the closer that person is drawn to God.

➤ The kingdom is not a country club.

Scenic Overlooks

"Gratitude is the memory of the heart."

—J. B. Massieu

The significance of gratitude for Jesus is primarily in the irony of who most often displays it. Jesus continues to make his central case that his followers will be those the world has rejected and those the religious establishment has branded as cursed. Jesus affirms that genuine faith does not see tragedy as the absence of God but as the context in which God is often found.

Jesus taught his disciples to remember that which matters most. He taught them to count their blessings. He asked them to keep his legacy imprinted upon their hearts. Jesus saw gratitude as a major energy source for building the kingdom. Gratitude fuels the faith required of those who build.

Points of Interest

Gratitude is an attitude. It is a way of approaching the day and a perspective on life. Gratitude sets the mood, establishes the tone, and frames the picture. It gives everything brightness and depth. It is a relationship to God.

Gratitude also is a choice. The one healed leper chose to come back. He chose to give thanks. I believe that this choice yielded satisfaction; this choice deepened his relationship to God and made him healthier, happier, and more hopeful. The other nine chose to walk away and follow the path of assumption and indifference.

Be Aware

Jesus often commented that people choose to be deaf and blind to the world around them. Jesus encouraged his followers to do the opposite:

➤ To keep their eyes and ears wide open

➤ To notice the beauty and majesty of creation

➤ To keep their minds open to the mysteries of life

➤ To keep their hearts open to the love that is displayed everywhere in everything

➤ To keep their souls open to the miraculous healing powers of faith

➤ To keep their spirits open to the transforming powers of the Holy Spirit

Jesus felt that the world, especially the religious establishment, encouraged the wearing of blinders and earplugs. The world wanted folks to be less and less open. In a sense, the world encouraged people to spiritually shrink and shrivel. The less you notice, the less you have to do. The less you see, the less you have to feel. The less you remember, the less you have to create.

Detours

The opposite spirit to gratitude is cynicism. The cynic never experiences anything as a gift because he doesn't believe that anything is genuine or truly good. The best faith for the cynic is no faith at all.

Jesus wanted his followers to notice, to pay attention. He did not want them to miss their lives. He wanted his followers to see their lives as marvelous adventures. He wanted them to expand, to keep on growing, to mature to the maximum.

The kingdom cannot be built by those who are in hiding. It cannot be constructed by individuals who are out of touch with their senses and who have no vision. The kingdom must be built in open spaces by folks with open eyes, ears, and hearts.

The Least You Need to Know

➤ In the Beatitudes, Jesus challenged the established idea of what it meant to be blessed.

➤ Jesus saw happiness as the satisfying result of service, making a difference, improving the world, and choosing to be a genuinely good human being.

➤ Jesus told his followers to love the outcast, the lost, the poor, and the enemy, as well as neighbors.

➤ In his comments concerning the leper who expressed gratitude for being healed, Jesus established the importance of gratitude in faith.

➤ Jesus encouraged his followers to keep their eyes, ears, hearts, spirits, and souls open to God and the world around them.

Chapter 10

What Not to Be

> ### In This Chapter
>
> ➤ The difference between acting religious and being faithful
>
> ➤ The importance of leaving judgments to God
>
> ➤ The lack of love in the religious establishment

Please take the time to read the Chapter 23 of Matthew. Each time I read this powerful section of scripture, I am shocked by the courage of Jesus. I cannot comprehend the risk that he took in speaking to the religious elite in such fashion. If I translate it to my own life and career, it gives me shivers. In this section of scripture, Jesus held up the religious establishment as an example of how *not* to be. He held up the Pharisees as the prototype of a false and destructive faith, a faith that would not only fail to build the kingdom, but might even encourage its destruction.

Don't Be Arrogant and Self-Important

In Matthew 6:7–13, Jesus told his followers that prayer should not be a vehicle for proving their religious importance. He asked them not to pray from a posture of arrogance, which was to fill the air with babble. Babbling prayer was an excellent example of the arrogance and self-importance that Jesus uncovered in the religious establishment.

The following are the marks of a babbling prayer:

➤ The person praying is concerned about how he or she looks while praying.

➤ It requires a human audience.

➤ It works at sounding holy.

➤ It makes every effort to impress others.

➤ It seeks to impress God with sheer magnitude.

Major Highways

"'And in praying do not heap up empty phrases as the Gentiles do; for they think that they will be heard for their many words. Do not be like them, for your Father knows what you need before you ask him. Pray like this:

'Our Father, who art in heaven,
Hallowed be thy name.
Thy kingdom come,
Thy will be done, On earth as it is in heaven.
Give us this day our daily bread;
And forgive us our debts, As we also have forgiven our debtors;
And lead us not into temptation, But deliver us from evil.'"

—Matthew 6:7–13

Jesus advocated prayer that came straight from the heart and was plain and simple. There is no need to posture before God, because God already knows what we need. The Lord's Prayer is offered as such a prayer. It says it all with no effort to impress anyone by its creativity or number of words. It's just a basic request that God grant all that is needed to enjoy the day.

Jesus' message was simple. Get the focus off of the self. We are not in charge. We are not in control. Prayer is not the human effort to convince God. Prayer is never impressive to God and should never be used to display faith.

Prayer is just one example of how the religious establishment became spiritually self-important and arrogant. The Jews prized prayer. Many rabbis spoke of their desire to pray all day long. Jesus' contemporaries had prayers for almost every conceivable occasion, and praying was thought of as a primary spiritual duty. For Jesus to condemn how the Pharisees prayed, or at least to scold them for filling the air with meaningless utterances, was a bold and harsh attack. Jesus was rebuking the Pharisees for being too busy trying to impress others by the wordiness of their prayers and spending no time building the kingdom. Jesus told his followers bluntly that it was far easier to act religious than to be faithful.

Don't Be Judgmental or Self-Righteous

Is there anything harder to do than to refrain from judging others? Is there any topic on which Jesus was more blatant? Jesus put the act of being judgmental in a particularly harsh light.

Being judgmental is the expression of self-righteousness, and self-righteousness equals spiritual elitism. Part of being judgmental is falsely believing that one can rank sin and sinners. Jesus never ranked sin or sinners because he knew that everyone was equal in the eyes of God.

Sadly, Jesus found that those who thought of themselves as most religious were often those who were most judgmental as well. The closer you are to God, the better you should know your own sin, and the more unwilling you should be to critique others. The truly faithful know that all righteousness is God's alone and that all judgment should be left to God.

Scenic Overlooks

"In prayer it is better to have a heart without words than words without a heart."

—John Bunyan

Major Highways

"'Judge not, that you be not judged. For with the judgment you pronounce you will be judged, and the measure you give will be the measure you get. Why do you see the speck that is in your brother's eye, but do not notice the log that is in your own eye? Or how can you say to your brother, 'Let me take the speck out of your eye,' when there is the log in your own eye? You hypocrite, first take the log out of your own eye, and then you will see clearly to take the speck out of your brother's eye.'"

—Matthew 7:1–5

Scenic Overlooks

"People judge you by your actions, not your intentions. You may have a heart of gold, but so has a hard-boiled egg."

—*Good Reading*

"Only God is in the position to look down on anyone."

—Sarah Browne

"I have never for one instant seen clearly within myself. How then could you have me judge the deeds of others?"

—Maurice Maeterlink

"Moral indignation is jealousy with a halo."

—H. G. Wells

Jesus worked hard not to judge others, yet he did judge some people. His judgments are of those folks of whom he expected the most and are issued forth from a place of pain and disappointment. He is hurt and offended by the failure of those he loves: his family, the disciples, the religious establishment, and all who fail to be the people he believes they were created to be.

However, his judgments were never cruel, manipulative, or secret. He issued them infrequently, in the open, and never in a mocking tone. He addressed the Pharisees in a voice of conviction and challenge. He made his comments and then moved on without grudge, quickly returning to his message of grace.

Detours

Vindicating our judgments is so easy. It is second nature to claim our right to judge others. Many of our harshest attacks are masked under the excuse of honesty. Self-righteousness and being judgmental are the most common, most defended, and most covered-up sins.

Don't Be Spiritually Hollow and Bankrupt

Jesus had a bottom line: The kingdom would never be built by the religious establishment. It had grown spiritually empty. It was consumed in details and had lost sight of the big picture. Those of the religious establishment talked the talk but did not walk the walk. Their religion was an act without loving action. Their spiritual lives had shriveled to monotonous routine and the wearing of legalistic blinders. They had become hopelessly devoid of loving.

I cannot think of a stronger spiritual image than the one Jesus used to describe the religious establishment: a whitewashed tomb. This tomb appears to be holy and pure, yet it is filled with nothing but lifeless bones. It is a passionless, deadening place.

Jesus saw the kingdom as a place filled with the genuine good life. It would be a sacred spot filled with joy, hope, and faith. It would be jammed with those who lived to love and loved to live. It would be a busy place of peacemaking, the passionate pursuit of justice, the preaching of good news to the poor, and the seeking out of the outcast. The kingdom outlined by Jesus would be loaded with the faith action of love.

Major Highwways

"'Woe to you, scribes and Pharisees, hypocrites! For you cleanse the outside of the cup and of the plate, but inside they are full of extortion and rapacity. You blind Pharisee! First cleanse the inside of the cup and of the plate, that the outside also may be clean.'"

—Matthew 23:25–26

Scenic Overlooks

"It is good enough to talk of God while we are sitting here after a nice breakfast and looking forward to a nicer luncheon, but how am I to talk of God to the millions who have to go without two meals a day? To them God can only appear as bread and butter."

—Mohandas K. Gandhi

The Least You Need to Know

➤ Jesus rebuked the religious establishment for being arrogant. He felt that the Pharisees were more interested in demonstrating how religious they were instead of truly living in a faithful manner.

➤ Jesus condemned those who were judgmental or self-righteous. He felt that God was the only one who should make judgments.

➤ Jesus warned that becoming immersed in details and religious rules and regulations would drain the love out of faith.

➤ The kingdom would never be built by the religious establishment because it had become spiritually empty.

Part 5

Jesus the Storyteller

Jesus was a born storyteller. He did most of his preaching and teaching in story form. Why did Jesus tell so many stories? Why did he use parables as his chief means of spiritual instruction?

Jesus was aware that good teaching is filled with good stories. People are best taught by the sharing of real life and can easily identify with a tale that comes out of their own history and tradition. Jesus was conscious that the lessons he wished to impart would best be shared through the medium of storytelling.

I suspect that Jesus was a great storyteller. He must have spoken with a strong, clear voice that could capture a crowd's attention. He wove tales from the fabric of the day-to-day lives of his listeners. He used common, everyday images. His parables were inviting to the ear because they sounded so familiar. His stories spoke a language of faith that was neither judgmental nor self-righteous. The faith that inhabited his stories was a plain and simple truth, available to all. The following chapters reveal Christ's parables and show why they were such strong messages to the people.

Parables: The Kingdom Is Like ...

Describing a person or place is difficult enough; describing a spiritual notion is even harder. Jesus used parables as a means to shed light on the concept of the kingdom. He wanted his followers to feel what it would be like to experience it.

The Kingdom: A Multifaceted Concept

Jesus used parables to tell people what the kingdom was like. He sought to share with his followers the essence of the place and the idea itself. He wanted his disciples to feel familiar with the territory, to feel at home on this spiritual land.

From my perspective, the kingdom was, for Jesus, a multifaceted conception:

➤ The dwelling place of God

➤ The presence of the sacred in the profane, the extraordinary in the ordinary, and the eternal in the everyday

➤ The truth, the home of the word, and the sanctuary of the heart of God

➤ Heaven come to earth

➤ The world living according to the will of God

Jesus used the concept of the kingdom strictly in a spiritual sense. He wanted the idea to maintain its mystery and elusive nature. He did not want humanity to believe it could own or contain it. He wanted to set the kingdom apart: not so distant as to be unseen, but not so close so as to cast a shadow. Jesus held the kingdom up as a goal, a spiritual aim, and a destiny.

Major Highways

"Another parable he put before them saying, 'The kingdom of heaven is like a grain of mustard seed which a man took and sowed in his field; it is the smallest of all seeds, but when it has grown it is the greatest of shrubs and becomes a tree, so that the birds of the air come and make nests in its branches.'"

—Matthew 13:31–32

Like a Mustard Seed

Jesus worked diligently to contrast the kingdom to the world. His use of the mustard seed as a defining image for the kingdom offered a stark contrast to a world in love with big things. Jesus knew that the world was impressed by size, that larger meant better. Anything God-like was thought to be grandiose.

Jesus disagreed that God and the kingdom should be represented in large-scale. The kingdom could be found in something as small and seemingly insignificant as a mustard seed. Jesus argued that it takes only a morsel of faith to transform a life, a relationship, or even a world. The mustard seed was traditionally the smallest seed used by the farmers of Christ's time. Nothing could have served better to illustrate his point that it only takes a little to yield great results.

Like Yeast

Jesus also compared the kingdom to yeast (Matthew 13:33). Though yeast looks like a small and insignificant ingredient, it permeates the whole loaf. Likewise, the kingdom will grow and expand despite its small beginnings.

Scenic Overlooks

"We find great things are made of little things,
And little things go lessening till at last
Comes God behind them."

—Robert Browning ("Mr. Sludge, 'The Medium'" from *Dramatis Personae*)

I suspect that Jesus' followers were looking for a major and complete transformation of the world. After all, the Messiah should be able to build the kingdom in the twinkling of an eye. However, Jesus was clear with his listeners that the kingdom would start small. The kingdom would be almost invisible in its very beginnings. Only over time would it rise up and expand into greatness.

Like Hidden Treasure

The parable of hidden treasure is short and quirky. By accident, a man stumbles upon a treasure hidden in a field. He reburies the treasure and buys the whole field to get it.

Jesus was letting his disciples know that this treasure was the most valuable thing they could possess. It was worth any price. If it required buying the whole field, so be it.

Jesus saw faith in God as the top priority in life. Nothing was of greater value, and only faith could produce lives of genuine worth.

Major Highways

"'The kingdom of heaven is like treasure hidden in a field, which a man found and covered up; then in his joy he goes and sells all that he has and buys that field.'"

—Matthew 13:44

Like a Pearl of Great Price

With the parable of a precious pearl, Jesus used a simple but striking poetic image for the kingdom. He was telling his disciples that they would have to value the kingdom above all things. The kingdom is rare, precious, and of eternal value.

Why is something as small as a tiny pearl of such great value? Only the heart of faith can know and understand. Jesus asked his followers to be on the lookout for such choice pearls. He also declared his expectation that if they found one, they would have to sacrifice everything to own it. Without faith, without God, and without truth, life has no value or worth; that is at the heart of Jesus' message.

Major Highways

"'Again, the kingdom of heaven is like a merchant in search of fine pearls, who, on finding one pearl of great value, went and sold all that he had and bought it.'"

—Matthew 13:45–46

Like Good Soil

Jesus taught his followers by comparing something familiar to something unfamiliar. His parables invited his listeners to discover the truth, but at the same time, they concealed the truth from those too spiritually lazy to think and feel.

The parable of the sower and the good soil was Jesus' way of asking his followers whether they were ready to find the kingdom. It queried their readiness to pay the price. Four different soils are used to compare those who are ready to become disciples and those who are not:

1. Seed that falls upon the hardened footpath is quickly eaten by birds. A hard heart or a hard head is never receptive to faith.

2. Seed that falls on shallow, rocky ground grows quickly, but it does not have the strong roots needed to withstand the light of day. This soil represents quick and easy faith that requires no cost, no sacrifice, and no endurance. It wilts just as quickly as it grows.

3. Seed that falls upon thorny ground is unable to breathe and blossom. It is strangled. With this image, Jesus describes how the worries and wishes of the world can suffocate the spirit.

4. The seed that falls upon fertile soil is able to yield an abundant crop.

Jesus followed with an explanation of what it meant (Matthew 13:10–23). This sort of explanation was rare, and I believe it emphasized the importance of this parable. Of course, the key to understanding this parable is understanding what Jesus meant by fertile soil. Such soil …

➤ Was fruitful.

➤ Was receptive to the presence of God.

➤ Made growing love its sole priority.

➤ Was receptive to building the kingdom.

Major Highways

"That same day Jesus went out of the house and sat beside the sea. And great crowds gathered about him, so that he got into a boat and sat there; and the whole crowd stood on the beach. And he told them many things in parables, saying: 'A sower went out to sow. And as he sowed, some seeds fell along the path, and the birds came and devoured them. Other seeds fell on rocky ground, where they had not much soil, and immediately they sprang up, since they had no depth of soil, but when the sun rose they were scorched; and since they had no root they withered away. Other seeds fell upon thorns, and the thorns grew up and choked them. Other seeds fell on good soil and brought forth grain, some a hundredfold, some sixty, some thirty. He who has ears, let him hear.'"

—Matthew 13:1–9

Jesus wanted his followers to search for the kingdom. If necessary, he wanted them to dig down deep to find it. He wanted them to be willing to pay any price to build the kingdom. He asked a full commitment of his disciples because he believed the building of the kingdom would require it.

Jesus could not paint a detailed, realistic landscape of the kingdom. Instead, he chose to offer an impressionistic rendering. He gave us the feel of the kingdom.

Jesus made it clear that the kingdom would not come in big packages. Instead, it would be tiny but valuable. The kingdom was worth any price and needed to be a person's top, if not sole, priority. Though Jesus indicated that the kingdom was hidden, he made it equally clear that it could be found.

The Least You Need to Know

➤ Parables offer poetic images that strive to illuminate or capture the spirit of the kingdom.

➤ The kingdom may at first appear to be tiny and insignificant, but it will eventually grow and expand.

➤ If you locate the kingdom, be willing to pay any spiritual price to make it yours.

➤ Searching for the kingdom is a disciple's highest calling.

➤ The kingdom can be planted only in those hearts and minds that have made themselves ready to receive.

Parables: Lost and Found

One of the primary themes of the ministry of Jesus was to find those who were lost. He believed that in the kingdom everyone would have a physical and spiritual home. All people would be of value, and everyone's gifts would be cherished.

Jesus Empathized with the Lost

I can only speculate about this, but I suspect that Jesus came from a family who welcomed strangers. He must have been raised in the belief that everyone has value and that all are equal in the eyes of God. Jesus had a bold belief in the willingness of faith to search for those who are lost and to bring them safely home.

I further contend that Jesus knew from experience what it was like to be left out, rejected, and scorned. The lost-and-found parables were told with insight and compassion. Jesus knew the pain of rejection. He knew the agony of watching close friends and family turn their backs. He also knew what it was like to lose faith and to question the meaning of everything. To ask God the question, "Why have you forsaken me?" while on the cross, Jesus had to have experienced the loss of intimacy, life, love, and faith.

Jesus did not just talk about welcoming the outcast to his table; he went out and extended the invitation. The difference here is the one between delivering a turkey to a homeless shelter at Thanksgiving and inviting the diners at the shelter to your home. Jesus did the latter.

Scenic Overlooks

"You never really understand a person until you consider things from his point of view."

—Harper Lee (from *To Kill a Mockingbird*)

Jesus was offensive to the people of his time, especially the religious establishment, because of his close association to those the world chose to reject and ridicule. Jesus befriended and associated with the following:

➤ Sinners

➤ Tax collectors

➤ Women

➤ Prostitutes

➤ Samaritans

➤ The poor

➤ Lepers

➤ The mentally ill

Jesus was fearless in his belief that those scorned by society must be affirmed by people of faith. He challenged his followers not only to find the lost and the outcast, but also to bring them home and back to life. His was a ministry of recovery, and he recovered souls. He gave the lonely and despised a will to live.

Points of Interest

I have found that if you speak today of the experience of being lost physically, emotionally, or spiritually, you immediately have the audience in the palm of your hand. No other theme resonates so dramatically and deeply with the soul of modern men and women.

The Lost Sheep

When Jesus is criticized for eating with sinners, he tells the parable of the lost sheep (see the following Major Highways sidebar), in which a shepherd leaves his flock of 99 sheep to go look for one that has wandered away. When he finds the lost sheep, he is overjoyed. This parable illustrates that the kingdom and the world did not use the same math. In the kingdom, 1 was larger than 99. From the perspective of the world, as Jesus understood it, 99 were not only much more important than 1, but 1 also could easily be left behind and lost forever. From the world's perspective, going after the one who was lost was unnecessary. If they got themselves lost, they could get themselves found. The one was just not the world's problem.

Major Highways

"Now the tax collectors and sinners were all drawing near to hear him. And the Pharisees and the scribes murmured, saying, 'This man receives sinners and eats with them.' So he told them this parable: 'What man of you, having a hundred sheep, if he has lost one of them, does not leave the ninety-nine in the wilderness, and go after the one which is lost, until he finds it? And when he has found it, he lays it on his shoulders, rejoicing. And when he comes home he calls together his friends and his neighbors, saying to them, "Rejoice with me, for I have found my sheep which was lost." Just so, I tell you, there will be no more joy in heaven over one sinner who repents than over ninety-nine righteous persons who need no repentance.'"

—Luke 15:1–7

The Lost Coin

Palestinian women were given 10 silver coins as a wedding gift. These coins thus became objects of great sentimental value. To lose one would create heartbreak. The search to find a missing coin would be in earnest and extensive. Every possible effort would be made to locate the missing coin. Every nook and cranny would be examined.

Major Highways

"'Or what woman, having ten silver coins, if she loses one coin, does not light a lamp and sweep the house and seek diligently until she finds it? And when she has found it, she calls together her friends and neighbors, saying, 'Rejoice with me, for I have found the coin which I had lost.' Just so I tell you, there is joy before the angels of God over one sinner who repents.'"

—Luke 15:8–10

Jesus describes such a search in a passage known as the parable of the lost coin. I don't believe the content of the lost coin parable is as significant as is its placement, which is immediately following the lost sheep parable. Its placement seems to underline the importance of the theme that the lost must be found.

Jesus stressed the importance of each individual. He made his followers aware that every soul was important to God. Because most of his followers were those who felt powerless, even pointless, his message must have felt like cool water on parched lips. The idea that everyone was precious was and is a radical idea, especially if you live it as your faith.

The Lost Son

The parable of the prodigal son (Luke 15:11–32) is probably the most famous story taken from scripture. I would venture a guess that it is the topic of more sermons than any other. This story seems to speak eternally to the heart of the human race.

Here's the gist of this tale: A father works with his two sons on a farm. The younger son grows bored with life on the farm and demands his inheritance early. This son literally tells his father to drop dead and give him what he has coming. Amazingly, the father gives him the money.

This son heads off for the big city and the bright lights, determined to make a name for himself. He squanders his fortune while the father waits and the elder son works the farm. Famine strikes the land, and the younger son becomes homeless and hungry. He hits bottom—he is found eating at a pig trough.

The younger son finally comes to his senses and heads home with a repentant heart. His father runs to greet him and welcome him home and throws a huge block party in his honor. The dutiful elder son is furious. The father tries to teach the elder son of the spiritual significance of welcoming home the lost, but the elder son doesn't buy it.

This parable has three primary characters and an equal number of points. Understanding this parable is crucial to understanding the faith of Jesus.

The Younger Son

The younger son represented those who listened to Jesus. He was tempted to follow the path laid out by the world. He was looking for the good life. He wanted to be something special and make a name for himself, a big name. He wanted more of everything. He wanted his share of the pie.

In the process of trying to become a somebody, he spiritually becomes a nobody. He sells his soul. He gains the world, but he loses everything that matters. He hits bottom big time. He falls flat on his spiritual face and is lost.

The Father

The father is God. He loves his younger son enough to let him go. He gives him the freedom to fall on his face. His love is without conditions.

He waits patiently and expectantly, and he prays for his son's return. When he sees the son returning down the road, he runs to meet him. His forgiveness is a celebration. His forgiveness is full, with no strings attached. The party he throws displays the grace he offers his children.

The Elder Son

The elder son symbolizes the religious establishment, those folks who have worked hard to do good and have done so for a long time. They cannot understand the father's treatment of this wandering son. They cannot tolerate the throwing of a party for a spoiled brat. They are furious with the special attention given those who do not deserve it. They feel entitled to determine who does and does not deserve God's grace.

This parable sheds great light on the faith of Jesus:

➤ Jesus believed that God's love was unconditional.

➤ Jesus believed that everyone can and must be forgiven, even those who have walked away from God and God's work.

➤ Forgiveness is a celebration.

➤ Forgiveness is seldom earned or deserved.

➤ If you do God's work, you should expect no other reward but the work itself. You shouldn't demand money or sulk because no one throws you a party.

Detours

Do we all secretly harbor that adolescent need to feel the power of leaving someone out? I suspect we do, more often than we care to admit.

The faith of Jesus required deep compassion. His faith was offensive to the people of his time because it was quick to forgive and actively sought out the outcast. Jesus' party-throwing faith was scandalous to the religious establishment.

Scenic Overlooks

"He who cannot forgive others destroys the bridge over which he himself must pass."

—George Herbert

"Forgiveness is a gift of high value. Yet its cost is nothing."

—Betty Smith (from *A Tree Grows in Brooklyn*)

"One of the most lasting pleasures you can experience is the feeling that comes over you when you genuinely forgive an enemy—whether he knows it or not."

—O. A. Batista (from *Quote* magazine)

The Least You Need to Know

➤ Jesus was appalled by how the world, and the religious establishment, treated many folks as though they did not matter.

➤ In the kingdom, nobody would be an outcast.

➤ Jesus believed that a strong faith would seek out the lost in the world.

➤ Jesus believed that all of us are lost at one point, and only by the grace of God are any of us found.

Chapter 13

Parables: Upside Down

In This Chapter

➤ When saving isn't smart

➤ How to respond to God's invitation

➤ Why the good Samaritan is a radical image

The followers of Jesus thought of him as extremely wise. Most of the people with whom he came in contact thought he was a fool. The religious establishment thought he was nuts. At one point Jesus told folks that they should give him their burdens and that he alone could give them rest. How scandalous! How could this guy with no money, no power, and no social or religious rank or privilege claim to give anyone anything, let alone rest? The world had declared that he had nothing to offer. The religious establishment had declared that what he offered was a lie.

Jesus confronted the wisdom of the world by declaring it foolishness. He also elevated those whom the world had branded as fools to the rank of the wise. Jesus turned over the tables of the money-changers at the temple, and he deliberately sought to turn the world on its proverbial ear.

Jesus made it clear that the kingdom of God was nothing like the kingdoms of the world. He boldly stated that faith in that kingdom was totally unlike the hypocritical religiosity of the Pharisees. Jesus' teachings came out swinging, and he used his parables to pack the knockout wallop.

The Rich Fool

With the parable of the rich fool (Luke 12:13–21), Jesus caused a stir right from the get-go. If you were rich, you were thought to be blessed by God. If you were blessed by God, you must be wise. Wrong! Jesus severed the tie between wealth and wisdom.

The parable begins with someone asking a question usually asked of a rabbi. Jesus does not appear to answer the question, but his response points to an even deeper issue. Jesus challenges the wisdom of spending one's life accumulating worldly wealth; he makes the point that the good life has nothing to do with wealth. In Jesus' view, the good life is all about building the kingdom and being on good terms with God. With the parable of the rich fool, Jesus makes the point that you can't take it with you.

Jesus is here challenging the wisdom of the world, which …

➤ Encourages saving money as the way to security.

➤ Tells us that we are secure if we have enough in the bank, or in the rich fool's case, barn.

➤ Asks us to spend all of our time and energy on becoming financially secure.

Scenic Overlooks

"Never mistake knowledge for wisdom. One helps you make a living; the other helps you make a life."

—Sandra Carey

Jesus turns that logic upside down:

➤ Money does not make a person secure.

➤ Material good does not last.

➤ Only God offers genuine security.

➤ Life should be spent in the pursuit of God, not money.

➤ Faith is our fortune.

The Great Feast

In the parable of the great feast (Luke 14:15–24), Jesus issues a direct confrontation to the religious establishment. The story goes that there was a great banquet being held, and all the A-list guests (the religious establishment) came up with paltry excuses for not attending. The host (God) will not and cannot cancel the party. He sends his servants (the followers of Jesus) out into the streets to invite the poor, the crippled, the lame, and the blind.

The host is clearly not pleased with the excuses offered by the A-list guests. The Z-list guests are treated like A-list guests and thus become A-list guests. Here, again, the message is transparent. Jesus turns the religious establishment's notion of favored status with God upside down. The Z-list has become the A-list and vice versa.

The Good Samaritan

The parable of the good Samaritan (Luke 10:25–37) is an outstanding parable. It stands out because it is such a slap at the religious establishment.

In this parable, a Jewish man is traveling from Jerusalem to Jericho. This route is notoriously dangerous and swarming with thieves. The Jewish man is stripped, beaten, robbed, and left for dead at the side of the road. A Jewish priest walks by the man and ignores him. A temple assistant also walks right on by, noticing but failing to stop. A Samaritan, who was despised by the Jews, stops to care for the wounded man. The Samaritan attends the man's wounds, takes him to an inn, and pays the bill. So extravagant is the Samaritan in his care for the man that he tells the innkeeper that he will also pay any other bills the next time he is there.

This parable is painfully obvious. Its razor-sharp message turned everything the world and the religious establishment held dear upside down. In the parable, the religious establishment miserably fails a test of true faith when both the priest and the temple assistant fail to stop and attend to the person in need.

The Samaritans were the people the religious establishment saw as least likely to respond in faith and do the right thing. But in this parable, the Samaritan is lifted up as the hero. The Samaritan proves to be a kingdom builder. He demonstrates extravagant love for his enemy, a Jew.

Detours

When God calls, most of us have many excuses for failing to pick up the phone. We may even hear the message being delivered, but we still don't pick up. We are just too busy and too important and cannot be bothered. This spiritual issue of Christ's time is just as robust in our own.

Jesus was fearless. His faith came from a place of pure conviction. He spoke the truth. He chose to say what needed to be heard, not what folks hoped to hear. He attacked those who saw themselves as beyond reproach. Because he entrusted power to and showered love upon those the world thought of as fools, the world could not accept his wisdom.

Remember that in the times in which Jesus ministered, the poor, the lame, the crippled, and the blind were all believed to be cursed by God. Jesus turned that notion upside down. Those who were called losers by the world became winners in the kingdom. Those whom the world saw as unworthy of God's love were to be known as God's most cherished children.

The Least You Need to Know

➤ Jesus' parables reflected values that were in stark contrast to those of the world around him.

➤ Jesus criticized those who focused on money at the expense of their spirit.

➤ Jesus attacked the religious establishment for failing to live according to God's wishes.

➤ Jesus saw deeds as far more important than creeds and held out the Samaritan as an unlikely hero.

➤ The parables taught by Jesus infuriated the religious establishment by painting it as faithless and indifferent to human need.

Part 6
Jesus the Healer

Whatever your faith or perspective on the topic, clearly some things did happen that Christ's followers considered of a miraculous nature. Whether those happenings were actually miracles or not is left to you and your faith to judge.

I will say, though, that Jesus did not distinguish miracles. For Jesus, all of life was a miracle. The events recorded in scripture may have caught the attention of his followers, but may have been of little importance to Christ. Jesus was likely to have viewed the act of falling in love to be every bit as miraculous as walking on water—and a good deal more dangerous.

Many miracles are attributed to Jesus. I cannot prove them. I cannot explain them. I will not try to defend them. In these chapters, though, I share with you those events of his ministry that were called miracles.

Chapter 14

The Healing Powers: Faith and Forgiveness

In This Chapter

➤ Fear destroys and faith heals

➤ Tenacity and faith work miracles for a paralyzed man and two blind men

➤ Blind Bartimaeus and the bleeding woman believe they can be healed

➤ A Roman centurion becomes an example of strong faith

The time in which Jesus lived and ministered must have been a frightening one. Poverty was extensive. Disease was rampant. War was either on the horizon or had already arrived. Earthquakes, famines, and eclipses were seen as ominous signs from an angry God. Few appeared to be blessed by God; many seemed to be cursed by him. The enormous fear of the unknown drove many to cult religions or insanity. The belief system of many was based on the notion of a God who was frequently ruthless.

Faith vs. Fear

As you read about the miracles of Jesus, think for a moment about the enormous power of fear. Physically, emotionally, and spiritually, fear is the opponent of faith. It robs faith of any power or purpose. Fear has the capacity to do the following:

➤ Paralyze people

➤ Send people into lives of hiding

➤ Worry people sick

➤ Break people's spirit

➤ Haunt people with bad memories

➤ Give people nightmares

➤ Make people's lives living nightmares

Jesus was a man of faith. He was convinced that faith could build the kingdom. He saw faith as possessing miraculous powers of courage and transformation. As you might suppose, he also saw faith as healing. Just as fear can be physically debilitating, emotionally wounding, and spiritually scarring, faith has the capacity to promote health.

Your beliefs about miracles are most likely directly linked to your understanding of faith. Jesus was always quick to point out the power of faith to his followers. He did so in such a way as to make that power seem ordinary. The power of faith was not abnormal to Jesus, so in many respects, he would not have thought of it as a miracle. His followers were those who branded this power as miraculous.

Remember that to Jesus the whole human body was a miracle, as was the earth itself. Therefore it was unnecessary to make one event more miraculous than another. He simply called attention to the capacity of faith to transform an attitude, a life, a love, a friendship, a family, or a world.

A Paralyzed Man

Most miracle stories are quite sparse in terms of detail. They give little information as to the backgrounds or motivations of those healed. For example, the Gospel of Mark never explains why or how the paralyzed man came to be paralyzed. What the story does tell us is that a man's paralysis moved his friends to do something (Mark 2:1–12).

The paralyzed man's friends had heard that Jesus was in Capernaum, so they brought their friend to see him. Jesus was well-known by this time, and his dwelling place was jammed with visitors. Undeterred, and remarkably bold, these friends carried the paralyzed man to the roof. The roofs of that time were flat and made of mud mixed with straw. They cut out an opening and lowered the paralyzed man in on a mat. Jesus was startled—and I bet a bit amused—by the tenacity and faith of these four friends.

The first thing Jesus told the paralyzed man was that his sins were forgiven. Some of the Pharisees who were there were appalled to hear him claim to forgive sins. Jesus next told him to get up and walk and announced that he was healed.

This story captures the twin themes of almost all scriptural miracle accounts:

➤ Faith has miraculous powers to heal.

➤ Forgiveness is the dynamic core of all faith.

Jesus was said to have been impressed by the determination of the four friends to get the paralyzed man to him. Their love for their friend and their faith that Jesus could help were overwhelming. He was struck by the rawness of their faith, a faith that would not be stopped and that broke all rules of decorum.

The forgiveness of sin was critical in this story, as was the role played by the Pharisees. The Pharisees were so consumed in the law that they came to represent a paralyzing fear of sin. Whether the man's paralysis was purely physical or coated in a deep fear of being unforgivable is not the point. Either way, the Pharisees were more interested in the man's sin than in healing his paralysis. They would have been quicker to point out his supposedly divinely sanctioned state of immobility than to have offered him the grace of movement.

Jesus freed this man to walk. The man may have been trapped in a sin he felt no God could forgive. He could have been paralyzed by the fear of hell. He could have been stopped cold by the scorn and ridicule of everyone but these four men. He also could have fallen and damaged his spine. I don't know. What I do know is that Jesus offered the man faith, hope, and love. It was apparently exactly what was needed.

Two Blind Men

The miracle story of the two blind men (Matthew 9:27–31) again reveals the importance Jesus placed on tenacity and faith in creating miracles. The two men ask for healing and mercy. Jesus listens, but he initially does not respond. The two men follow Jesus back to where he is staying and walk in without an invitation. Jesus is clearly impressed by their boldness and disregard for protocol.

Jesus then asks the men directly if they have faith. They assure him that they do. Jesus touches their eyes and tells them that they are healed. They can see. Jesus tells them to keep this miracle quiet, but they tell everyone they can.

This miracle story makes five graphic points:

➤ Jesus pays attention to those who follow him.

➤ Jesus is very impressed by faith that will not be stopped.

➤ Jesus loves faith that has no regard for religious or political protocol.

➤ Jesus believes that faith can and will heal.

➤ Jesus is touched by the plight of these men, and he touches them. His touch is said to transfer healing. Therefore, healing means being deeply touched.

Most people would have chosen to stay away from these two men. Their blindness would have been seen as a sign from God of their sinful status. These two blind men were likely treated as repulsive. Jesus not only spoke with them, but he also did so on intimate terms. He asked them about their faith and was touched by their fierce will to be healed. He then touched their eyes. I wonder when the last time was that anyone had touched these symbols of sinful shame? Jesus touched the part of them they believed to be untouchable.

Blind Bartimaeus

Hordes of beggars filled every town of Jesus' time. Bartimaeus (Mark 10:46–52) was a beggar because he was blind and could not work. His disability had left him penniless. As far as religious status went, he was on the bottom rung. Again, blindness was thought of as a curse from God, and begging was thought to be an act of shame.

Major Highways

"And they came to Jericho; and as he was leaving Jericho with his disciples and a great multitude, Bartimaeus, a blind beggar, the son of Timaeus, was sitting by the roadside. And when he heard that it was Jesus of Nazareth, he began to cry out and say, 'Jesus, Son of David, have mercy on me!' ... And Jesus stopped and said, 'Call him.' And they called the blind man, saying to him, 'Take heart; rise, he is calling you.' And throwing off his mantle he sprang up and came to Jesus. And Jesus said to him, 'What do you want me to do for you?' And the blind man said to him, 'Master, let me receive my sight.' And Jesus said to him, 'Go your way; your faith has made you well.' And immediately he received his sight and followed him on the way."

—Mark 10:46–52

Bartimaeus addressed Jesus as "Son of David." This address was a popular way of calling Jesus the Messiah. Because Bartimaeus recognized Jesus as the Messiah even though Bartimaeus could not see him, Jesus respected him. Bartimaeus begged for sight, and Jesus granted his wish.

This story contains a few striking insights about the miracles of Jesus:

➤ Even though the scriptures were clear about the importance of caring for the needy, the religious establishment had failed to do so.

➤ The desire to be healed had to be passionate, even obsessive.

➤ Jesus never claimed to have performed the healing. He gave all the credit to the man's faith.

➤ Jesus did not see the miracles as a waving of some magic wand of health, but rather an affirmation of the power of human faith to heal. Bartimaeus had sufficient faith to seek healing, and to do so confident that he would receive it.

➤ The miracles do not come from the outside in, but from the inside out.

The Healing at the Pool

The healing at the pool (John 5:1–18) is a strange miracle story with many implications. In this story, Jesus returned to Jerusalem for a celebration and noticed a man waiting by the Pool of Bethesda, a pool that was believed to contain healing waters. It was held that the first person into the pool when the waters rippled would be healed. This man had been sick for 38 years and had been going to the pool ever since becoming ill.

Jesus asked the man whether he sincerely wanted to get well; the sick man replied that nobody has been there to help him into the pool. Jesus told him to pick up his mat and walk; the man did and was healed. Jesus also told the man to stop sinning, or something worse would happen to him. This miracle occurred on the Sabbath, on which no one was to work. The fact that the man walked and carried his mat was considered work, and this action upset the Pharisees.

I love this story. It is chock-full of symbolism and insight and is wide open for interpretation. This story makes these points about sickness and miracles:

➤ Some people want to be sick.

➤ Some people wait endlessly for others to make them well and blame others for not healing them or for making them sick.

➤ The fact that a person has been visited with a miracle does not guarantee that his or her future life will be problem-free. Worse things can happen if one doesn't choose to live as a person of faith, the very faith that makes one well.

Jesus was skeptical of the man at the pool. Jesus needed to know that this man was sincere, that he really wanted to get well and that his sickness had not become a way of life for him. Jesus made sure that the person's faith was authentic. Like Jesus' other healings, this healing required no magical waters. It required the aid of nobody else but the sufferer. In addition, the healing was grounded in the forgiveness of sins. Jesus may have been initially skeptical of the man, but the religious establishment was so far off the mark that they were more concerned about the man breaking the law of working on the Sabbath than about celebrating his healing.

The Bleeding Woman

A major factor in Jesus' miracle stories is not the miracle itself, but who receives them. Mark 5:21–34 tells about a woman who is bleeding constantly. This symptom means she likely had a menstrual or uterine disorder, which made her ritually unclean. Socially, she would have been considered untouchable. Anyone who touched her wouldn't be able to go near God. Jesus revealed the opposite to be true.

The woman was convinced that if she could simply touch the robe of Jesus, she would be healed. She did so. Jesus was somehow aware of her touch and searched for her in the crowd. She came to him in total fear, certain that she had done a shameful thing. Instead, she was affirmed for her reaching out to touch his garment and was told that she was healed. The bleeding stopped.

Like the story of the two blind men, this miracle account places heavy emphasis on touch. To me, the point is clear: Jesus wants his followers to know that when they feel most out of touch with God and most unworthy of his embrace that is exactly the time they should reach out for God. God touches those whom the world does not go near and heals those whom the world rejects. God cares passionately about those the world despises.

Another important point of this story is that faith is action. The bleeding woman came to Jesus and reached out to him. She risked touching his garment. Her faith is what cured her, and it was a faith in action. No miracle can be found in a dormant faith.

The Roman Centurion's Servant

I read the miracle story of the Roman centurion's servant (Luke 7:1–10) as a subtle slam on the religious establishment. It is more veiled than Jesus' other critiques of the Pharisees, but the criticism is still piercing.

Major Highways

"Now a centurion had a slave who was dear to him, who was sick and at the point of death. When he heard of Jesus, he sent to him elders of the Jews, asking him to come and heal his slave. And when they came to Jesus, they besought him earnestly, saying, 'He is worthy to have you do this for him, for he loves our nation, and he built us our synagogue.' And Jesus went with them. When he was not far from the house, the centurion sent friends to him, saying to him, 'Lord, do not trouble yourself, for I am not worthy to have you come under my roof; therefore I did not presume to come to you. But say the word and let my servant be healed ....' When Jesus heard this he marveled at him, and turned and said to the multitude that followed him, 'I tell you, not even in Israel have I found such faith.' And when those who had been sent returned to the house, they found the slave well."

—Luke 7:2–10

In this story, a Roman *centurion*—who would ordinarily have been hated by the Jews, except that this one had been helpful to them—sends his Jewish friends to plead for his servant, who is ill. The centurion believes the Jewish leaders would have more credibility with Jesus than he would (although the opposite is the case), and he passes on the message that he does not feel worthy of a visit from Jesus. His concern for his slave is far greater than the compassion shown by the religious establishment for the poor and needy.

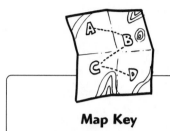

Map Key

A **centurion** was a leader of a division of Roman forces.

The centurion's faith is absolute. Even if Jesus is not there, he is convinced that all Jesus needs to do is say the word. This miracle is one where the presence of Jesus (and that of the centurion, for that matter) is not required.

The religious establishment showed Jesus little or no faith. They neglected those in need. They oppressed the poor. They appeared to despise the sick or disabled. Any faith they had seemed to come from either following the dictates of the law to the letter or from seeing some proof of God's presence firsthand. They also treated Jesus with disdain.

The centurion showed great faith. He cared deeply for his slave and went to great lengths to help him. He showed Jesus respect by sending Jewish leaders and by not demanding an audience with him. He demonstrated full faith by saying that he knew that a mere word from Jesus would be sufficient. His treatment of Jesus displayed true reverence.

The Least You Need to Know

➤ Fear is the main obstacle to faith and, thus, to miracles.

➤ Miracles come to those who are sincere in their desire for one.

➤ Miracles come to those who feel that Jesus can indeed forgive sins.

➤ Miracles come to those who have great and authentic faith, a faith that will risk almost anything.

➤ Miracles are created inside the human soul by the transforming powers of faith. Jesus does not claim to perform miracles.

➤ Miracles never come by command or demand.

Chapter 15

Demon Demolition Derby

In This Chapter

➤ Jesus acts as an agent of grace

➤ Jesus denies dealings with the devil

➤ Pigs are possessed by a legion of demons

➤ The disciples try to exorcise

In Joseph Heller's little-known book *Something Happened,* he describes a middle-aged man's attack of the "willies." The "willies" is a swarming emptiness, sadness, and grief. It is the experience of having lived a lie or, worse yet, of being a lie. It is the feeling of being lost and having lost out on life. It is a belief that the worst is yet to come.

The "willies" is another name for demons. For those who feel haunted by demons, they are real. The folks of Jesus' time had little or no understanding of a mental break-down, a psychotic episode, neurotic or compulsive behavior, addiction, or attacks of anxiety. They had no names for these maladies other than demons. All they knew was that demons made people act in bizarre ways that were frightening and alarming. This chapter explains how Jesus dealt with these demons.

Jesus as Therapist

Carl Rogers (1902–1987) has often been called the most influential psychologist in American history. He was the founder of *client-centered therapy.* Rogers outlined five specific tasks of a good therapist:

1. The therapist must be genuine.

2. The therapist must establish a relationship of trust with the client.

3. The therapist must offer unconditional, positive regard (love and forgiveness) in ample doses.

4. The client must be seen as a work in progress. Healing is an ongoing process.

5. There is no room for giving up on an individual.

Detours

Does it bother you to have Jesus called a therapist? Why? Does that label seem to make him less than godlike? Therapy, in my experience, is loaded with the presence of God. Good therapy and good faith are after the same thing: a healthy, whole person who can live life to the fullest. Jesus surely did not think of himself as a therapist—there was no such category of thought or profession then—but he did function as one, according to Rogers's job description.

A good therapist is an agent of grace. Though Rogers would not have used the word grace to describe his approach, I don't think he would have been offended by it either.

Jesus was a good therapist. His approach was analogous to Rogers's in every respect, except one. Jesus would expect those he healed to believe. Faith was a prerequisite to all these healings.

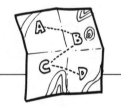

Map Key

A **demon** is a living lie; a lie lived.

Satan (also known as Beelzebub) is the author of all lies and the advocate for living them.

Jesus and Satan

The Gospel of Luke states that Jesus cast out the *demon* that had kept a man from speaking (Luke 11:14–23). We do not know if this man's speechlessness had been since birth or was a more recent phenomenon. We do know that Jesus freed this man so that he could speak. We are not sure whether he granted the man the physical freedom to speak or removed emotional and spiritual barriers to his speech.

After witnessing this miracle, the Pharisees made an astonishingly offensive accusation, saying that the only reason Jesus was able to remove demons was because he worked for *Satan*. We can only imagine how offensive this charge was to Christ.

Jesus responded angrily and firmly. He said that it was crazy to think that an agent of the prince of demons would work to eradicate the presence of demons. He also said that you couldn't be on the side of God and Satan. You must have allegiance to one or the other.

Jesus makes the following clear:

➤ He is casting out demons in the name of God.

➤ If you believe Jesus is an agent of Satan, you have in fact turned your back on God, and *you* have become the agent of Satan.

➤ The power of God is much stronger than the power of Satan. Against faith, Satan cannot win.

At the close of this passage, a woman yells out a blessing on the womb of Jesus' mother—a sign of deep gratitude for his having been born. Jesus diverts the blessing. He states that the truly blessed are those who hear the word of God and do it.

Major Highways

"Now he was casting out a demon that was dumb; when the demon had gone out, the dumb man spoke, and the people marveled. But some of them said, 'He casts out demons by Beelzebub, the prince of demons'; while others, to test him, sought from him a sign from heaven. But he, knowing their thoughts, said to them, 'Every kingdom divided against itself is laid waste, and a divided household falls. And if Satan also is divided against himself, how will his kingdom stand? For you say that I cast out demons by Beelzebub. And if I cast out demons by Beelzebub, by whom do your sons cast them out? Therefore they shall be your judges. But if it is by the finger of God that I cast out demons, then the kingdom of God has come upon you.'"

—Luke 11:14–20

A Mob of Demons

The story of the mob of demons (Mark 5:1–20) is fascinating. It tells of a man who was believed to be possessed by demons. In modern terms, the man was mentally ill. He was a wild man who could not even be restrained by chains.

Clearly, he was a source of great fear to the people of the area known as Gerasenes. He lived in what was the equivalent of a cemetery, housed in a tomb. He was known to scream wildly at night and hit himself with stones.

This man saw Jesus pulling ashore by boat and ran to meet him. Jesus had most likely already heard stories of the man, because he was not shocked by the craziness he witnessed. The man told Jesus that his demons were legion.

Several things strike me about this story up to this point:

➤ The mentally ill man was alone and had been completely shunned. Everyone was terrified of him.

➤ The only human contact he appeared to have had was to be shackled.

➤ He lived in a tomb, which would certainly only serve to worsen his condition.

➤ His misery was obvious and enormous. He wailed into the night and was bloodied by his own efforts to pound the demons into submission.

➤ He ran to meet Jesus, who was either known to be accessible or gave off that aura.

➤ Jesus showed no fear. He spoke calmly with the man. He did not run or hide.

➤ Jesus became his confessor, as the demon-possessed man revealed the nature of his mental illness.

➤ The man claimed that his demons were legion, which was the largest unit in the Roman army, consisting of 3,000 to 6,000 soldiers.

The next aspect of the story is classic. Jesus ordered the demons out of the man's body and charged them to enter a herd of swine that grazed nearby. The demons came out of the man and entered the pigs, and then all 2,000 pigs ran wildly over the edge of a bluff to drown in the sea below. Jesus then told the man to tell people about his healing.

The demon-possessed pigs are an excellent example of what psychologists call transference. Transference is the idea behind having a person beat a pillow to vent their anger. In this case, Jesus used pigs, notoriously unclean animals that Jews could not eat or touch. The only reason pigs were present was that the Gerasenes was a Gentile area south of the Sea of Galilee.

I consider this story to be an exorcism. The exorcism was successful because …

➤ Jesus believed that the man was possessed by demons.

➤ The man believed that Jesus could help.

➤ The man believed that the demons had entered the pigs.

I am hard pressed to explain why Jesus tells the healed man to tell people about his healing. He requested that most miracles be kept quiet. I suspect that because this

140

area was a Gentile region, he may have been less wary of the religious establishment and their incessant criticizing.

A Boy with a Demon

In the story of a boy with a demon, a passionately compassionate father brought his son to Jesus. The boy suffered from seizures and fits and was a danger to himself. He often fell. He had fallen into the sea and even a fire.

The boy had been brought to the disciples, but they had failed to heal him.

Jesus attributed the failure of the disciples to heal this boy directly to their lack of faith. This statement was Jesus' clearest and boldest claim to the centrality of faith in healing. In his frustration, he went so far as to say that if the disciples had faith the size of a mustard seed, they could have cast out the boy's demon. The healing performed by Jesus is swift and complete. The "demon" was eradicated.

For me, this story describes Jesus dealing with an epileptic child. Epilepsy was a terrifying disease for the people of this time. Obviously, we no longer associate epilepsy with demons, but it is understandable that this illness would have appeared to have been possession by a demonic force then.

Major Highways

"And when they came to the crowd, a man came up to him and kneeling before him said, 'Lord, have mercy on my son, for he is an epileptic and he suffers terribly; for often he falls into the fire, and often into the water. And I brought him to your disciples, and they could not heal him.' And Jesus answered, 'O faithless and perverse generation, how long am I to be with you? How long am I to bear with you? Bring him here to me.' And Jesus rebuked him and the demon came out of him, and the boy was cured instantly. Then the disciples came to Jesus privately and said, 'Why could we not cast it out?' He said to them, 'Because of your little faith. For truly, I say to you, if you have faith as a grain of mustard seed, you will say to this mountain "Move from here to there," and it will move; and nothing will be impossible to you.'"

—Matthew 17:14–21

The Least You Need to Know

➤ Jesus dealt with demons as real.

➤ Jesus showed demon-possessed folks mercy and compassion.

➤ Those people suspected of demonic possession trusted Christ and sought him out.

➤ Jesus ordered the demons out. Jesus took charge of the situation and claimed a power greater than the demon.

➤ The power Jesus exclusively claimed was faith.

➤ A demon was no match for a mustard seed of faith.

Chapter 16

Wombs and Tombs

In This Chapter

➤ Believing in resurrection

➤ Dying spiritually

➤ Being born again

➤ Raising the dead

Speculation about the great beyond is rampant in today's world. There are many stories of those who have actually died for a short time and then been revived. These tales of tunnels to white light are becoming more and more numerous and certainly stand up to the test of consistency. The Shroud of Turin, which some claim bears the tracings of a risen Christ, appears to be authentic but leaves ample room for doubt and ongoing skepticism.

I think, for many people, a belief in resurrection stems from an inability to believe that life just ends here. I don't think this is simply a wish for immortality, but rather a conviction grown in the consciousness of life's vast mystery.

Faith in the Resurrection

Jesus saw the power of faith to be unlimited. A strong faith could conquer anything, even death. This contention is a major obstacle to many who seek faith. The idea that Jesus raised people from the dead and was raised himself demands a huge leap of faith. There is certainly no possible way it can be proved in any scientific sense.

A faith in the *resurrection* is not, however, blind faith. It is a faith that is created from the heart and is born of trust and intuition. It is a faith inspired by a deep confidence that a creator does not just disappear after a creation. Those who have learned to surrender to God on a daily basis often make this leap of faith. For them, this is not all that risky a jump.

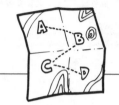

Map Key

Resurrection is the reuniting of the human spirit with the Holy Spirit following death. This reunion does not mean endless life or time. It means an entry into eternity, which has no such categories. To be resurrected is to be with God—whatever that reality may be.

Points of Interest

The greatest fear we need to realize in this modern world is the fear of dying spiritually before we die physically. We can become so numbed, crazed, burned out and up that we are nothing more than a spiritual carcass.

Spiritual Death

In today's highly stressful world, many of us often wish for a far more peaceful life. We long for a world without pain, worry, or problems. The irony of getting pain-free, problem-free lives, however, is that we literally kill our spirits. Spiritual death is the direct result of trying to eliminate those human experiences that are present to stimulate our maturation.

Jesus stressed that faith could bring people back to life spiritually. When people choose to leave life, spiritually speaking, where do they go? They go to any of the following:

➤ In search of fame and fortune

➤ To make a name for themselves

➤ Into the rat race

➤ To climb the ladder of success

➤ In search of the fountain of youth

➤ Into hiding or denial

➤ Into a bottle of booze or pills

➤ Into a TV screen

➤ To get more and more stuff

➤ To try to be in charge and perfect

➤ To try to be saints

➤ Into romance and sex

➤ Into rigid, legalistic religions

It is the will of God for human beings to be human. Being human does not mean that we are hell-bent on being evil, but we foolishly cling to the notion that we are in charge and can be perfect like God. The effort to play God is lethal to our spirits. Spiritual death is the result of worshiping the triune god of ...

➤ Perfectionism.

➤ People pleasing.

➤ Performance.

When you treat the human spirit as a machine, it is bound to break down. Human beings are created in the image of God, and God lays claim to all kinds of vulnerability. Biblically speaking, God weeps, doubts, explodes with anger, and grieves often and deeply. Robots are created in the image of the perfect human being, and they are adequate for every task except faith, hope, and love.

Nicodemus Is Born Again

As with most faith stories, the story of Nicodemus (John 3:1–21) is deceptively simple. This story is about a spiritual search. Nicodemus was a Pharisee and a member of the Sanhedrin, the ruling council, yet he still yearned for something deeper and more fulfilling. He was trying to find that which would ignite a spark of joy in his life, give him hope, inspire his love, and enable him to be the person he believed he was created to be.

Major Highways

"Now there was a man of the Pharisees, named Nicodemus, a ruler of the Jews. This man came to Jesus by night and said to him, 'Rabbi, we know that you are a teacher come from God; for no one can do these signs that you do, unless God is with him.' Jesus answered him, 'Truly, truly, I say to you, unless one is born anew, he cannot see the kingdom of God.' Nicodemus said to him, 'How can a man be born when he is old? Can he enter a second time into his mother's womb and be born?' Jesus answered, 'Truly, truly, I say to you unless one is born of water and the Spirit, he cannot enter the kingdom of God. That which is born of the flesh is flesh, and that which is born of the Spirit is spirit. Do not marvel that I said to you, "You must be born anew." ... For God so loved the world that he gave his only Son, that whoever believes in him should not perish but have eternal life.'"

—John 3:1–7; 16

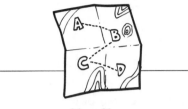

Map Key

The **Holy Spirit** is the active presence of grace, the unconditional love and forgiveness of God in the world. This force cannot be controlled, but faith alone can open the door to its arrival in our lives.

He came to Jesus by night, because he was afraid of the response of his peers. The Pharisees saw Jesus as a threat to their power and as a prophetic pest. During his visit, Nicodemus questioned the notion that he must be born again to see the kingdom by asking if that means he would have to crawl back into his mother's womb. Jesus told him not to take him literally; to be born again meant that Nicodemus must experience a spiritual awakening.

A spiritual awakening is granted by the *Holy Spirit* and enables a person to experience the kingdom. This spiritual awakening is likened to a coming into the light. This light is the fuel of faith and is that which makes our faith glow. It radiates eternally, and those who bask in it can see forever. The kingdom is a place of light, and to enter into the kingdom is to enter eternity, for everything that is of the kingdom is that which will last forever.

The light is ...

➤ The living presence of God, or Holy Spirit.

➤ The word of God, or gospel truth.

➤ The force that gives life meaning, purpose, and hope.

For his followers, Jesus was the light of the world, and the light does the following:

➤ Enables us to see the truth of who we really are

➤ Exposes the heart of humanity, both individually and as a community

➤ Points the way that we need to go

Living in darkness is the root cause of spiritual death. To live in darkness is to live a lie. It is to deny the truth of our existence. It is to be dishonest with ourselves, our families, and our friends. It is to follow a way of life that we know leads nowhere or, worse yet, to a place that systematically destroys the spiritual presence of the kingdom. Nicodemus was called out of the darkness into the light.

The Widow's Son

The widow's son is a sweet story. In it, Jesus had arrived in the village of Nain with a throng behind him. He encountered a funeral procession of the only son of a widow and was overwhelmed with compassion. Jesus knew the widow's pain. As a woman without a husband or child, she risked being penniless and alone. His compassion was born of his awareness of her plight. Jesus embraced her very real fears of a bleak future.

This description gives us crucial information about the life of Jesus:

➤ Jesus feels.

➤ Jesus is empathetic to the pain of others.

➤ Jesus is a presence of mercy.

After expressing his compassion for the widow, Jesus touched the casket and asked the young man to get up. The young man did. The mourners and followers of Jesus were dumbstruck as Jesus returned the young man to his mother.

Such miracles can only be comprehended by faith. Faith is able to hear these stories as tales filled with many layers of truth. The layers that I experience within this account are as follows:

➤ Compassion can raise a person's spirits and hopes.

➤ The compassion of God is enormously powerful.

➤ God's mercy can heal a broken heart, revive a wounded spirit, or return the dead to the living.

➤ The power of God is amazing. To be amazed is to recognize that we are not in control and that a power far greater than our own is in charge.

➤ Awe is the consciousness of not being able to explain something.

Major Highways

"Soon afterward he went to a city called Nain, and his disciples and a great crowd went with him. As he drew near to the gate of the city, behold, a man who had died was being carried out, the only son of his mother, and she was a widow; and a large crowd from the city was with her. And when the Lord saw her, he had compassion on her and said to her, 'Do not weep.' And he came and touched the bier, and the bearers stood still. And he said, 'Young man, I say to you, arise.' And the dead man sat up and began to speak. And he gave him to his mother. Fear seized them all; and they glorified God, saying, 'A great prophet has arisen among us!' and 'God has visited his people!' And this report concerning him spread through the whole of Judea and all the surrounding country."

—Luke 7:11–17

Just as people in a 12-step program will tell you that they cannot explain why or how the program works, so it is with those who have experienced miracles. I have no idea why or how the compassion of God works, but I have heard more stories of God's miraculous healing powers (many from doctors) than I care to count.

Points of Interest

I was just reading an article about heart transplant patients. In the article, a scientist tells of a psychiatrist who had been working with an 8-year-old girl who had received the heart of a 10-year-old murder victim. The psychiatrist tells a convention of scientists that her patient had numerous nightmares about the murder and the murderer. She further went on to say that as a result of those dreams, she and the child's mother had been able to tell the police the name of the murderer and the details of the crime. The convention was said to be speechless, but there was not a dry eye in the house.

Lazarus

The story of Jesus raising Lazarus from the dead is a sophisticated and multilayered tale. It is far more extensive than many of the miracle accounts and appears to be far more significant because of the cast of characters involved.

Lazarus, who was a good friend of Jesus, lived in Bethany with his sisters Mary and Martha. Mary and Martha are the two infamous sisters who hosted Jesus. Martha busied herself with the chores of hosting while Mary sat and listened at the foot of Christ. From a faith perspective, Mary was thought to be the wise one (Luke 10:38–42).

Martha and Mary sent word to Jesus that Lazarus was quite ill. Remember how unusual it was that two women would feel free to request anything of Jesus. Upon getting this message, Jesus expressed his faith that Lazarus would not die.

A few days later, Jesus asked his disciples to go with him to visit Lazarus, which meant heading back to Judea. The disciples were leery of returning to Judea because Jesus had almost been killed the last time he was there. Jesus then told them that Lazarus was dead and hinted that he would have an opportunity to demonstrate his divine power. Doubting Thomas showed great faith and courage at this point, stating his expectation that all of the disciples would accompany Jesus on his return.

Martha and Mary were furious with Jesus for his delayed arrival. They felt that he could have saved their brother from dying. Jesus assured them both that hope was not lost. Jesus then asked Martha if she had faith that he was the Messiah and that Lazarus could indeed be brought back from the dead. Martha showed tremendous faith and declared her utter confidence in Christ's capacity to raise Lazarus.

Jesus had the rock rolled away from Lazarus' tomb, and he called Lazarus to come out. Lazarus appeared enshrouded in burial attire, which Jesus demanded to be removed.

This story has many twists and turns:

➤ Jesus chooses to delay his arrival. The delay of Jesus' visit is attributed to Jesus not wishing to heal Lazarus, but rather to much more dramatically raise him from the dead.

➤ Doubting Thomas turns out to be the bravest disciple.

➤ Busy Martha is shown to be a woman of deep and abiding faith.

➤ Jesus and his followers are shown to be alternately compassionate and courageous, indignant and frustrated, and faithful and faithless.

Major Highways

"Then Jesus, deeply moved again, came to the tomb; it was a cave, and a stone lay upon it. Jesus said, 'Take away the stone.' Martha, the sister of the dead man, said to him, 'Lord, by this time there will be an odor, for he has been dead four days.' Jesus said to her, 'Did I not tell you that if you would believe you would see the glory of God?' So they took away the stone. And Jesus lifted up his eyes and said, 'Father, I thank thee that thou has heard me. I knew that thou hearest me always, but I have said this on account of the people standing by, that they may believe that thou didst send me.' When he had said this, he cried with a loud voice, 'Lazarus, come out.' The dead man came out, his hands and feet bound with bandages, and his face wrapped with a cloth. Jesus said to them, 'Unbind him, and let him go.'"

—John 11:38–44

The bottom line of this saga is that Jesus raised Lazarus. This is a bold story of the power of Jesus. This story unequivocally declares the following:

➤ Jesus is the Messiah.

➤ Jesus is God come to earth.

➤ Jesus possesses the power of God.

➤ The power of God can take the sting out of death's bite.

➤ Faith unleashes God's power in our lives and world.

The importance of this miracle account is its directness about Jesus being the Son of God. There is no wavering here. Jesus arrives in Bethany determined to show himself for who he is: the Messiah. To those who believed, God's glory was revealed. In this case, believing enabled seeing.

The Least You Need to Know

➤ Jesus felt that the power of faith was unlimited. A strong faith could even conquer death.

➤ Those who sought to control things and be perfect suffered spiritual death.

➤ Nicodemus experienced a spiritual awakening through the Holy Spirit.

➤ The story of the widow's son demonstrated that Jesus was empathetic.

➤ Bringing Lazarus back from the dead suggests that Jesus was the Messiah.

Chapter 17

The X Files

In This Chapter

➤ Miracles become myth

➤ A few loaves and fishes become food for thousands

➤ The sea becomes a sidewalk

➤ A storm becomes calm

➤ Water becomes wine

Some miracles recorded in scripture have a mythic quality to them. By this I mean that they have a deeper meaning than what might appear on the surface of the story. These miracles can be understood simply as demonstrations of God's power, but I doubt that was what Jesus intended. If that were the case, I think Jesus would have done an unlimited number of such acts of awesome power; he would have been wowing the crowds on a daily basis. That was not what happened. Jesus seldom, if ever, tried to impress people with his powers. Instead, he tried to transform them with the truth of his message and ministry.

Understanding Miracles as Myths

It is possible, and not blasphemous, to take Biblical miracles as myths. Consider the following:

➤ Feeding 5,000 people with a few fish and a couple of loaves of bread (John 6:1–14)

➤ Walking on water (John 6:15–21)

➤ Calming the storm (Luke 8:22–25)

➤ Turning water into wine (John 2:1–12)

I am not saying these events did not happen. I am in no position to make such a judgment. What I am saying is that these miracles are much more than displays of God's miraculous powers. I would further contend that, taken as myths, these four miracles reveal an even deeper and fuller power than if they are understood as mere physical feats.

Points of Interest

The great poets often wrote about subjects like love and death, heaven and hell, and the meaning of life. Their words were never written to prove their message as fact. Their words were meant to inspire, to share a feeling, and to invite the reader to enter an experience. Poems are not facts, nor are they fiction. They reveal a truth poets have known with their heart and soul. In this way, poems are like myths.

What do I mean by taking these miracles as myths? I mean that if Jesus did feed 5,000, walk on water, calm a storm, and turn water into wine, what then? What is the point of the story? Is it simply to prove that Jesus is God? Jesus never felt such need before, why the change? Why didn't he perform a huge number of such extraordinary displays?

If these miracles are divine magic shows, then I don't think they have much to say. Jesus walking on water is a fascinating, even entertaining, mystery, but I doubt it has much to say about how we live. I could argue that it might make someone believe, but Jesus seemed to seldom want anyone to have faith in him simply on the basis of some miraculous display of power. Jesus demanded conviction from his followers. He wanted them to invest heavily in the building of the kingdom.

If we take these miracles as myths, we are free to examine them for poetic truths. We can seek out the kingdom hidden in their telling. We can spiritually play with the imagery and see how it speaks to our modern lives. We are free to enter the miracle on an emotional and spiritual basis and explore the story for the sacredness it contains.

Feeding Five Thousand

At the time of the miracle story of the feeding of 5,000 people (John 6:1–14), Jesus was attracting large crowds as word of his miracles spread. He crossed the Sea of Galilee and was resting with his disciples on the top of a hill. Crowds came. Jesus asked Philip where they could buy some food. (Philip was from Bethsaida, a nearby town, and was likely to have known where they could have acquired food.) But Philip said that it would cost a fortune to feed this size of gathering.

Jesus was told of a small boy who had five barley loaves and two fish. Jesus blessed the child's offering, distributed the bread and fish, and everyone ate until they were full. Jesus asked for the leftovers to be saved so that nothing would go to waste.

If the story is to be taken solely as a literal account, then it is a tale of God's power to multiply bread and fish at whim. I have no problem with someone choosing to believe that this miracle happened just as it says. However, I do have a problem if the point of the story is simply to prove God's power.

Taken as a myth, this sacred story has other meanings:

➤ This event may have been similar to a celebration of holy communion, in which a single bottle of wine and a loaf of bread can spiritually feed hundreds and leave their souls full and satisfied.

➤ Could the real miracle here be that people who were hoarding what they had were moved by the young boy to share? Is this a miracle of spiritual transformation from selfish to generous? Now that would be a miracle!

➤ Is the boy with the loaves and fishes central to the story? Is he another reminder that what the world views as small and insignificant is in the eyes of God capable of extraordinary things?

➤ Is this miracle a story of Jesus' faith? First, he asks his disciples where they can buy food, but then he tells everyone to be seated and blesses the offering of the small child. He trusts that God will provide. He believes in the contagious power of the Holy Spirit. He expects it to spread, and it does.

➤ Is this a miraculous story of God's faith in us? Does Jesus display here an absolute confidence in this gathering to do the right thing and share what they have in order to make sure everyone has something?

➤ Is this a story of the kingdom coming to earth in which a mere morsel is more than enough and true satisfaction comes from spiritual food?

The issue is not how or what you believe or even if you believe, as long as you give this miracle story full access to your soul. When we examine this story as a myth, we are free to consider the multiplicity of messages contained within the sacred confines of the miracle itself.

Walking on Water

The miracle story of Jesus walking on the water (John 6:15–21) began with the disciples waiting on shore for Jesus. Night fell, and the disciples grew impatient. They boarded a boat and headed out on the Sea of Galilee toward Capernaum. A storm whipped the sea into a froth. Three to four miles out, they saw Jesus walking toward them across the sea. They immediately took Jesus aboard and were said to instantly arrive at their destination.

Did this actually happen? I don't know. I do know that faith is capable of accepting such divine power. Yet I believe that this miracle story is a myth and, as such, has many dynamic lessons to teach. It is loaded with powerful metaphors concerning faith and Jesus:

➤ The followers of Jesus need to be patient.

➤ When we try to go it on our own, we run into stormy seas.

➤ If we seek Jesus, he will come.

➤ Jesus responds to faith and will walk on water to find it.

➤ When we have Jesus on board, we are bound to get where we are going.

The poetic appeal of this story is that it reveals so many spiritual challenges. As a myth, this miracle can be understood as a proclamation: Jesus will go to any lengths to find people of faith. Trust in him and patiently wait, and he will come.

Calming a Storm

As I was writing this book, my wife Christine died following complications after surgery. Her death was brutal, and her pain was immense. The time she spent hooked to machines was interminable, and the outcome was a disaster. During this time, I repeatedly questioned God's absence. I could not fathom how God could witness this good woman dying at such a young age.

In the story about the calming of the storm (Matthew 8:23–27), the disciples were on a boat during a storm. Jesus was sleeping on the boat, but they woke him up and asked him to save them. He asked them why they were afraid and said they had little faith. He then calmed the storm.

Major Highways

"And when he got into the boat, his disciples followed him. And behold, there arose a great storm on the seas, so that the boat was being swamped by the waves; but he was asleep. And they went and woke him, saying, 'Save us, Lord; we are perishing.' And he said to them, 'Why are you afraid, O men of little faith?' Then he rose and rebuked the winds and the sea; and there was a great calm. And the men marveled, saying, 'What sort of man is this, that even winds and sea obey him?'"

—Matthew 8:23–27

The miracle of Jesus calming a storm is obviously metaphorical:

➤ Fear has the power to consume faith.

➤ Often when we feel abandoned by God, God is in truth right next to us in the same boat.

➤ Faith alone can calm the stormy seas of our lives.

➤ The daily spiritual choice is between fear and faith.

We often feel that God is sleeping on the job while we are riding out stormy seas. Our faith is overwhelmed with fear. Our faith evaporates under a blistering attack of doubt, disappointment, and despair. We internally rant at God for his disappearing act. We are furious with him for abandoning us just when we need him most.

Still, it takes only a pinch of prayer and an ounce of faith, and our seas do miraculously settle. Whenever I was able to admit to myself that God knew and understood my fear and pain concerning my wife, I was swept by an amazing calm. I am still amazed at how true it is that when there is nowhere else to turn, we turn to God, and in so doing we find the peace we sought in the first place.

Turning Water into Wine

Weddings in Jesus' time were huge events. The celebrations usually lasted a full week, and often the entire town was invited. It was considered bad manners to refuse a wedding invitation. Guests were invited to numerous festive parties or banquets, all of which required a significant degree of planning. Being a good host was considered an almost sacred duty. If you ran out of wine, it was a terrible reflection upon the wedding and the family name.

During the celebration of the wedding at Cana (John 2:1–12), Jesus' mother expresses her concern to him that there is no more wine. Jesus basically tells her that this is not his problem and not to expect a miracle out of him. It is hard to understand Jesus' response to his mother unless the story is taken as a myth. Jesus' mother then tells the servants to do whatever her son says. Mythically speaking, Jesus' mother has asked the servants to have faith in her son.

Jesus tells the servants to fill six pots that are normally used for ceremonial washing with water. These pots are enormous, holding up to 30 gallons. Jesus then asks the servants to take a ladle of liquid from the pot to the master of ceremonies. The master of ceremonies is stunned to taste the very best wine and asks the host why he had saved the best for last.

Again, I stress that I doubt this miracle is simply about Jesus' ability to turn water into wine. The mythic lessons of this miracle seem to be of far greater spiritual impact and relevance:

➤ We often go last to God for what we need.

➤ Jesus always turns things upside down, as with saving the best wine for last.

155

➤ You cannot demand a miracle, but if you have faith, you can expect one.

➤ Jesus is in control of the situation.

➤ If God is present, you are never empty.

➤ If God is not present, you will always fall short.

The Least You Need to Know

➤ Miracles may have occurred as the Gospels described, but the true power of miracle stories came from the insight they provided about Jesus' faith.

➤ Jesus showed that God would provide when he fed the 5,000.

➤ Jesus taught his followers that if they had faith, he would always come to them; he would walk on water if he had to.

➤ Jesus taught his followers to trust that he could calm any storm in their lives.

➤ Jesus taught his followers that they could not demand miracles, but if they had total trust, they could expect miracles to happen.

Part 7

Jesus the Messiah

The Jews had been waiting for the coming of the Messiah for a long, long time. Over the years, a conception of the Messiah developed. The Jews anticipated that the Messiah would be like …

- ➤ *David, a great warrior king.*
- ➤ *Melchizedek, a great priest.*
- ➤ *Elijah, a great prophet.*

The operative word here is "great." The Jews yearned for a Messiah who would be much larger than life. Jesus did not meet any of their expectations. He was not only life-size, but maybe even on the small side. As for greatness, well, think about it: Jesus was a nobody who came from nowhere. He knew Jewish law inside out but was quite cavalier in his attitude toward it. He had no religious rank. He associated with prostitutes, tax collectors, lepers, Samaritans, and thieves. He called the religious establishment a bunch of hypocrites. He told people they had to love their enemies. His followers were a rather small group of illiterates, revolutionary rabble, the lost and the suffering—literally the walking wounded.

As proof positive that Jesus was not the Messiah after his crucifixion, the religious establishment simply cited the state of the world: There was still poverty and disease; wars continued to sprout like weeds; fear and famine raced across the countryside. If the Messiah had come, the world would have changed. Those who followed Jesus, however, heard and saw the story differently. The next four chapters explain their version.

Chapter 18

The Imperfect Storm

In This Chapter

➤ Jesus appears with Elijah and Moses

➤ Jesus rides into Jerusalem to meet his fate

➤ Jesus washes his disciples' feet

➤ Jesus shares prayers and food during the Last Supper

➤ Pilate gives in to an angry mob

The events leading to the crucifixion of Jesus are like the proverbial snowball rolling down the hill. They build and build, gain powerful momentum, and are seemingly out-of-control. Everything and everyone appear to conspire to bring Jesus to a brutal death on the cross. For Jesus, there is nowhere to run or hide. He has no other choice but to go to Jerusalem and face the cross.

The Transfiguration

The transfiguration is for me a poetic interpretation of Jesus' revelation that there was no possible way for him to avoid being crucified. At the beginning of this story, Jesus takes Peter, James, and John, who are three of the disciples, to the top of a mountain to serve as witnesses to what Jesus expects to occur.

At the top of the mountain, Jesus is said to be transformed, and the three disciples can clearly see his aura. Then Moses and Elijah appear. Peter expresses his desire to memorialize the event with the building of three shrines. While he is talking, a bright cloud descends and enshrouds Jesus. Then God speaks and declares that Jesus is his beloved Son.

Afterward, when Jesus and the three disciples are coming down the mountain, the disciples ask Jesus about the belief of the religious establishment that Elijah must come before the Messiah could arrive. Jesus declares that John the Baptist has served that prophetic role.

Major Highways

"And after six days Jesus took with him Peter and James and John his brother, and led them up a high mountain apart. And he was transfigured before them, and his face shone like the sun, and his garments became white as light. And behold, there appeared to them Moses and Elijah, talking with him. And Peter said to Jesus, 'Lord, it is well that we are here; if you wish, I will make three booths here, one for you and one for Moses and one for Elijah.' He was still speaking, when lo, a bright cloud overshadowed them, and a voice from the cloud said, 'This is my beloved Son, with whom I am well pleased; listen to him.' When the disciples heard this, they fell on their faces and were filled with awe. But Jesus came and touched them, saying, 'Rise and have no fear.' And when they lifted up their eyes, they saw no one but Jesus only."

—Matthew 17:1–8

The transfiguration is a vision, a revelation. This confirmation of destiny by two great Jewish prophets is a further declaration of Jesus' deep Jewish roots and his steadfast adherence to the fulfillment of scriptural prophecy. Jesus visually demonstrates to designated disciples that there is no way to avoid Jerusalem and crucifixion. They must move forward and must trust God.

I believe Jesus told his followers not to tell of this vision because he was sure they did not truly understand it. The risk of offering confusing or false information was too high. Although they were Jesus' chosen disciples, they were not on the same spiritual plane as he was, which was often displayed in their lack of awareness and faith.

The Plan

Jesus has a plan. He sends two of his disciples ahead to get a donkey and a colt. This action is a fulfillment of a prophecy in Zechariah 9:9. Jesus states that if anyone questions the disciples, they should simply say the Lord has need of these animals. This story (Matthew 21:1–16) clearly follows a preordained script.

Jesus arrives in Jerusalem on the back of a donkey's colt. This is a sign of his being the Messiah and the humility of his earthly reign. A good-sized crowd welcomes him; he is heralded as the Son of David. The crowd lays palm branches down before him (an event that Christians celebrate as Palm Sunday). Though the crowd welcomes Jesus with open arms, they soon bow to political and religious pressure and retreat from any claims that he is the Messiah.

The drama that has unfolded in Jerusalem is a plan to avow that ...

➤ Jesus is the Messiah.

➤ Old Testament prophecies have been fulfilled.

➤ The crowds would recognize him as the one who comes in the name of the Lord.

By establishing and entering into this plan, Jesus has taken his boldest and broadest leap of faith. He has leaped into the certain chaos of being claimed the Messiah.

The Washing of Stinky Feet

The Last Supper is preceded by a significant act: Jesus washes his disciples' feet (John 13:1–20). This act is upsetting to Peter, because Peter sees it as an inappropriate act for a Messiah. Jesus makes it clear that this washing of feet is symbolic:

➤ It demonstrates humble service, which is to be the calling of all of Jesus' followers.

➤ It illustrates a new kind of kingship. Jesus is not of this world and does not adhere to its goals or dreams.

➤ It represents God's unconditional love for his followers.

The act of washing feet becomes miraculous when it is performed by a kneeling, serving God. Remember that these feet had walked down dung-covered, dusty roads. By washing his disciples' feet, Jesus shows that he accepts the whole of who his disciples are, even those parts that they consider most foul.

The call to servanthood declared by this act is Jesus' most brazen rejection of the standards of the world. To wash his disciples' feet is to turn his back on the world's call to power, wealth, and winning. Jesus has chosen a different path. His path is far more difficult, but it is spiritually and eternally far more rewarding.

The Last Supper

The Last Supper (John 13:21–17:25) is an extraordinary event. During this memorable meal, Jesus predicts his betrayal by Judas and Peter's denial of him, but more importantly, he passes on his legacy to his followers. I am moved when I think of Jesus pouring out these words of wisdom and love to the very same men he knows will abandon him. It is the single greatest example of his unconditional love for these men.

Imagine an upper room quiet with fear, despair, and the first whiffs of grief and a table lit only by candles. In this dim light, Jesus speaks quietly to his closest friends and lays out before them a legacy he hopes they will live. In gentle tones, Jesus sets out the following hopes and prayers:

➤ Quit worrying!

➤ Jesus declares that he has already prepared a place for them in eternity.

➤ In spite of their denials, doubts, betrayals, and squabbles over heavenly rankings, Jesus guarantees his eternal love for his disciples.

➤ Jesus discloses that he is the way to God.

➤ To know Jesus is to know God because Jesus reveals the heart and mind of God.

➤ If you have great faith, you will do even greater works than Jesus.

➤ Jesus promises that the Holy Spirit will come as a counselor and will function as a guardian angel for Jesus' followers.

➤ The works of the Holy Spirit will be known by the experience of a peace that passes all understanding. The peace that the world offers is not anything like that brought by the Holy Spirit.

➤ The world seeks security in money and material things; Jesus seeks security in faith.

➤ Jesus conveys that he is the vine and his followers are the branches. If they are cut off from that vine, they will wither and die.

➤ Jesus commands his disciples to love each other.

➤ Jesus states that love will be the one way that others recognize his followers.

➤ Jesus warns of the hatred of the world and acknowledges the hatred he has known.

➤ Jesus does not promise a tragedy-free or pain-free future for his disciples.

➤ Jesus admits to his sadness at having to leave them and how much more he wishes he could teach them.

➤ Jesus states that he had to speak in parables, but that this will not always be the case. His message will become more obvious and direct.

➤ The disciples will grieve over the loss of Jesus, but the world, he says, will rejoice.

➤ Jesus reminds his disciples that they belong to him and not the world.

➤ Jesus prays that his followers will know joy and that the Holy Spirit will guide and protect them.

➤ Jesus prays that the world will someday know that he was sent by God to save the world.

At the close of this meal, Jesus shares with his disciples what is now commonly referred to as communion. He breaks bread as a symbol of his body, and he pours wine as a symbol of his blood. He asks his disciples to perform this ritual as a sign of remembrance. What they are asked to remember is that if you choose to follow Jesus, it will take all of you, flesh and blood.

The Crucifixion

I recall a young man in a confirmation class I taught asking me why Jesus had to die in such an awful way. He thought it would have been a good bit smarter on God's part if Jesus had lived to a nice old age, maybe 90, and just died peacefully in his sleep. Then, he postulated, we could have learned a lot more, and Jesus would not have had to endure the nails and the cross.

I had to admit the same thought had crossed my mind. It also made me aware that it is hard to teach 13-year-olds why tragedy and pain are sometimes required ingredients in life. (Maybe confirmation classes should begin when we are at least 30. The notion of a crucified Messiah might make a bit more sense then. Even the ideas of mercy and grace would be easier to comprehend in your 30s.)

The crucifixion is a true stumbling block to faith. Death by crucifixion is long, slow, and tortuous, and the crucifixion is indeed a brutal finale to the life of a man of peace, love, and mercy. It is amazing that a man of such gentle goodness could have met such a horrible ending. Through his crucifixion, Jesus offers his disciples a most realistic portrait of a life of discipleship. He makes sure they know that the cost of following him may be expensive indeed.

I don't believe that crucifixion was God's plan. I believe crucifixion was the response of humanity to the gospel truth. The challenge Jesus posed to the religious establishment, as well as to the political leadership of that time, was extreme, so extreme measures were used to silence him. The crucifixion is nothing more than humanity's rejection of anyone who threatens the established order and seeks to build a kingdom not by the standards of the world, but by a blueprint designed in heaven.

Scenic Overlooks

"Jesus needn't have died. Presumably, he could have followed the advice of friends like Peter and avoided the showdown. Instead, he chose to die because he believed that he had to if the world was to be saved. Thus the cross stands for the best that men can do as well as for the worst."

—Frederick Buechner (from *Wishful Thinking*)

The story of the crucifixion (Luke 22–23) is laid out as a vast conspiracy. This conspiracy involves a rich and varied cast of characters, all of whom have become infamous over time.

Points of Interest

I don't believe that Judas betrayed Jesus for the money. I suspect that he believed Jesus had given up on the ministry. He was livid with Jesus for allowing a woman to anoint him with expensive perfume. That perfume could have been used to help the poor, which was supposed to be their mission. Judas did not recognize the use of the perfume as a foreshadowing of Jesus' death and the eventual anointing of the corpse. Instead, Judas felt Jesus had given up on him and their cause, which was preaching good news to the poor. I can't imagine that Judas would have committed suicide if he were only after the money. I think Judas realized his mistake on a spiritual basis and took his life in grief.

When the events leading up to the actual crucifixion were set into motion, religious leaders had been plotting to find a way to get rid of Jesus. Angry with Jesus, Judas found them and agreed to lead them to Jesus when he would be alone. After the Last Supper, Jesus went to the garden to pray. He prayed for God to remove this yoke from him, and he accepted whatever was God's will. Jesus then became furious with his disciples for falling asleep while he agonized over his fate.

Points of Interest

"A six-pointed star, a crescent moon, a lotus—the symbols of other religions suggest beauty and light. The symbol of Christianity is an instrument of death. It suggests, at the very least, hope."

—Frederick Buechner (from *Wishful Thinking*)

Next, Judas arrived with a mob and kissed Jesus to signal that Jesus was the person they wanted. Jesus was then arrested for acts of treason to the state. When questioned about whether he knew Jesus, Peter denied that he knew him three times.

When Jesus was brought before the religious leaders, he claimed to be the Son of God. The religious leaders then took Jesus to Pilate, the Roman governor of Judea. Pilate was very unpopular with the Jews. He had used temple money to build an aqueduct, and he had brought imperial images into the city. Pilate considered appeasing the religious establishment who had made his tenure so shaky.

Jesus next was brought before Herod, the part-Jewish leader of Galilee and Perea. Herod and Pilate had long been enemies, but they were united in their use of Jesus as a means of dealing with the religious establishment. Herod and Pilate initially concurred that Jesus had done nothing worthy of death.

Points of Interest

The crown of thorns is a stirring symbol of the crucifixion of Jesus. The religious establishment wanted a Messiah who would reign like a king. The crown of thorns was used to mock Jesus and symbolize that he was a king with no power, only pain. To the followers of Jesus, the crown was a different kind of symbol. It represented Jesus' final rejection of the powers and principles of the world. Jesus was the King of Kings, but his was to be a reign of peace and justice for all, and that would require his blood. The thorny crown declares that Jesus is a king whose only power is grace.

Pilate wanted to release Jesus, but he was swayed by the intensity of the mob and the ongoing accusations shouted by the religious establishment. The religious establishment was threatened by Jesus and made it clear that it would report Pilate to Rome if he did not execute Jesus. The last thing Pilate wanted was for the mob to riot. Out of a deep desire to protect his political position, Pilate condemned Jesus to die and released Barrabas, who stood accused of the same political insurrection with which Jesus was charged. Jesus was handed over to the mob and was executed between two thieves on a hill called Golgotha, or The Skull.

The whole world stood at the foot of the cross and mocked Jesus. They cried out to him, "If you are the Messiah, then come on down! Show us your miracle powers. Free yourself from this agony." Those who claim to believe in Jesus today attest to believing in him because he did not come down. Christians claim to understand and know why they call Good Friday, the day of his crucifixion, good.

The Least You Need to Know

➤ The transfiguration illustrates Jesus' destiny; during this vision, Moses and Elijah affirmed his movement to Jerusalem.

➤ Jesus rode into Jerusalem during the Passover on the back of a donkey's colt, which was a sign that he was the Messiah, according to the prophecies of Zechariah.

➤ Jesus washed his disciples' feet to symbolize the disciples' call to serve others.

➤ At the Last Supper, Jesus offers words and prayers of comfort and hope to his disciples. The disciples are assured of the ongoing care and guidance of the Holy Spirit.

➤ The meal of bread and wine became the sacrament of Holy Communion, a reminder that choosing to follow Jesus requires everything you are.

➤ Jesus was executed for political treason at Golgotha, a place better known as The Skull.

Chapter 19

It Is All About Appearances

In This Chapter

➤ Angels and an empty tomb

➤ The women's revelation

➤ Two men and a Messiah

➤ The disciples' duty

A member of my congregation lost his sister to a brutal murder. He had warned her that she was being too kind to a man in her building, who he feared was stalking her. This man turned out to be his sister's killer.

The brother then awoke one morning in tears and felt compelled to get in his car and drive. He drove a great distance to a cottage his family had often stayed in when he was growing up. Memories of his beloved sister rushed in like a flooding river, and he burst into torrential sobs. He entered the cottage, walked to the living room, and looked out the enormous picture window to behold the sun setting over the still lake. Seemingly out of nowhere, he screamed, "I am so angry with you Sis; you have even ruined the sunsets. Why didn't you listen to me?" He then claimed to have heard the unmistakable sound of his sister's laugh, followed by her voice saying, "You big dope, I am the sunset!" She had always called him a big dope.

About a year after his sister's death, he asked me what I thought about these events. I told him this story was not about thinking; it was about believing, and I believed him. I found his story to be too good not to be true. I could write a hundred plus such stories that I have heard over my 25 years of ministry. It may not be a surprise to you to know that most of these stories are kept secret because folks fear being branded as "nuts." Isn't that a shame?

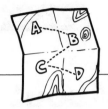

Jesus Rises from the Dead

Women were the first ones to discover the resurrection, a fact that may be even more amazing than the resurrection itself. I am sure that this fact was scandalous to the exclusively male religious establishment. Not only did the religious establishment not believe Jesus to be the Messiah, but if he were, he would not have died on a cross. However, even if they could have accepted the radical notion of a crucified Messiah, they would never have tolerated the idea that his rising would have been first noticed by a group of women.

The story goes that a number of women went to the tomb, including Mary Magdalene, Joanna, and Mary, the mother of James (Luke 24:1–12). They found the tomb empty. At the tomb, the women were greeted by two *angels* who asked why they had come. The angels told the women that they were looking for the living among the dead.

Map Key

Angels are emissaries from God who bring vital messages. When we hear these messages, we often get goosebumps, a lump in the throat, or a shiver up and down the spine, or we are moved to tears. Our bodies tell us when angel wings are touching us.

Major Highways

"But on the first day of the week, at early dawn, they went to the tomb, taking the spices which they had prepared. And they found the stone rolled away from the tomb, but when they went in they did not find the body. While they were perplexed about this, behold, two men stood by them in dazzling apparel; and as they were frightened and bowed their faces to the ground, the men said to them, 'Why do you seek the living among the dead? Remember how he told you, while he was still in Galilee, that the Son of man must be delivered into the hands of sinful men, and be crucified, and on the third day rise.'"

—Luke 24:1–7

Many of us still look for God among the dead. We may participate in some religious ritual, yet we have no expectation that God has anything to do or say to our lives in the present. Many of us treat God as we would a fine antique. We look upon it occasionally and dust it off. We know it has value, so we seldom pick it up for fear of breaking it. We pass it on, but we have no idea of its real worth.

Jesus Appears to Two Women

The Gospel of Matthew describes Jesus himself appearing to Mary Magdalene and the other Mary. As they are scurrying off to report the emptiness of the tomb to the disciples, they confront the risen Christ. He greets them, and they run to him and fall on their knees to worship. Jesus tells the women not to be afraid. Clearly, Jesus knows that spiritual experience of all kinds can be frightening. Fear is once again declared the enemy of a full and receptive faith. It closes the door on God's arrival in our lives.

This passage packs a powerful message:

➤ The risen Christ appears first to women.

➤ These women appear to be receptive to the presence of Christ and show a fullness of faith—like that first shown by Mary, the mother of Jesus.

➤ These women saw with their hearts, and they trusted what they saw.

➤ Their male counterparts (such as Thomas) tended to see with their minds and therefore needed more physical proof.

Jesus Appears to Two Men

The appearance of the risen Christ to two men is a fascinating story. The two men are followers of Jesus who are heading west to Emmaus from Jerusalem. They are headed into the sunset, which may be why they cannot recognize Christ's appearance at first. The two men are in despair and totally confused by the events that have led up to the crucifixion. Jesus makes sense out of those events and reminds the two men that all that happened had been predicted in scripture. The two men do not recognize Christ until he breaks bread.

Scenic Overlooks

"But all God's angels come to us
  disguised;
Sorrow and sickness, poverty and
  death.
One after other lift their frowning
  masks,
And we behold the Seraph's face
  beneath,
All radiant with the glory and the
  calm
Of having looked upon the front
  of God."

—James Russell Lowell (from "On the Death of a Friend's Child")

Major Highways

"So they departed quickly from the tomb with fear and great joy, and ran to tell his disciples. And behold, Jesus met them and said, 'Hail!' And they came up and took hold of his feet and worshiped him. Then Jesus said to them, 'Do not be afraid; go and tell my brethren to go to Galilee, and there they will see me.'"

—Matthew 28:8–10

169

They cannot keep the good news to themselves and race back the seven miles to Jerusalem to tell of their miraculous experience. This story also states that Jesus appears to Peter. The story itself is left untold, but this single line underlines Peter's importance to Jesus.

Major Highways

"And he [Jesus] said to them, 'Oh foolish men and slow of heart to believe all that the prophets have spoken! Was it not necessary that the Christ should suffer these things and enter into his glory?' And beginning with Moses and all the prophets, he interpreted to them in all the scriptures the things concerning himself."

"So they drew near to the village to which they were going. He appeared to be going further, but they constrained him, saying, 'Stay with us, for it is toward evening and the day is now far spent.' So he went in to stay with them. When he was at table with them, he took the bread and blessed and broke it, and gave it to them. And their eyes were opened, and they recognized him; and he vanished out of their sight."

—Luke 24:25–31

Detours

It is so easy to live our lives in hiding. If we never ask what God wants from us, we can remain in isolation, doing and being nothing. The contemporary term for hiding is denial. Spiritually, the two terms mean the same.

Jesus Appears to the Disciples

The account of the appearance of Jesus to the disciples (Luke 24:36–49) is blunt and specific. It stresses that the resurrection of Jesus was no fantasy. It was real! It also stresses that the crucifixion was unavoidable. It had to happen. The truth of the scripture declared the spiritual necessity of the cross.

Jesus tells the disciples that they have work to do and that they must go out into the world. They cannot live off of memories of when Jesus was with them. They must create new memories, because a new resurrected Jesus is with them. However, they must wait to go into the world until they are ready, and that readiness includes the reception of the Holy Spirit. When they are full of faith, they will be ready to continue Jesus' ministry.

Points of Interest

Readiness is crucial to spirituality. When we are ready to learn, grow, and mature, we will be presented with the opportunity to do so. That opportunity is often a crisis.

The Least You Need to Know

➤ Jesus' followers believed he was raised from the dead.

➤ Women were the first to experience the empty tomb.

➤ Jesus appeared to two women, two men, and to all of his disciples.

➤ Jesus commissioned his disciples to go and make new disciples after they were filled with the Holy Spirit.

Chapter 20

The Holy Spirit: Amazing Grace

In This Chapter

➤ Jesus as a sacrifice

➤ Jesus as soul food

➤ Jesus as water and light

➤ Jesus as a path and a plant

Believing that we can truly understand anything about Jesus is often difficult. He is gone from the earth. We can't see him or touch him, and if we claimed to hear him, we'd be rushed off to a rubber room in Dubuque. His followers admit to a deep desire to feel his presence, to sense what it was like to have him near, and to know him with some degree of intimacy.

The author of the Gospel of John clearly knew the wish to understand the heart, mind, and soul of Jesus. This gospel was written some 70 years after the crucifixion to meet a growing need to keep the essence of Jesus alive, to make known the real spiritual presence of the Christ. The Gospel of John strives to unpack the mind of Jesus by having Jesus himself characterize his nature by using poetic imagery. These images offer us a glimpse into the event of grace, Jesus Christ.

The author of John knew that mere words could not contain the spirit of Christ, but they could embrace the core of the man. The metaphors Jesus chose as labels for his spirit are filled with meaning. For believers, each of these metaphors is thought to release the dynamic powers of the Holy Spirit. The amazing power of grace, which is the ongoing work of the Holy Spirit, is grounded in these powerful poetic images.

The Lamb of God

The metaphor of Jesus as a lamb is no longer as easy to grasp as it would have been at the time of Christ. To grasp the full spiritual impact of the metaphor, you must understand the following:

➤ A shepherd with his sheep was a common sight in biblical times.

➤ A lamb was sacrificed daily at the temple to atone for the sins of the people.

➤ A lamb was sacrificed at Passover.

➤ On the night when the Jews were to flee Egypt, the blood of the lamb was smeared on the doorposts of their homes. It was believed that the angel of death would see the sacred blood and pass over their houses.

➤ Both Jeremiah and Isaiah, two famous Jewish prophets, referred to the Messiah as a lamb being led to the slaughter (Jeremiah 11:19 and Isaiah 53:7).

Major Highways

"The next day he [John the Baptist] saw Jesus coming toward him, and said, 'Behold, the Lamb of God, who takes away the sin of the world! This is he of whom I said, "After me comes a man who ranks before me, for he was before me." I myself did not know him; but for this I came baptizing with water, that he might be revealed to Israel.'"

—John 1:29–31

Jesus did not want his followers to take him literally. He wanted them to understand the will of his mind and the wish of his heart. The image of the Lamb of God spoke on many levels:

➤ A lamb was thought of as a lowly animal; this beast had no grandeur.

➤ A lamb would have been common to that time and place and was certainly not thought of as extraordinary in any way.

➤ The lamb was not an aggressive or violent animal. As a creature of zero malice, the lamb was a worthy symbol of innocence.

➤ The flock consumed the lamb.

➤ Only the shepherd knew the lamb as an individual.

➤ The lamb was used as a symbol of sacrifice.

➤ The innocent blood of a lamb was thought to atone for sins and have other miraculous powers.

Jesus effectively used the symbol of the lamb to speak to his own nature. He was a man of no rank or privilege who would be hard to pick out in a crowd. He was a man of peace and meant nobody harm. Jesus was wholly innocent of any crime and was crucified for no other reason than the world's hatred of the truth. Jesus was sacrificed for the sins of the world, the major sin being the rejection of the grace of God.

This metaphor, the Lamb of God, reveals much about the essence of Jesus. It speaks to his followers of his gracious nature and the nature of grace. In this image, grace is expressed as unconditional love and forgiveness, a mercy so great that it serves only to magnify the heart of God. The Holy Spirit continues to teach the followers of Jesus about the sacrificial nature of his amazing love and of the completeness of the forgiveness that he offers.

Scenic Overlooks

"The Christian character is the flower of which sacrifice is the seed."

—Fr. Andrew SDC (from *The Gift of Life*)

The Bread of Life

Remember that a metaphor is not to be taken literally. When Jesus called himself the Bread of Life, he was not equating himself to Wonder Bread. Jesus again chose something most common to reveal his most uncommon nature. In the ordinariness of bread, which was the primary staple of everyone's diet in those times, he sought to disclose the extraordinary power of the Holy Spirit.

Why was bread chosen as a spiritual symbol? What does this poetic image have to say then and now? By calling himself the Bread of Life, Jesus was …

➤ Speaking to the deep human hunger for meaning and hope.

➤ Affirming that faith alone can feed this hunger.

➤ Stating that spiritual nourishment comes only to those who swallow the truth of his life and ministry.

➤ Acknowledging that faith is a daily decision and that spiritual nourishment must be taken on a regular basis.

The Lord's Prayer asks for our daily bread to be supplied. Yes, this request may mean that our physical hunger must be met, but most assuredly, it also means that our spiritual hungers need to be satisfied. To the followers of Jesus, spiritual nourishment was thought to give both strength and endurance during times of crisis and courage to face the crosses that may need to be carried in the future. When he called himself the Bread of Life, Jesus stated categorically that he alone could feed the soul.

Major Highways

"Jesus said to them, 'I am the bread of life; he who comes to me shall not hunger, and he who believes in me shall never thirst. But I said to you that you have seen me and yet do not believe. All that the Father gives me will come to me; and him who comes to me I will not cast out. For I have come down from heaven, not to do my own will, but the will of him who sent me; and this is the will of him who sent me, that I should lose nothing of all that he has given me, but raise it up at the last day. For this is the will of my Father, that every one who sees the Son and believes in him should have eternal life; and I will raise him up at the last day.'"

—John 6:35–40

Without a good spiritual diet, the soul withers and weakens. Jesus presents himself as the original well-balanced meal:

1. He offers us a healthy and happy physical life.

2. He creates the capacity for emotional wholeness.

3. He enables spiritual maturation and growth.

Major Highways

"Cast your bread upon the waters, for you will find it after many days."
—Ecclesiastes 11:1

"... 'It is written, "Man shall not live by bread alone, but by every word that proceeds from the mouth of God."'"
—Matthew 4:4

Jesus as the Bread of Life is a metaphor that addresses the human hunger for lives of genuine value and eternal hope.

Major Highways

"On the last day of the feast, the great day, Jesus stood up and proclaimed, 'If any one thirst, let him come to me and drink. He who believes in me, as the scripture has said, "Out of his heart shall flow rivers of living water."' Now this he said about the Spirit, which those who believed in him were to receive; for as yet the Spirit had not been given, because Jesus was not yet glorified."

"When they heard these words, some of the people said, 'This is really the prophet.' Others said, 'This is the Christ.' But some said, 'Is the Christ to come from Galilee? Has not the scripture said that the Christ is descended from David, and comes from Bethlehem, the village where David was?' So there was a division among the people over him. Some of them wanted to arrest him, but no one laid hands on him."

—John 7:37–44

The Ever-Flowing Stream

Consider the central importance of water in Palestine. The Palestinians were both a desert and agrarian people. A drought meant disaster and was experienced as a sign from an angry God. The Bible often describes the power of a drought to bring a man to his knees—the Prodigal Son.

Consider the powerful imagery of water in your own life: a hot bath after a hard day's work, a cool shower on a hot and sticky summer day, the feeling of freshness evoked by a spring rain, or the goose bumps that sprout at the first leap into an ocean wave. Water is a natural metaphor. It is a perfect symbol for God's endless love and forgiveness and the endless presence of the Holy Spirit.

Points of Interest

Have you ever known an all-consuming thirst? This kind of thirst is the kind of desire for faith that Jesus seeks to ignite in his followers. It is also the only thirst he claims to be able to quench.

Detours

Jesus warns his followers that they think they are drowning in knee-deep water and that they sit by pools of mercy with parched lips and shriveling souls. Jesus offers himself as an oasis, but people consistently choose to go on across the desert in search of another Promised Land.

Jesus effectively uses this metaphor, an ever-flowing stream, to express the nature of his being:

➤ Jesus is a verb.

➤ The Holy Spirit flows eternally.

➤ The grace of God cleanses the heart, refreshes the soul, rinses away the slime of sin, and quenches the thirst for truth.

➤ The Holy Spirit moves us along (matures us) as we flow into an ocean of grace.

Jesus wants his followers to thirst for him. He wants them to admit their thirst for lives of energy and enthusiasm. He wants them to feel their deep, burning desire to enjoy life again. He wants people to know that he is the swollen cloud, and that he alone can grant the rain needed for a fruitful crop.

Major Highways

"Again, Jesus spoke to them, saying, 'I am the light of the world; he who follows me will not walk in darkness, but will have the light of life.' The Pharisees then said to him, 'You are bearing witness to yourself; your testimony is not true.' Jesus answered, 'Even if I do bear witness to myself, my testimony is true, for I know whence I have come and whither I am going, but you do not know whence I come or whither I am going. You judge according to the flesh, I judge no one. Yet even if I do judge, my judgement is true, for it is not I alone that judge, but I and he who sent me. In your law it is written that the testimony of two men is true; I bear witness to myself, and the Father who sent me bears witness to me.' They said to him therefore, 'Where is your Father?' Jesus answered, 'You know neither me nor my Father; if you knew me, you would know my Father also.' These words he spoke in the treasury, as he taught in the temple; but no one arrested him, because his hour had not yet come."

—John 8:12–20

The Light of the World

I love children's sermons, and adults often like my kid talks better than my pulpit efforts. A children's sermon is short, sweet, and to the point, and it usually includes an easily identifiable visual aid. A good children's sermon is one in which the kids are able to explain exactly what they have learned.

For one children's sermon, I brought in a night-light and a flashlight. I held each up and asked the kids to explain their uses. They did so with ease. I then asked the children whether they still used a night-light. Every kid but one named Toby said yes. Toby kept a "whole lamp" on all the time. I then asked when they had last used a flashlight. The responses varied: A few had used one during a recent thunderstorm blackout; a few used one while camping and needing to find the bathroom; and a few used a flashlight to explore attics, barns, garages, and basements.

Scenic Overlooks

"An age is called dark, not because the light fails to shine, but because people refuse to see it."

—James A. Michener

"In the end, the poem is not a thing we see; it is, rather, a light by which we may see— and what we see is life."

—Robert Penn Warren

"In faith there is enough light for those who want to believe and enough shadows to blind those who don't."

—Blaise Pascal

"Joy seems to me a step beyond happiness—happiness is a sort of atmosphere you can live in sometimes when you're lucky. Joy is a light that fills you with hope and faith and love."

—Adela Rogers St. John

I explained that Jesus functions in our lives like a night light and a flashlight. He helps us feel safe and secure, even during our darkest hours. He also helps us find what is vital or missing in our lives. I was not at all surprised that the adults got more out of this message than the kids. The kids could tell me what they had learned, but the adults understood the wisdom packed in this little message.

I think Jesus chose to call himself the Light of the World for the following reasons:

➤ Faith demands awareness and insists on full honesty and disclosure; faith is unwilling to deny the truth.

➤ The Holy Spirit is often dragging us kicking and screaming into the bright light of day.

➤ The Holy Spirit is the catalyst for maturation, and maturity requires seeing the light.

➤ The Holy Spirit is ceaselessly expanding our consciousness.

➤ To live in the dark is to live in fear; to choose the darkness is called denial.

➤ Jesus does not want to be followed out of blind faith.

➤ Only those who are aware of the blueprints Christ has left us can build the kingdom.

➤ The mustard seed of faith needs light to grow.

➤ Everything that matters in life—love, joy, and hope—can happen only if our eyes are wide open.

I have often thought of the darkness known by the people of Palestine and Galilee. They had no streetlights, neon signs, or lamps gilding windows; there was only an occasional lamp or candle under a sky that often hung like tar. The blackness must have felt thick and omnipresent, and the night must have seemed frightening.

To these folks, Jesus' words must have had great meaning. Light did ease fear. The light of day was met with gratitude and a sigh of relief. Jesus was calling his followers to a deep faith to overcome an equally strong fear. The poetic image of him as the Light of the World would have spoken volumes to his listeners.

The Good Shepherd

The metaphor of Jesus as the Good Shepherd is rooted in the culture in which he lived. Shepherds and their sheep were a common sight. However, they were held in low esteem by the religious establishment. Shepherds were dirty, and they stunk. Because of their profession, they could not observe many of the ceremonial laws, especially those revolving around cleanliness. Shepherds were therefore not welcome at the temple.

Why then did Jesus choose to call himself by what at face value might seem an offensive image? The following are all reasons:

➤ Jesus identified with the lowly shepherds because he also was rejected by the religious establishment.

➤ Jesus was impressed by the utter devotion of a shepherd to his flock. Jesus knew that a good shepherd would do anything to protect his sheep from harm or to locate one that was missing.

➤ Jesus respected that a good shepherd knew each of his sheep individually and felt that each one mattered.

Major Highways

"'I am the good shepherd. The good shepherd lays down his life for the sheep. He who is a hireling and not a shepherd, whose own the sheep are not, sees the wolf coming and leaves the sheep and flees; and the wolf snatches them and scatters them. He flees because he is a hireling and cares nothing for the sheep. I am the good shepherd; I know my own and my own know me, as the Father knows me and I know the Father; and I lay down my life for the sheep.'"

—John 10:11–15

Jesus saw himself as a good shepherd. He promised his followers that he would go to any length to keep them safe or to find them if they were lost. He promised each one a personal relationship, a genuine bond of intimacy. He made it clear that he was devoted to his followers, as he hoped they would be devoted to him.

To the followers of Jesus, the Holy Spirit is also thought to function like a good shepherd. The Spirit encases them in a protective coating of grace and is tireless in tending to the needs of the faithful flock. The Spirit speaks to the heart of the amazing love God has for those who are open and ready to receive it.

The Way

A metaphor speaks on many levels; it can affect us intellectually, emotionally, and spiritually. At times, a poetic image will escape the minds of those we call intelligent, but fasten itself as wisdom to the hearts of many we call fools.

Jesus chose common imagery to reveal uncommon truths. He wanted his followers to find the extraordinary in the ordinary, the miracle in the mundane. The Way is yet another metaphor that speaks on several planes:

➤ **Physically.** Transportation during biblical times was rough, dangerous, and downright frightening. Most good folks never traveled or did so only when their faith demanded it. A road in Palestine could be wiped away by a single sand squall. Many of the roads surrounding Jerusalem were hangouts for robbers and thieves. The roads themselves were not well-marked, and it was easy to get hopelessly lost. Being lost in desert country was terrifying and potentially terminal.

When Jesus called himself the Way, he was expressing to his followers that he would give their lives direction. He would make sure they arrived at their destination. With Jesus as their guide, they would not get lost.

➤ **Emotionally.** To be depressed or in despair is like falling down a deep well. You cannot move. You have no energy. You feel stuck. Jesus tells his followers that he will help them out of the well. He will get them unstuck and moving again.

➤ **Spiritually.** To grow spiritually requires traveling new roads, taking detours, and even constructing your own way. Jesus inspires his followers to believe that they are on the right track and that their destination is worthy of their effort to travel.

Major Highways

"'Let not your hearts be troubled; believe in God, believe also in me. In my Father's house are many rooms; if it were not so, would I have told you that I go to prepare a place for you? And when I go and prepare a place for you, I will come again and will take you to myself, that where I am you may be also. And you know the way where I am going.' Thomas said to him, 'Lord we do not know where you are going; how can we know the way?' Jesus said to him, 'I am the way, and the truth, and the life; no one comes to the Father, but by me. If you had known me, you would have known my Father also; henceforth you know him and have seen him.'"

—John 14:1–14

Detours

We are a fast-moving culture, a culture that has walked on the moon. Still, we have no idea where we are going. Worse yet, we have no idea why we are moving at all. We talk a good game about progress, but we secretly feel as though things are getting worse. At times, we brag about the pace of our lives, but we spiritually feel like lemmings. Progress isn't a noble journey if it only means a fatal leap into the sea.

Jesus calls himself the Way. What is offered in that image is spiritually profound:

➤ Jesus offers his followers a point and a purpose—direction.

➤ He offers his followers a reason for the journey—a destination.

➤ He tells his followers that he will be their guide and offers his life as a map.

Scenic Overlooks

"A glimpse is not a vision. But to a man on a mountain road by night, a glimpse of the next three feet of road may matter more than a vision of the horizon."

—C. S. Lewis

"A place is yours when you know where all the roads go."

—Stephen King

"Discoveries are often made by not following instructions, but by going off the main road, by trying the untried."

—Frank Tyler

"A road twice traveled is never as long."

—Rosalie Graham

Major Highways

"'I am the true vine, and my Father is the vinedresser. Every branch of mine that bears no fruit, he takes away, and every branch that does bear fruit he prunes, that it may bear more fruit. You are already made clean by the word which I have spoken to you. Abide in me, and I in you. As the branch cannot bear fruit by itself, unless it abides in the vine, neither can you, unless you abide in me. I am the vine; you are the branches. He who abides in me, and I in him, he it is that bears much fruit, for apart from me you can do nothing. ...'"

"'This is my commandment, that you love one another as I have loved you. Greater love has no man than this, that a man lay down his life for his friends. You are my friends if you do what I command you.'"

—John 15:1–5; 12–14

Points of Interest

It takes so little to stay connected with our faith. A mere half-hour of genuine devotion can create a hope-filled perspective to an entire day. Making conscious contact with God, however you understand God, can make the difference between a day lived in fear, worry, or anxiety and a day that is spent sailing on the gentle seas of God's grace.

The Vine

For another children's sermon, I brought in a vine almost 20 feet long. After the kids oohed and aahed at the length of the vine, they were stunned silent when I cut the vine into 10 two-foot pieces and handed them out. I asked the kids what would happen now that the vine was cut. Tommy, a bubbly five-year-old with a three-inch cowlick said, "This sucker will be deader than a doornail in about an hour." Kids tell the gospel truth.

After the laughter subsided, I was able to explain to the kids why it is so critical to not be cut off from God, the source of all life. They understood what I meant by keeping a close connection to Christ. I think many of the adults were thinking about how cut off they felt from Christ.

Jesus uses another common image, a grapevine, to make an uncommon point. A grapevine was a most familiar sight in Palestine and Galilee. The agricultural folks in these lands knew how things grew, and they knew how to help them to grow. They knew that nothing grew if it was cut off from its supply of sun, soil, and water.

Jesus used this poetic image to remind his followers what happens if they are cut off from the Vine:

➤ Faith withers.

➤ Love and hope rots.

➤ The soul dies.

Jesus also used this image to clarify for his disciples the importance of staying connected to the Vine so that Jesus could …

➤ Infuse their faith.

➤ Inspire them to love extravagantly and hope with courage.

➤ Embolden their soul sufficiently to work on the task of building the kingdom.

The choice of faith is simple: You either turn your back on God, or you run down the road to meet him who has already run more than half the distance to meet you. This choice can mean the difference between having a life or losing one.

Detours

In our culture, becoming disconnected from God is easy. You can see this disconnection in our relationship to time: We spend time, kill time, make time, buy time, or beat the clock, but we take all the punches. By trying to own time, we wind up disowning God. In America, finding time for faith is hard.

The Least You Need to Know

➤ Jesus utilized metaphors to reveal his nature. These metaphors spoke to people on many levels.

➤ Jesus referred to himself as the Lamb of God, the Bread of Life, the Everflowing Stream, the Good Shepherd, the Light of the World, the Way, and the Vine.

➤ These poetic images unpacked the mind of God and defined the essential tasks of the Holy Spirit.

➤ These metaphors all addressed the amazing transforming power of grace, as witnessed in the life of Jesus Christ.

Revelation: The Apocalypse

From the very beginning, Christians anticipated the coming of a new age. They held to the notion that eventually Jesus would complete his transformation of the world. As time progressed, the community was forced to struggle with sagging morale, incessant persecution, and a world that seemed to be getting worse.

The Christian community in Asia Minor clung firmly to the belief that a final struggle was coming: a battle between the city of Earth (Rome) and the city of God. This particular faith community produced John the Prophet, the author of the Book of Revelation. Though the book, the last in the New Testament, is attributed to John the Disciple, it seems highly unlikely that the beloved fisherman would have composed such a fiery and prophetic text. The main issue confronting the Christian community at this time was emperor worship. John the Prophet knew that this issue was only the tip of the iceberg. Underneath lay the enormous conflict between the forces of good and evil. He viewed the crisis surrounding emperor worship as the mere foreshadowing of an impending battle of far more epic and eternal proportions.

The Book of Revelation was written during the reign of Roman Emperor Domitian, the sadistic successor to Nero. Christians were being fed to the lions at the Roman Circus as a form of entertainment. The heads of Christians were lit afire like street lamps to lead the way to the Circus. During these vicious times, John the Prophet wrote the Book of Revelation as a means of offering his suffering flock some much-needed hope.

Apocalyptic Literature

Apocalyptic literature was a form of writing with a certain style and structure. A piece of apocalyptic writing was easily recognizable by the following attributes:

➤ It was set in the midst of great crisis.

➤ Its world was dualistic and had two competing forces, such as Satan and God, light and dark, and good and evil, vying for power.

➤ Redemption was not thought of as a process, but as a singular event.

➤ The victory of the light was guaranteed.

➤ God was not seen as immanent, but transcendent and holy.

➤ The writing was laden with code because of the surrounding crisis.

➤ Cycles were a common theme in apocalyptic literature; the stories formed a grand spiral continuing upward toward the fulfillment of God's purpose.

Apocalyptic Code

Apocalyptic literature contained symbolic numbers, creatures, and colors. Various other objects and phenomena portended significant events. The following are the significant numbers used in apocalyptic literature and their corresponding symbolic meanings:

Number	Meaning
3	This number is of the spirit world.
$3^1/_2$	Half of 7, this number symbolizes incompleteness; 42 months or 1260 days is used to represent the dark side.
4	This number is of the material world (4 corners of the earth).
6	This human number falls short of 7.
7	The perfect number, 7 is the unification of earth (4) and spirit (3).
12	This number symbolizes God's redeeming company, as in 12 Jewish tribes and 12 disciples. It also is the product of 4 (earth) × 3 (spirit).

These apocalyptic creatures also had symbolic meanings:

Animal	Meaning
Lion	Great strength
Bear	Stealth
Goat	Coarse evil
Lamb	Sacrifice
Ox	Patient and devoted service
Eagle	Lofty spirituality

These apocalyptic colors have symbolic meanings as well:

Color	Meaning
White	Triumph
Red	Strife and war
Black	Famine
Green-gray	Death

The following are the various apocalyptic portents:

Solar eclipse

Bloody moon

Falling stars

Rainbows

All-seeing eye

Throne

Precious stones and metals

Apocalyptic Influences on Revelation

Several ancient religious texts influenced Revelation. The Book of Enoch predicted the coming of the Son of Man and referred to him as the righteous or anointed one. The Apocalypse of Baruch predicted the fall of Jerusalem. Fourth Esdras, like the Book of Job, dealt with the theme of enduring great suffering; only the end of the world could solve all the problems being faced. This work, Fourth Esdras, had the greatest influence on the Book of Revelation.

Apocalyptic Literature in the Bible

The Book of Revelation is not the only apocalyptic writing in the Bible. The following biblical texts contain good examples of writing in the apocalyptic style:

- ➤ Daniel 2, 7, and 12
- ➤ Isaiah 24–27
- ➤ Zechariah 12–14
- ➤ Ezekiel 1
- ➤ Book of Jude
- ➤ 1 Thessalonians 4:13–18
- ➤ 2 Thessalonians 2:1–12
- ➤ Mark 13
- ➤ Matthew 24
- ➤ Luke 17:22–37 and 21:5–36

Apocalyptic writing offers the hope of an end to suffering and a coming glory. The end of the world is not seen as a climax, but as a judgment. The old world is completely gone. There is no continuity in apocalyptic literature. The end is the end of history.

Apocalyptic Jesus

The Book of Revelation tells of a new age and a new world. Nothing of the old world remains. Everything that is past is past. The line of demarcation is as wide and deep as a canyon: You are either a new creature or an old one. If you are new, you are brand new. If you are old, you are no longer worthy of notice.

This apocalyptic perspective gives Jesus a whole new look. The life of Jesus is understood in a totally altered way. The intimate Jesus of the Gospels becomes the grand holy victor of the Book of Revelation. Jesus is now both the lion (5:5) and the lamb (5:6). The kingdom of God has been built, but the kingdoms of the world have been destroyed.

The Jesus found in the Book of Revelation is a wholly new character from the one portrayed in the Gospels. The Jesus of the Book of Revelation is ...

- ➤ At the end of his rope and angry.
- ➤ Far more concerned with victory in a more traditional sense.
- ➤ Less concerned with the power of love than the declaration of what is right.
- ➤ Far more obsessed with the powers of Satan.
- ➤ Weary and increasingly impatient.
- ➤ No longer willing to love enemies, if those enemies are spiritual enemies.
- ➤ No longer focused on the poor and outcast, because everyone is now the recipient of persecution and oppression.
- ➤ Exclusive and not inclusive.

190

➤ A believer in a grace that is yet to come, unlike the Gospels' presentation of Jesus as the event of grace itself.

The Jesus of Revelation is worthy of a closer examination. He bears only a slight family resemblance to the man and Messiah described in the Gospels.

The Letters to the Churches

The Book of Revelation begins with letters to the seven churches in Asia (1:1–3:22). These letters contain more than general comments and information. Each one targets specific issues of each church. From the perspective of this book, it is fascinating to see how the message of Jesus is applied in these letters to the problems facing these early Christian communities. As I review the main points addressed in each letter, take note of the application of the life of Christ to these problems.

The Message to the Church in Ephesus

The prophet John gently scolded the church in Ephesus for failing to treat one another in a loving spirit. In the early stages of the church, love had been abundant. As is so often the case even today, more conflicts arose as time passed, and the love began to diminish. Jesus taught his followers to love in a spirit of forgiveness, unconditionally, even to the extent of embracing an enemy. John issued the same charge to the community at Ephesus.

The Message to the Church in Smyrna

John the Prophet asked the Christian community in Smyrna to be strong in faith. He acknowledged that this church would face tough times and extensive persecution. Suffering was a major aspect of the ministry and message of Jesus. Jesus did not paint a pretty picture for the faithful. He told his followers that the road of faith would be long, difficult, and strewn with obstacles of every kind. Disciples of Jesus were told to expect suffering. The prophet John echoed that message.

Major Highways

"'But I have this against you, that you have abandoned the love you had at first. Remember then from what you have fallen, repent and do the works you did at first. If not, I will come to you and remove your lampstand from its place, unless you repent.'"

—Revelation 2:4–5

Major Highways

"'Do not fear what you are about to suffer. Behold, the devil is about to throw some of you into prison, that you may be tested, and for ten days you will have tribulation. Be faithful until death, and I will give you the crown of life.'"

—Revelation 2:10

Major Highways

"'But I have this against you, that you tolerate the woman Jezebel, who calls herself a prophetess and is teaching and beguiling my servants to practice immorality and to eat food sacrificed to idols. I gave her time to repent, but she refuses to repent of her immorality. Behold, I will throw her on a sickbed, and those who commit adultery with her I will throw into great tribulation, unless they repent of her doings; and I will strike her children dead. And all the churches shall know that I am he who searches mind and heart, and I will give to each of you as your works deserve.'"

—Revelation 2:20–23

The Message to the Church in Thyatira

This letter to the church in Thyatira is scathing. In it, John the Prophet condemns a female prophet in the church who he believes is leading many in the community astray. Jesus often warned his followers to beware of false prophets, and John the Prophet reiterates that warning in this letter. The attack on the woman is particularly strong and gives evidence of how seriously John took this threat.

Major Highways

"'And to the angel of the church in Sardis write: The words of him who has the seven spirits of God and the seven stars.'"

"'I know your works; you have the name of being alive, but you are dead. Awake, and strengthen what remains and is on the point of death, for I have not found your works perfect in the sight of my God.'"

—Revelation 3:1–2

The Message to the Church in Pergamum

Pergamum was a contaminated faith community. Some members of the community were known to worship idols and pay homage to the Roman emperor. In his letter to the church in Pergamum, John the Prophet applied a basic principle of Christian faith: There can be only one God.

The Message to the Church in Sardis

In earlier chapters, we witnessed the rigorous honesty of Jesus. He spoke a blistering truth, the gospel truth.

John the Prophet maintained this tradition. In his letter to the church in Sardis, John blatantly told the members of the church that their faith was a sham. They were spiritually bankrupt. Their faith was dead because it was not filled with the life of compassion and mercy to which they were called.

Major Highways

"'But I have a few things against you: you have some there who hold the teaching of Balaam, who taught Balak to put a stumbling block before the sons of Israel, that they might eat food sacrificed to idols and practice immorality. So you also have some who hold the teaching of the Nicolaitans. Repent then. If not, I will come to you soon and war against them with the sword of my mouth.'"

—Revelation 2:14–16

The Message to the Church in Philadelphia

The letter to the church in Philadelphia is a letter of encouragement. This message asks the faith community to persevere. Perseverance was another critical theme in the ministry of Jesus Christ. When the followers of Jesus were at the end of their rope, Jesus would ask them to tie a knot and hang on. John the Prophet delivered an identical message to the church in Philadelphia.

The Message to the Church in Laodicea

Laodicea was the wealthiest of all seven cities mentioned here. It was well known for manufacturing wool and as a banking center. The church here had grown lazy, complacent, and far too comfortable. In his letter to the church in Laodicea, John

Major Highways

"'Because you have kept my word of patient endurance, I will keep you from the hour of trial which is coming on the whole world, to try those who dwell upon the earth. I am coming soon; hold fast what you have, so that no one may seize your crown.'"

—Revelation 3:10–11

the Prophet tells the members of the church that they stand for nothing. He blasts them with the accusation that they are lukewarm. This potent image of something that is neither hot nor cold and has little taste sure sums up a faith that has lost its edge.

Major Highways

"'I know your works: you are neither cold nor hot. Would that you were cold or hot! So, because you are lukewarm, and neither cold nor hot, I will spew you out of my mouth. For you say, "I am rich; I have prospered, and I need nothing"; not knowing that you are wretched, pitiable, poor, blind, and naked. Therefore I counsel you to buy from me gold refined by fire, that you may be rich, and white garments to clothe you and to keep the shame of your nakedness from being seen, and salve to anoint your eyes, that you may see. Those whom I love, I reprove and chasten; so be zealous and repent.'"

—Revelation 3:15–19

All seven churches received messages from John the Prophet, but one can see that these words could have just as easily flowed from the lips of Jesus. The life of Jesus was brief. However, the impact of his message and ministry appear to be eternal. The imprint of Jesus' life onto his followers was deep, so much so that John the Prophet spoke as if possessed by Christ's spirit.

The Seven Visions

The remainder of the Book of Revelation is composed of a series of seven visions. The number seven is crucial here because seven was thought to be the perfect number and therefore represents the concept that this prophecy is staged in eternity. In other words, John the Prophet was not writing only for his time in history, but also for all time.

The seven visions and their symbolic meaning are as follows:

1. **The Seven Seals** (6:1–8:1). The Lamb, Jesus Christ, breaks open the seals to seven scrolls. These scrolls contain the gospel truth and are thought to reveal the will of God for our lives.

2. **The Seven Trumpets** (8:2–11:15). The trumpet was often used in scripture to announce the intervention of God. The trumpet was used to sound the alarm as a warning, to announce the presence of royalty, or to call people to battle.

3. **The Seven Visions of the Kingdom of the Dragon** (11:6–13:18). The dragon is the archenemy of God. The dragon has 7 heads and 10 horns, which signifies that it is a mighty power. It is thought to represent the Antichrist. God is the creator of order, but the dragon creates chaos.

4. **The Seven Visions of the Coming of the Son of Man** (14:1–20). The 144,000 followers of Jesus all bear the mark of Christ. This mark is a mark of ownership and protection. These followers of Jesus will face great pain and suffering, but they will remain safe. The Son of Man will come again and reign victorious, and those who bear his mark will share in the glory of that victory.

5. **The Seven Bowls** (15:1–16:21). The scene is heaven, and the seven bowls are bowls of judgment. They are filled with the wrath of God and spell natural disaster for the peoples of the earth. The world is beset by plagues: ulcerous sores appear on the men, water turns to blood, the sun becomes scorchingly hot, darkness covers the kingdom of the dragon, and violent earthquakes and hailstorms occur.

6. **The Seven Visions of the Fall of Babylon** (17:1–19:10). Babylon is another name for Rome. Rome's wealth has come from taking advantage of other nations, the poor, and the needy. The fall of Rome is predicted here as the revenge of the angels and the followers of Jesus.

7. **The Seven Visions of the End** (19:11–21:4). For the first time, God speaks. God can take a human being and re-create him, make him or her brand new. This same God will create a whole new universe for the saints who have been restored. The saints and Christ will reign for 1,000 years.

Taking these seven cycles as history or as if they are to occur in chronological order is foolish. Revelation is written from a spiritual time and place and is set against a heavenly backdrop. Revelation is not to be taken as literal history, but as an expression of the daily battle between the forces of the light and those of darkness. The story that unfolds in Revelation does not speak exclusively to one moment in time, but to time eternal.

The Beast

The beast is a powerful and pointed metaphor for the Roman Empire. This beast has the mouth of a lion, the feet of a bear, and the body of leopard. Its seven heads represent seven emperors: Tiberius, Caligula, Claudius, Nero, Vespasian, Titus, and Domitian. The 10 horns are these emperors plus three who only reigned for brief times: Galba, Otha, and Vitellius. During the reigns of these emperors, the worship of Caesar became prominent.

Major Highways

"And I saw a beast rising out of the seas, with ten horns and seven heads, with ten diadems upon its horns and a blasphemous name upon its heads. And the beast that I saw was like a leopard, its feet were like a bear's, and its mouth was like a lion's mouth. And to it the dragon gave his power and his throne and great authority. One of its heads seemed to have a mortal wound, but its mortal wound was healed, and the whole earth followed the beast with wonder. Men worshiped the dragon, for he had given his authority to the beast, and they worshiped the beast, saying, 'Who is like the beast, and who can fight against it?'"

"And the beast was given a mouth uttering haughty and blasphemous words, and it was allowed to exercise authority for forty-two months ...."

—Revelation 13:1–5

For a long time, Rome was witnessed as a friend of the Christian community. Paul often sought the help of the Roman government. Paul acknowledged that he was frequently saved from the fury of the Jews by the Roman authorities and went so far as to ask Christians to be obedient to Roman authority (Romans 13:1–6).

In Revelation, this perspective on Rome is totally altered. When Revelation was written, the Christian community held Rome in contempt. Why?

➤ Rome had become the champion of worshipping Caesar.

➤ Rome strived to crush the Christian faith and all those who did not swear allegiance to the emperor.

➤ Rome was an empire that had become the agent of the devil.

➤ Rome was anti-God and established its authority by brute force.

➤ Rome had no moral authority.

➤ Rome was the bastion of decadence and decay, the powers of death.

The Book of Revelation is a startling departure in tone and style from the Gospels. The Gospels are often painted in lovely shades of gray, meaning that there is ample room for interpretation. The words invite reflection. The love that pours out of the words is extravagant and unconditional. The overall feeling exuded is one of an encounter with an extraordinarily gracious and generous Jesus.

In contrast, the Book of Revelation is completely black and white. There is no room for interpretation. The love of Jesus is selective and scalpel sharp. Rome is pure evil, death incarnate, and a beast of unparalleled ugliness.

The beast in the Book of Revelation was marked. A marking held great significance in the Roman Empire and within the Jewish faith:

➤ Slaves were marked to claim ownership.

➤ Soldiers wore the mark of their general.

➤ All contracts held the seal of the emperor.

➤ All coinage held the inscription of the emperor.

➤ The burning of incense to Caesar was rewarded with a certificate; thus, the certificate became the mark of emperor worship.

➤ To distinguish themselves, the Jews wore phylacteries (leather boxes containing scripture) on their left arms and foreheads while praying.

The beast wore the number 666. This number is the Latin numerical equivalent for Nero, probably the most vile and evil of all the Roman emperors. John the Prophet predicts the coming of the Antichrist, Nero, who is the incarnation of evil.

Major Highways

"'Rejoice over her, O heaven, O saints and apostles and prophets, for God has given judgment for you against her!' Then a mighty angel took up a stone like a great millstone and threw it into the sea, saying, 'So shall Babylon the great city be thrown down with violence, and shall be no more; and the sound of harpers and minstrels, of flute players and trumpeters, shall be heard in thee no more; and a craftsman of any craft shall be found in thee no more; and the sound of the millstone shall be heard in thee no more; and the light of a lamp shall shine in thee no more; and the voice of bridegroom and bride shall be heard in thee no more; for thy merchants were the great men of the earth, and all nations were deceived by thy sorcery. And in her was found the blood of prophets and of saints, and of all who have been slain on earth.'"

—Revelation 18:20–24

The Fall of Babylon

It is difficult for Americans to give the Book of Revelation an honest reading. The similarity between the nation of Rome and the United States of America is too obvious to ignore. It is hard for us to recognize that when we sing or hear "The Hallelujah Chorus," these words are sung by the angels over the smoldering ruins of Rome, the greatest, wealthiest, and most powerful nation on the face of the planet.

John the Prophet took an enormous risk in composing the Book of Revelation because he offered the following depiction of the Roman Empire:

➤ Spiritually speaking, Rome was a necrophiliac nation, a people possessed by death.

➤ Rome gained her wealth off the backs of the poor.

➤ Rome treated those in need with disdain.

➤ Rome was all about pleasure and the avoidance of pain.

➤ Rome asked its citizenry to serve nobody but Caesar.

➤ Rome displayed no ethics or morality.

➤ Rome showed a bloodlust; it was incessantly involved in wars and battles to acquire more land and riches.

➤ Rome did not know the word *enough*. They could not do enough conquering or own enough stuff. Enough was never enough.

➤ Rome found death and violence to be entertaining. The Roman Circus became a bastion for evil where Christians were slaughtered by wild animals and gladiators fought to the death.

➤ Rome was faithless and void of humility.

➤ The citizenry of Rome was heavily invested in playing God.

As you can see, Rome represented the opposite of the will and wishes of Jesus. It bore no resemblance to the kingdom that Christ asked his followers to build. The kingdom of God is one where enough is enough; service, sacrifice, and humility generate their own spiritual rewards; all worship is focused on God alone; love is the dominant force; and forgiveness is the name of the game.

The Book of Revelation is the most political treatise of the New Testament. It makes a strong attack on the politics, economics, and moral impoverishment of Rome. The fall of Rome is applauded in heaven, because Rome was a nation that did not care for those who were hungry, homeless, sick, shattered, frail, disabled, lonely, or alone. America can learn a great deal from the Book of Revelation, but first the church will need to become courageous enough to preach the gospel truth of its message.

The New Age

Throughout the Book of Revelation, we are told that ultimately the Lamb of God, Jesus Christ, will come again to reign victorious with the saints. This victory is not the winning of a battle; it is the claim of the ultimate triumph of good over evil.

Major Highways

"And I saw the holy city, new Jerusalem, coming down out of heaven from God, prepared as a bride adorned for her husband; and I heard a loud voice from the throne saying, 'Behold, the dwelling of God is with men. He will dwell with them, and they shall be his people, and God himself will be with them; he will wipe away every tear from their eyes, and death shall be no more, neither shall there be mourning nor crying nor pain any more, for the former things have passed away.'"

"And he who sat upon the throne said, 'Behold, I make all things new.' Also he said, 'Write this, for these words are trustworthy and true.' And he said to me, 'It is done! I am the Alpha and the Omega, the beginning and the end. To the thirsty I will give from the fountain of the water of life without payment.'"

—Revelation 21:2–6

The Book of Revelation describes this new age as the making of all things new; the transformation is total. The new age will produce a new Jerusalem, which is the kingdom of God; a new people, which is the communion of the saints; a new heaven; and a new earth. In this new age, a magnificent temple where God alone is worshipped will be built.

This new age is an eternal time and place where

➤ Suffering, pain, and death do not exist.

➤ The truth flows like a pure, crystalline river.

➤ Light always shines and darkness has been vanquished.

➤ The saints, those followers of Christ who have persevered, are rewarded.

➤ All needs, both physical and spiritual, are met.

➤ Christ reigns without threat.

The depiction of this new age is filled with magnificent poetry and imagery. The images of precious stones and metals are abundant. I realize now that many of the images I had of heaven as a child, including pearly gates and streets of gold, were inspired by the Book of Revelation. The main theme of the new age is that it will be a time of peace and tranquility when the true riches of grace and mercy will be owned exclusively by the followers of Jesus.

The Book of Revelation is inspiring and troubling. The poetic imagery and potent metaphors that dot its pages can be taken as literal signs that call for some pretty horrific actions. More than a few nuts have found their demonic callings on the pages of Revelation. I encourage you to consider these as the main points of the Book of Revelation, as written by John the Prophet:

➤ Evil exists, and it often exists as a nation or a people.

➤ Evil is grounded in a disrespect for life and a fascination with death. Evil also has a lot to do with money, greed, and power.

➤ Morality is not primarily about sex; it is primarily about the treatment of the poor and outcast. All Christian communities are called to stand up for the poor, the oppressed, and the people in the greatest physical and emotional need.

➤ At times the powers of darkness will appear to be winning the war. The faithful must remain strong and continue to follow; they also must stand up for what they believe.

➤ The rewards for having led a good life are often granted in eternity as the legacy an individual may leave.

➤ Jesus is the ultimate declaration of victory for the forces of goodness and light. He will ultimately build the kingdom.

➤ Jesus calls his followers to be a new people who live in a new world, and he demands that they let go of all that is past.

➤ Jesus wipes away all sin from the face of the earth.

➤ Less is more in the kingdom.

➤ The good life is one lived in the spirit of grace, which is unconditional love and forgiveness.

➤ Grace is the transforming force of the Book of Revelation; it makes all things new.

The Least You Need to Know

➤ John the Prophet wrote the Book of Revelation.

➤ The Book of Revelation was written during a time of horrific persecution of Christians by the Roman Empire.

➤ The Book of Revelation challenged the churches of Asia to remain faithful and strong and to persevere.

➤ The Book of Revelation depicted Rome as a brutal beast, one that would ultimately be felled by a lowly lamb.

➤ The Book of Revelation stated that Jesus, the lamb and the lion, would return to usher in a new age of peace, tranquility, and abundant faith, which would give rise to a New Jerusalem. The Book of Revelation also revealed the look and feel of the kingdom of God.

Part 8

The Ministry Continues

What did Jesus do for a living? What was his vocation? What was his job? He was a minister/rabbi. Yes, he was a healer and a storyteller, and he was claimed to be the Messiah. However, it was ministry that was the focus of his adult life on earth.

Ministry is defined by the life of Jesus Christ. His life gives meaning to the concept and is the lens through which we can see the nature of ministry. In this part I present what Jesus Christ taught about ministry.

Chapter 22

Acts: Faith in Action

In This Chapter

➤ Luke continues the story of Christ

➤ Luke gives history a new framework

➤ The Holy Spirit arrives at Pentecost

➤ Peter plays a prominent role in Jerusalem

➤ Stephen suffers

➤ Paul preaches in Antioch

Acts is the sequel to the Gospel of Luke and is a reasonably accurate historical accounting of the early church. Acts is also what is called an apologetic work in which Luke offers a strong defense of the claims of the life and ministry of Jesus Christ.

Luke's Purpose

In Acts, Luke confronts a very real problem for the early church. The *Second Coming* had not come and did not appear to be on the horizon. Mark's gospel and the writings of Paul had spoken of the Second Coming as if it were right around the corner. By the time of Luke's writings, however, it was clear that this wasn't the case. For this reason, Luke had to cast history in a new framework. He had to give a purpose for the early church other than waiting patiently and expectantly for the Second Coming. Luke had to take the focus of the followers off the future and place it back in the here and now. He had to offer a mission and ministry (in other words, a reason for being) to the early church.

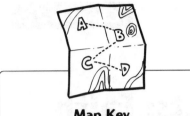

Map Key

The **Second Coming** is the be-lief that Jesus will return to Earth. Earlier Christians believed this to be imminent.

Detours

If a reader doesn't have a proper understanding of history, the Book of Acts can be read as anti-Semitic and hateful toward Jews.

Acts is set in Jerusalem. Jerusalem becomes the dwell-ing place of the followers of Jesus, who hold to a be-lief in the resurrection. The first task of these followers was to replace Judas, who had in effect defected from the 12 disciples (by betraying Jesus and then commit-ting suicide). A system of lots was used, and Matthias was chosen. Once the original number of apostles was restored, the followers of Jesus took on the formidable task of reestablishing the powerful position of Israel. The Hebrew scriptures play a critical role in Acts, be-cause Luke seeks to demonstrate that the faith of the followers of Jesus is rooted in a deep and passionate understanding of God's chosen people and their sa-cred history. Luke is determined to present a strong case to convert the Jews.

Pentecost and the Role of the Holy Spirit

Early on in the Book of Acts, its lead actor, the Holy Spirit, is introduced. The Holy Spirit becomes the dominating presence both for the Book of Acts and the building of the early church. It is described as a rushing and mighty wind that transforms many lives by infusing them with and inspiring them to new faith. The Holy Spirit is the resurrected presence of Jesus Christ, and it has the power to turn lives around.

Pentecost is the Greek name for the Jewish Festival of Weeks, a time to celebrate the harvest as well as to mark the Jewish reception of the law at Sinai. The receiving of the law was believed to be God's clear declaration that the Jews were a chosen people. For the early Christian community, Pentecost celebrates the harvesting of new believ-ers by the Holy Spirit as well as the moment God declares the specialness of his new followers.

In the Gospels, the Holy Spirit worked on individuals. In the Book of Acts, the Holy Spirit works on many people at once and becomes a genuine force for unification. This theme of unity is also demonstrated in the accounting of the gift of tongues, which accompanies the Pentecost events. In the story of the Tower of Babel, found in Genesis 11, the human drive to play God by building a tower that would enable hu-mans to see God face to face is confounded by God, who destroys the tower and turns languages into babble. At Pentecost, however, this confusion is replaced by comprehension. The followers of Jesus are now able to communicate in one another's foreign tongues. The walls of language that had long divided them have been brought down by the winds of the Holy Spirit.

Major Highways

"When the day of Pentecost had come, they were all together in one place. And suddenly a sound came from heaven like the rush of a mighty wind, and it filled all the house where they were sitting. And there appeared to them tongues as of fire, distributed and resting on each one of them. And they were all filled with the Holy Spirit and began to speak in other tongues, as the Spirit gave them utterance."

"Now there were dwelling in Jerusalem Jews, devout men from every nation under heaven. And at this sound the multitude came together, and they were bewildered, because each one heard them speaking in his own language."

—Acts 2:1–6

The Holy Spirit, as presented in the Book of Acts, is thought to be ...

➤ The counselor and guide promised by Jesus.

➤ The eternal power and presence of the risen Christ.

➤ A force of faith, inspiring new believers.

➤ A force of unification, breaking down old barriers.

➤ The definer of the purpose of the early church.

➤ The motivator of the mission of the early church.

➤ The catalyst for the growth of the early church.

The Prominent Role of Peter

Peter preached to the crowd that had gathered during the Pentecost experience. He told them that they should believe in the risen Christ. He explained that Jesus was the fulfillment of the prophecies of Hebrew scriptures. He claimed Jesus was the Messiah and that the Holy Spirit could transform their lives. (He used Psalm 16:8–11 to defend his position and noted that David was not writing of himself in the passage but was prophesying the resurrection of the Messiah.)

Major Highways

"Now when they heard this they were cut to the heart, and said to Peter and the rest of the apostles, 'Brethren, what shall we do?' And Peter said to them, 'Repent, and be baptized every one of you in the name of Jesus Christ for the forgiveness of your sins; and you shall receive the gift of the Holy Spirit. For the promise is to you and to your children and to all that are far off, every one whom the Lord our God calls to him.' And he testified with many other words and exhorted them, saying, 'Save yourselves from this crooked generation.' So those who received his word were baptized, and there were added that day about three thousand souls. And they devoted themselves to the apostles' teaching and fellowship, to the breaking of bread and the prayers."

—Acts 2:37–42

Peter's sermon put an emphasis on two major themes:

➤ The Holy Spirit filled these men with a new faith and the will to lead new lives.

➤ The work of the Holy Spirit was both predicted and endorsed by the Hebrew scriptures.

According to Acts, Peter's sermon converted 3,000 individuals. Remember, however, that these new believers did not believe they were rejecting their Jewish faith. They were convinced of being witnesses to the fulfillment of the prophetic word of God. They would continue to attend the temple and go to synagogue. The only difference, major as it may have been, was in their acknowledgement that the Messiah had come. They were not Jews in waiting; they were Jews whose hopes had been fulfilled.

Early on, Luke makes it clear that Peter will be a pivotal leader in the formation of the early church. His powerful preaching and the dramatic conversion of 3,000 souls lay the groundwork for Peter's spiritual role in the life of the Jerusalem church. Peter is the reigning spiritual leader in the first 12 chapters of the Book of Acts.

The Jerusalem Church

The establishment and expansion of the church in Jerusalem is the subject of nearly half of the Book of Acts. Through the bold *witness* of Peter and John, the church expanded and became well known for being a loving and compassionate community of believers.

Peter was an apostle full of the Holy Spirit (Acts 3:1–11). He healed a crippled beggar and, together with the apostles, won 5,000 converts. (Note the use of the number 5,000, as in the gospel miracle of the loaves and fishes.) He made an impassioned appeal to the Jews to believe in the promised prophet, Jesus Christ (Acts 3:12–26), and warned that those who reject Jesus will no longer be considered part of God's Israel. Of course, these messages angered the religious establishment. The Sadducees (those of the high priestly party that controlled the temple) objected strongly to Peter's teachings, especially the notion of the resurrection (Acts 4:1–22).

Jesus' followers then chose seven deacons to help with the increasing workload. One of these deacons was Stephen (Acts 6:1–7). He offered the Sadducees a powerful summary of the teachings of Jesus and accused them of failing to obey God's law, the same law they took pride in claiming to follow to the letter (Acts 6:8–7). As a result, Stephen became the first martyr of the early church. The suffering and death of Stephen bore a striking resemblance to that of Christ's. The followers of Jesus were instructed that they might meet the same fate. Persecution scattered the believers (Acts 8:1–3).

Philip, Paul, and Peter

After the followers scattered, Philip went to Samaria to preach (Acts 8:4–40). The Holy Spirit dominates the account of the conversion of the Samaritans and continues to be portrayed as a unifying force (Acts 8:9–25).

In Chapter 9 of Acts, Saul, later to be called Paul, is converted on the road to Damascus. This conversion story is found in three places in the Book of Acts. Paul was on his way to Damascus to persecute the followers of Jesus when the risen Christ enlightened him.

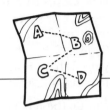

Map Key

To **witness** is to name and claim one's faith. Witnessing is traditionally thought of as verbally naming Jesus as Lord and Savior. I personally believe one can witness by thought, word, or deed.

Points of Interest

The early Christian church was a true socialist community. There was no such thing as private property because the followers of Jesus believed that all possessions must be shared (Acts 4:32–37). Ananias and Sapphira, two who refused to share all of their possessions, died as a result of their refusal (Acts 5:1–11).

Before Luke turns his full attention to the fascinating personage of Paul, he returns again to Peter. Peter healed Aeneas in Lydda and raised Tabitha (Dorcas) in Joppa. While in Joppa, he stayed at the home of Simon, a leatherworker. Because working with leather involves touching dead animals, Jewish law forbids it. In this setting,

Peter had a vision in which he was asked to eat unclean foods. Peter understood this vision as a calling to preach and minister to the "unclean" Gentiles.

Peter was then called to the house of Cornelius, the Roman commander of 100 soldiers. Peter shared the story of the risen Christ with Cornelius and his family, and all were converted to the faith. Peter later had to defend this conversion of a Gentile family to the church in Jerusalem. Though the Jerusalem church appeared to be convinced that his actions were inspired by the Holy Spirit, they had not considered the ramifications of including Gentiles within the faith family.

During the reign of King Herod Agrippa, the apostle James (John's brother) was killed, and Peter was imprisoned. Peter escaped from prison by the intervention of the Holy Spirit. As the story goes, an angel appeared to him in prison and guided him to freedom. Peter sought refuge in the home of Mary, the mother of Mark, and was met at the door by Rhoda, who was stunned to see him. She raced back to tell the gathering that Peter had escaped. They told her she was nuts. The early church, and the early Christians, still had a hard time believing in the power of the Holy Spirit.

Peter was an apostle of rare and exceptional faith and spiritual power. He converted thousands with his preaching. He healed people. He raised Tabitha from the dead. He also converted Cornelius and his family, all of whom were Gentiles. Luke placed Peter on a plane right below Christ. However, all of Peter's powers were said to be gifts of the Holy Spirit, which was an extension of the life of Jesus. Remember, Jesus told his followers they would do things much greater than he did!

Points of Interest

Barnabas offers a striking example of how to minister to new believers. He was not their judge or jury. He did not lecture them about what they were doing wrong. He did not offer himself up as having all the answers. He was excited for them. He listened and learned from their faith. He affirmed them, rejoiced in their belief, and embraced them with love.

The Role of the Church in Antioch

With a population of almost one million on the river Orontes, Antioch, the capital of Roman Syria, was one of the great cities of the Roman world. In such a large and cosmopolitan city, which hosted many diverse religions, Jews and Gentiles were bound to interact. It was in Antioch that followers of Jesus were first called Christians and that the church went worldwide. After Peter had convinced the church in Jerusalem that the Good News was also meant for Gentiles, the doors were open to the spreading of the Christian faith. It also became evident that Christianity was becoming a separate religion. The church at Antioch was declaring this independent spirit, and Antioch established the first Gentile church.

Barnabas—popular and well liked—was dispatched by the Jerusalem church to inspect the goings on in Antioch. He was overjoyed with what he saw, pleased with the passion of these new believers, and deeply moved by their enthusiastic spirit. Barnabas later carried famine relief sent by the church in Antioch to the Jerusalem church. The generosity and compassion of these new believers were certain to strike a positive chord.

It was Antioch that Paul used as his base for his missionary journeys. It was thought to be the headquarters of new beginnings, and it was there that the Holy Spirit was thought to be active and invested. Luke, the champion of the Holy Spirit, gives us numerous accounts of the powerful involvement of the Holy Spirit in the affairs of the church in Antioch.

The Prominent Role of Paul

Paul's ministry is covered in the Book of Acts 13:1–28:31, as the focus shifts to ministering to the Gentiles. Peter is replaced by Paul as the central figure in the book, and he completes three missionary journeys, is imprisoned in Jerusalem, and transported to Rome.

Paul is new to the faith. He has a history of persecuting the faithful, so his ministry to the church in Antioch is initially met with skepticism. Barnabas is treated with far greater respect than Paul is, and only much later does Paul prove his worth as a true spiritual leader.

Paul's First Missionary Journey

Paul, Barnabas, and Mark sail for Cyprus, where they preach and teach in Jewish synagogues, anxious to establish their Jewish roots both to gain an audience and to avoid persecution. It is in Cyprus that Paul confronts and denounces the powerful Jewish magician Bar-Jesus, declaring him to be a false prophet. Paul pronounces a punishment of temporary blindness and is thus himself declared to be a true prophet.

Paul is able to convert Sergius Paulus, the proconsul, a man of far greater significance than Cornelius, the Roman commander of 100 soldiers. This made for a powerful beginning in the winning of converts. However, Mark apparently becomes dissatisfied either with Paul's new role or the move toward Gentiles and returns to Jerusalem.

Paul and Barnabas preach of the newness of God's dealings with Israel. Three times, Paul repeats the story of his conversion and his commission as an apostle, making it clear that the light that struck him on the road to Damascus will soon shine upon the whole earth. However, their preaching is often met with rejection. The Jews struggle with their message, and once they even chase the apostles out of town.

At Lystra, Paul heals a man with crippled feet. The crowds declare that the apostles are gods, but Paul strongly condemns this notion. Jesus Christ is solely responsible for every morsel of their ministry, including miracles.

Paul successfully witnessed to the life of Jesus on this first pilgrimage of faith. He reveals the spirit of Jesus in the following events and acts:

1. Paul declares the difference between a true and false prophet in his dealings with Bar-Jesus.

2. Paul is capable of punishing Bar-Jesus with temporary blindness, and performing a healing.

3. Paul refuses to be equated to Jesus Christ.

The ministry of Jesus Christ continues in the personage and spiritual power of Paul.

The Council at Jerusalem

When Paul and Barnabas return to Antioch, a conservative group from the church in Jerusalem confronts them. This group believes that those who follow Jesus must be circumcised, as established by the law of Moses. Paul and Barnabas disagree. They present a strong case, but the debate rages on. Paul and Barnabas are sent to Jerusalem to discuss the issue with other elders and apostles.

Major Highways

"But some men came down from Judea and were teaching the brethren. 'Unless you are circumcised according to the custom of Moses, you cannot be saved.' And when Paul and Barnabas had no small dissension and debate with them, Paul and Barnabas and some of the others were appointed to go up to Jerusalem to the apostles and the elders about this question."

"... And after there had been much debate, Peter rose and said to them: 'Brethren, you know that in the early days God made choice among you that by my mouth the Gentiles should hear the word of the gospel and believe. And God who knows the heart bore witness to them, giving them the Holy Spirit just as he did to us; and he made no distinction between us and them, but cleansed their hearts by faith. Now therefore why do you make trial of God by putting a yoke upon the neck of the disciples which neither our fathers nor we have been able to bear? But we believe that we shall be saved through the grace of the Lord Jesus, just as they will.'"

—Acts 15:1–2; 7–11

It should come as no surprise that the early church went through such growing pains. The inclusion of Gentiles confronted them with the difficult task of determining what role the Jewish Law would play in the lives of those now called Christians. Though Paul and Barnabas paid respect to the law, they were clear that it was Jesus Christ alone, the event of grace, who was the source of all faith.

James, the brother of Christ, had assumed the leadership role in the church in Jerusalem and became the chief diplomat in resolving this dispute. Surprisingly, James was a religious pietist, unlike his brother, and was not all that fond of Paul's stress on faith over works. Still, in this case, he was able to offer a wider more inclusive view. Though the Gentiles would not be forced to be circumcised—a big relief to a good number of Gentile men—they would be asked to abstain from sexual misconduct and to follow certain basic Jewish laws regarding food—a compromise solution.

The Rift Between Paul and Barnabas

Unfortunately, Christians are notorious for not getting along. Feuds were frequent. Splits over spiritual matters were commonplace. Debates were waged as wars that often divided. Even in the early church, such conflict was the norm.

Paul and Barnabas split over three primary issues:

➤ Barnabas wished to include Mark in the next missionary journey, but Paul was still ticked off with him for leaving the first.

➤ Barnabas was struggling with pulling farther and farther away from his fellow Jews.

➤ There was a genuine clash of personalities. Barnabas was charismatic, warm, and friendly, even earthy. Paul was charismatic but stern and formidable, with a ferocious temper.

Barnabas takes Mark with him and sails to Cyprus.

The Second Missionary Journey

Paul's second missionary journey is made with Silas as his partner. It comes some three years after the first trip. They revisit many of the same cities visited on the first tour, and lay the foundations for the church in Greece.

It is on this second missionary journey that Paul and Silas meet Timothy, the son of a Greek father and a Jewish mother. Paul agrees to have Timothy circumcised as a sign of respect for the law. This is a smart move on Paul's part and displays a real go-with-the-flow attitude here.

Paul and Silas convert a woman named Lydia, who becomes the first female convert in Acts. Lydia invites Paul to dine with her. A Jew dining with a Gentile was risky business and a sharp break with Jewish custom. Paul again chose to adapt and to be flexible. He didn't make his decision based on the demands of law, but rather what the situation called for. In both cases, Paul demonstrated a far more gracious way of handling things.

It is said that Paul and Silas heal a demon-possessed slave girl. The girl's pagan pimps are enraged, as she had made them a lot of money, so the pimps protest to Roman officials, who treat the protest seriously because Paul and Silas pose an economic threat. This time they are arrested for going against Roman customs. These guys just can't win.

While Paul and Silas are imprisoned there is an earthquake, which loosens the prisoners' chains. The jailer thinks all of the prisoners have escaped, and, guilt-ridden, threatens to commit suicide. Paul overhears the threat while still hiding in a darkened passageway. Paul shouts and stops him, revealing the whereabouts of the prisoners; they could have escaped. This action leaves the jailer dumbstruck. Eventually, the jailer and his entire family are converted, and Paul and Silas win their freedom.

Paul goes on to preach at Thessalonica and Beroea. He continues to proclaim the Messiahship of the crucified and risen Jesus. Once again, Paul faces significant persecution and flees to Athens for his own safety. His ministry in all three places is linked by the claim of the resurrection, and the incomprehension of both Jew and Greek.

Paul meets Priscilla and Aquila, who were tent makers just like him, in Corinth. Priscilla and Aquila had been forced to leave Rome due to a decree by Claudius. This decree was probably the result of internal strife within the Jewish community over Christian teachings. Paul also encounters Apollos, a Jew, preaching in Ephesus. Apollos is a persuasive speaker and gifted apologist for the early church.

Once again, this second journey reveals the ongoing ministry of Jesus Christ. The Holy Spirit continues to inspire and empower new faith, as well as transform lives, attitudes, and beliefs. The legacy of Jesus lives on in the following key events from this second journey:

➤ Paul is willing to circumcise Timothy.

➤ Paul is willing to break bread with Lydia.

➤ Paul converts a Philippian jailer by a clear demonstration of loving your enemy.

➤ Paul faces rejection and persecution by his own people.

➤ Paul is imprisoned for being a prophet.

The life of Christ has been imprinted on the heart and mind of Paul, who lives as if he were a disciple walking at Jesus' side. The Holy Spirit moves and animates Paul's ministry.

The Third Missionary Journey

In Ephesus, where Paul adopts the regular practice of preaching in the synagogue first, he is confronted with the problem of lukewarm believers. Some only knew of the baptism of John, and others used Jesus' name as some magical talisman. Paul also continues to display the abundant presence of the Holy Spirit in his ministry, by performing many miracles and exorcisms.

Paul's ministry in Ephesus also threatens the economy. (Ephesus was a magnificent city that served as a religious center for a whole province in Asia.) The Greek goddess Artemis is worshipped here, and the city is the source of much commercial trade. Paul's preaching against the worship of idols poses a very real threat to many merchants who thrived on producing religious relics.

At this point Paul sets his face toward Jerusalem. Luke again is keenly aware of the comparisons that will be made to the passion of Jesus. Paul travels to Jerusalem by a weird route that takes him through Macedonia and Achaia. He is accompanied on his journey to Jerusalem by representatives of the congregations he had founded on his two previous evangelical excursions. (We also read of Paul delivering a sermon of great length, which even sends some of his closest comrades to sleep; this has never happened to me.)

The urgency of the trip to Jerusalem intensifies, and Paul does not go to Ephesus, where he was to deliver a major sermon. It is clear that Paul expects imprisonment. Paul's farewell discourse can be summed up as "it is more blessed to give than to receive." This is also a central message to the Book of Acts and a reminder by Luke of the inextricable link between Jesus and Paul.

At both Tyre and Caesarea, Paul receives messages from the Holy Spirit. Both reveal that Paul will suffer a fate similar to that of Jesus—he, too, will have to pick up his cross and carry it. The Spirit moves Paul toward Jerusalem, where suffering, or perhaps even Paul's death, awaits. Paul the prophet must journey from his missionary successes and miracles to face great pain in the holy city. He recognizes that there is no other way (his Gethsemane experience), as he decides to move forward to Jerusalem.

Luke, in both his Gospel and Acts, presents the Spirit of Jesus as often demanding great service, suffering, and sacrifice. Faith does not free someone from pain, but may in fact guide him or her to the center of it. Christians are asked not to pray for an easy life, but to be stronger and more courageous people.

Luke sees Jerusalem as a city on the decline, as he does the religious establishment that rules there. The Jewish converts in Jerusalem are first and foremost Jews. The church in Jerusalem finds Paul's missionary efforts to the Gentiles to be unsettling, even disturbing. When Paul arrives in Jerusalem, a riot breaks out, and Roman soldiers put Paul under protective custody.

Paul again recounts his conversion experience on the road to Damascus. He offers a vigorous defense of his convictions before the High Council. There is a plan hatched by some of the religious establishment to kill him, but Paul is saved by his Roman citizenship. Still in protective custody, he is transferred to Caesarea, which is under the control of Governor Felix, before whom Paul defends himself. Paul is then imprisoned.

Paul remains in prison for two years, until he defends himself before Festus, who had replaced Felix. Festus discusses the case with Herod Agrippa II, the ruler of northeastern Palestine, and Paul is sent to Rome courtesy of the Roman Empire.

There is a violent storm at sea, and the ship is wrecked upon the rocks. Paul comes ashore at Malta, off the coast of Sicily. Paul is bitten by a poisonous snake, but is unhurt. The people of Malta think he is a god.

Paul finally arrives in Rome. He preaches there that Jesus is a higher authority than Caesar. Luke abruptly ends the story with Paul under house arrest and free to speak and even preach to his captors.

As you can easily see, Paul's life, as presented by Luke, runs on a parallel track to that of Christ's:

➤ Paul preaches and converts followers, as did Jesus.

➤ Paul performs miracles and exorcisms, as did Jesus.

➤ Paul experiences his strongest persecution and rejection from his own people, as did Jesus.

➤ Paul is summoned to Jerusalem, as was Jesus.

➤ Paul prayerfully questions this decision, as he knows it will bring him significant pain and suffering—as Jesus experienced at Gethsemane.

➤ Paul must defend himself to the religious establishment, as was often the case for Jesus.

➤ A plot is hatched within the religious establishment to kill Paul—similar to the one in which Judas participated and sealed with a kiss.

➤ Paul appears before Felix and Festus to defend himself—Jesus appeared before Pilate and Herod.

➤ Paul appears before Agrippa to defend himself—Jesus stands again before Pilate.

➤ Agrippa, last of the Herod dynasty that ruled parts of Palestine from 40 B.C. to A.D. 100, fails to be convinced by Paul, and sarcastically rejects the gospel message.

➤ Agrippa does not find Paul worthy of imprisonment or death—as Pilate did not in the case of Jesus.

➤ Paul confronts Rome with the message that Jesus is a higher authority than Caesar, and he is placed under house arrest.

➤ Prison is used by Luke in like fashion to the tomb for Jesus.

➤ Paul's freedom to move about and preach while under house arrest in Rome is a mini-resurrection.

The Least You Need to Know

➤ Luke offers the church a mission statement in the Book of Acts—what to do now.

➤ The Holy Spirit is the dominant force of the Book of Acts.

➤ Peter makes significant efforts to evangelize the Jews.

➤ Paul focuses on the conversion of Gentiles.

➤ Paul leads three missionary journeys.

➤ The lives and ministries of Peter and Paul often mirror that of Jesus Christ.

Chapter 23

The Letters of Paul

In This Chapter

➤ The sin of religious perfectionism

➤ Grace, the creator of faith

➤ A church based in love, equality, and respect

➤ Paul's strong stand on money matters

Paul's letters are tricky turf, and I doubt that Paul ever thought these personal epistles would be published. They are often blatantly arrogant, at times downright rude, and frequently bigoted. Still, you also can find substantial wisdom in them and a permeating sense of love and affection. These letters speak directly to the practical and spiritual matters facing the early church.

I have often wondered why the letters from Paul were included in scriptural canon. They seem so specific to the times and the individual churches addressed, and the messages are often contradictory. Paul tells us that we are all children of God, but then tells slaves to be obedient to their masters. Paul tells us that in the eyes of God we are neither male nor female, but then goes on to tell women to be submissive to their husbands. He calls himself a humble servant of Jesus Christ, but endlessly boasts of his spectacular conversion on the road to Damascus. Paul was a most human apostle and author.

There are chunks of Paul's letters that I either struggle with or with which I completely disagree. I cannot read Paul apart from having examined the historical context that produced him. Knowing more about his history and the society in which he lived and worked enables me to tolerate some of his message that I would otherwise find intolerable, such as asking slaves to be obedient or asking women to go to the back of the church and to keep their heads covered and their mouths shut.

My reexamination of the Pauline letters for this chapter has led me to a deeper appreciation of the depth of faith reflected in Paul's words. I now see how he did in fact try to put the imprint of Jesus Christ onto the ministry and mission of the early church. I understand the formidable nature of his task of giving organization and spiritual meaning to these diverse congregations. I appreciate how radical his ideas were then, even if they appear archaic now. Most of all, I can see how Jesus Christ did live on in these letters from Paul.

Interpreting each of Paul's letters would make for another whole book. Instead, this chapter covers the primary issues that Paul addressed in these letters. I hope that from this chapter you will gain significant insight into the faith of Paul and how Jesus Christ animated his ministry and message.

Paul and the Law

The law of Moses is the Torah, the first five books of the Hebrew scripture. The intention of the law was to create righteous lives. Righteousness was simply seeking to do the will of God. Sin was thought to be direct defiance of the will of God. The law was meant to establish an intimate bond between God and man and woman. Over time, religious leaders interpreted the law, and rules and regulations were developed. The law soon became a vast network of "do's and don'ts" (but mainly don'ts). The closer the law was examined, the more laws were developed to dictate beliefs and behaviors. The more fanatic the scrutiny of the law became, the more extensive the piety demanded.

Major Highways

"O foolish Galatians! Who has bewitched you, before whose eyes Jesus Christ was publicly portrayed as crucified? Let me ask you only this: Did you receive the Spirit by works of the law, or by hearing with faith? Are you so foolish? Having begun with the Spirit, are you now ending with the flesh? Did you experience so many things in vain?—if it really is in vain. Does he who supplies the Spirit to you and works miracles among you do so by works of the law, or by hearing with faith?"

—Galatians 3:1–5

Paul had been a Pharisee and had tried to follow the law meticulously. He sought to become perfect in his faith. Ironically, Paul came to see that his religious perfectionism had become the source of his sin, and he became aware of the following:

➤ He was trying to be God.

➤ He was trying to be perfect through his own initiative and efforts.

➤ His drive to be perfect had replaced his desire to be merciful and loving.

➤ His self-righteousness was making him more and more judgmental of others.

➤ His own piety led him to persecute the people of the Way, the early Christians.

➤ The law was meant to serve until the Messiah came.

➤ He was trying to save himself.

Faith can easily become fanatic, obsessive, and rigidly defined. Likewise, religion can easily become intolerant and judgmental. Rules and regulations commonly kill off mercy and compassion. What Paul saw in the life of Jesus Christ was someone who refused to let anything be of greater importance than unconditional love and forgiveness. No rule, regulation, dogma, doctrine, creed, or cause was greater than grace. Jesus was in fact believed to be the event of grace itself.

In today's world, many wars are still fought over religion, many families are destroyed by religious squabbling, and many so-called Christians speak of other Christians as inferior. Moral judging goes on in the church on a daily basis, and often the church is the last place a sinner would ever go to know love and forgiveness. It's sad that the spirit of Christ is lost because religious protocol is put before people. Jesus would find it appalling that the church is often the bastion for intolerance, a catalyst for persecution, and the voice of judgment. Paul saw in his own life and faith that he was so busy pointing out the speck in the eyes of others that he had not even attempted to remove the log lodged in his own.

Paul and Grace

Grace is the unconditional love and forgiveness of God. God alone can offer such love and forgiveness because the absence of conditions reveals the divine nature of grace. Human love is always spoiled by some kind of condition. Human beings may strive to offer unconditional love, but it is not humanly feasible to do so.

Grace creates faith, which comes to us when we have been on our knees long enough to know we are not God. Faith is found when we realize that our efforts to climb the spiritual ladder of success have been thwarted. Jesus Christ knocks out all the rungs. He tells us that he will come down to us. We need not try to come up to him.

On the road to Damascus, Paul finally understood that he didn't need to try any longer to be perfect or to uphold every single facet of the law. Paul recognized that he was now loved, flaws and all. This enlightening experience led Paul to see that faith was not something earned, but something received. Faith is pure gift.

Major Highways

"Therefore, since we are justified by faith, we have peace with God through our Lord Jesus Christ. Through him we have obtained access to this grace in which we stand, and we rejoice in our hope of sharing the glory of God. More than that, we rejoice in our sufferings, knowing that suffering produces endurance, and endurance produces character, and character produces hope, and hope does not disappoint us, because God's love has been poured into our hearts through the Holy Spirit which has been given to us."

"... Not only so, but we also rejoice in God through our Lord Jesus Christ, through whom we have now received our reconciliation."

—Romans 5:1–5; 11

Paul's faith, as expressed in so many of his letters, was a fiery belief that God's love freed him to accept and embrace his humanness. Paul came to believe that the law had enslaved him. The law was his obsession, an addiction of sorts. Faith freed him from the bonds of trying to ...

➤ Be perfect.

➤ Prove that he was righteous.

➤ Play God.

➤ Save himself.

➤ Push others down (judgmentalness) to push himself up.

➤ Win God's approval.

➤ Win sainthood.

➤ Be holy.

In his letters, Paul expresses the conviction that grace alone can create a genuine and livable faith. Grace, from Paul's perspective, enables us to ...

➤ Accept and forgive ourselves.

➤ Accept and forgive our neighbors.

➤ Accept and forgive God.

➤ Receive the good news that we are loved.

➤ Receive the point and purpose of our lives.

➤ Receive the magnificent mercy of God.

➤ Receive our callings.

➤ Know our longings.

➤ Hear the truth.

➤ Find our true freedom, which is to be fully human.

➤ Worry more about loving and forgiving than about sin and sinning.

Paul and the Jews

At first glance, Paul's letters seem anti-Semitic. A deeper look shows that this is not the case. Paul's relationship with the Jewish community was strained and difficult because ...

➤ Paul was a Jew himself, and he expected more of his own people.

➤ Paul was easily frustrated with those with whom he shared deep spiritual roots.

➤ Paul's anger was displayed only with those he thought of as family.

➤ Paul considered the Jewish people to be addicted to the law and the works demanded by it.

➤ Paul experienced the Jewish faith as unwilling to receive the good news of a gracious God.

➤ Paul hoped that the establishment of the Gentile church would inspire the Jewish community to consider the good news of Jesus as the Messiah.

➤ Paul believed that the Gentile church would shame the Jewish community into conversion.

➤ Paul was convinced that faith alone could save and that works have no purpose other than to reveal that salvation.

➤ Paul saw the Jews as hopelessly trapped in a self-righteous and judgmental faith that prevented them from displaying their true heart.

However, Paul strongly believed that a few Jews would eventually come to faith in Jesus. Paul never fully gave up hope. Paul's hope was rooted in his faith in the power of God to graft the broken branch, the Jews, back onto the tree.

Remember, Paul's role was as evangelist to the Gentile church. He rejected his Pharisaic belief system and became the champion of the very people he had persecuted. By nature, Paul was prone to be tough on the Jews and to court the favor of the Gentiles. Paul was also human enough to respond to the fact that the Gentiles embraced his teachings, whereas the Jews either struggled with it or rejected it outright. People tend to go where they are liked. Paul was no exception.

Major Highways

"I ask, then, has God rejected his people? By no means! I myself am an Israelite, a descendant of Abraham, a member of the tribe of Benjamin. God has not rejected his people whom he foreknew. Do you not know what the scripture says of Elijah, how he pleads with God against Israel? 'Lord, they have killed thy prophets, they have demolished thy altars, and I alone am left, and they seek my life.' But what is God's reply to him? 'I have kept for myself seven thousand men who have not bowed the knee to Baal.' So too at the present time there is a remnant, chosen by grace. But if it is by grace, it is no longer on the basis of works; otherwise grace would no longer be grace."

—Romans 11:1–6

Paul and Women

During the time of Christ and the formation of the early church, the role of women stunk. Women were thought to be of less value than the family ox. Even the Bible tends to offer women one of two roles: virgins or whores. A good way to comprehend the hideous status of women in biblical times is to review the laws regarding divorce at that time. A woman could be divorced for any of the following reasons:

➤ Bad breath
➤ Cooking a poor meal
➤ Talking too loud
➤ Unattractiveness
➤ Failing to adequately meet her husband's sexual needs

The role of women within the early church was slight. They were allowed to attend, but they had no vote, power, or position. They were told to stay to the rear and keep their heads covered and their mouths shut. They were instructed to be submissive to their husbands. They were told that their menstrual cycle and labor pains were a punishment from God. (My wife agreed with that notion.) They were encouraged to raise children, keep a good house, and be pretty but not gaudy.

Major Highways

"So that the law was our custodian until Christ came, that we might be justified by faith. But now that faith has come, we are no longer under a custodian; for in Christ Jesus you are all sons of God, through faith. For as many of you as were baptized into Christ have put on Christ. There is neither Jew nor Greek; there is neither slave nor free; there is neither male nor female; for you are all one in Christ Jesus."

—Galatians 3:24–28

Paul was not nearly as radical as Jesus in his relationship to women. Jesus spent ample time with women. He clearly felt comfortable in their presence and considered several to be intimate friends. The Gospel of Luke is loaded with affirmations of the significant faith of women, as well as their spiritual gifts and insight.

Points of Interest

The ordination of women is still a raging debate in the contemporary Christian church. To me the issue is this: If the Bible is literally true, every letter to be followed as law, then women should not be ordained. If, on the other hand, we believe that the women who have been called to ministry are not liars, and that the Holy Spirit can override the letter of the law, then women must be ordained.

My wife was an ordained Presbyterian pastor and was the finest pastor I ever experienced. I came to know Christ more through her ministry than anywhere else. So as to the ordination of women, my choice was either to believe the Bible's legalisms or trust the Holy Spirit's relationship to my wife. I trusted the latter.

Paul gives only a slight nod of affirmation to the role of women in the early church. He does at least get them in the building, and he spiritually declares their equality. I see Paul as burdened in his relationship to women by his own background as a Pharisee and his admitted physical unattractiveness. His writing exposes a lack of comfort with women and an inability to accept their equality in practical matters. Paul is able to treat women with respect only when it is cloaked in faith, which may not be much, but it is something.

Paul and the Church

Paul was an effective spiritual leader of the Gentile church. He accomplished a great deal in establishing a church that ministered with a greater focus and mission. He was a sound organizer, a reasonably effective diplomat, and a tireless worker at creating a strong and vibrant church. Paul made every human effort to inspire the church to function like a family of faith, as congregations brought together as spiritual communities by the spirit of Jesus Christ. Paul worked hard to see these churches become faith-centered communities committed to ...

➤ Supporting one another.

➤ Respecting and refraining from criticism of the chosen leadership.

➤ Being peacemakers and consensus builders.

➤ Warning the lazy.

➤ Encouraging the timid.

➤ Assisting the weak.

➤ Being abundantly patient and kind.

➤ Resisting revenge.

➤ Being joyful.

➤ Being incessant in prayer.

➤ Being exceedingly grateful.

➤ Refusing to stifle the Holy Spirit.

➤ Refusing to belittle prophecies.

➤ Avoiding evil actions or words.

➤ Relying on the grace of God.

In Paul's hopes for the church, he best reflects the will of Jesus Christ. I cannot imagine Christ having any difficulty at all with Paul's words of encouragement in his letter to the church in Thessalonica. This same message is offered in each of his letters, with different words, style, emphasis, or focus.

Paul sought to inspire the early Gentile church to function as if inhabited by the spirit of Jesus Christ. Paul's letters offered these early churches a vision of a church filled with grace. It was no small or easy task, but Paul was up to it. I believe Paul did his best ministry in this arena.

Major Highways

"Therefore encourage one another and build one another up, just as you are doing."

"But we beseech you, brethren, to respect those who labor among you and are over you in the Lord and admonish you, and to esteem them very highly in love because of their work. Be at peace among yourselves. And we exhort you, brethren, admonish the idlers, encourage the fainthearted, help the weak, be patient with them all. See that none of you repays evil for evil, but always seek to do good to one another and to all. Rejoice always, pray constantly, give thanks in all circumstances; for this is the will of God in Christ Jesus for you. Do not quench the Spirit, do not despise prophesying, but test everything; hold fast to what is good, abstain from every form of evil."

—1 Thessalonians 5:11–22

Paul and Christ

Paul had a particular idea of what Jesus was like and what his ministry stood for. He also believed that we are often unable to be like Christ. Paul appreciated that at times humans cannot come up with the spiritual will to love, forgive, or be merciful, compassionate, generous, or gracious. Paul went further by saying that at such times we can wear Christ like a cloak and be covered in Jesus.

I love this idea. I think it expresses our true reliance on the grace of God. Paul captured something spiritually significant with this concept. The power of Jesus Christ can even coat over the human desire to get even, bear a grudge, or act hatefully. Jesus is such a vibrant and living presence that his followers can be encased in his spirit.

Paul was quite clear that a Christian outfitted head to toe in Jesus would be …

➤ Tenderhearted and merciful.

➤ Kind.

➤ Humble.

➤ Patient.

➤ Abundantly forgiving.

➤ Loving at all times.

➤ At peace with himself or herself, one another, and the world.

➤ Centered in calm.

➤ Full of a deep and abiding gratitude to God.

➤ Wise.

➤ Someone who counsels others during difficult times.

➤ Full of prayer and praise.

➤ Someone who reflects the will, wants, and wishes of Jesus Christ.

How many Christians do you know who resemble this description? Far too many Christians today come across as self-righteous, judgmental, divisive, combative, and willing to love only when it's convenient or when the other person agrees with everything they have to say. Loving those who are your spiritual clones is easy. The loving gets tough when you have to celebrate diversity, forgiveness, and equality.

I give credit to Paul for laying out a description of living in Christ that is true to the ministry and message of Jesus. Paul never held back; he never minced words. He told the gospel truth and challenged these early churches and Christians to follow a man named Jesus who was a most revolutionary role model.

Major Highways

"Put on then, as God's chosen ones, holy and beloved, compassion, kindness, lowliness, meekness, and patience, forbearing on another and, if one has a complaint against another, forgiving each other; as the Lord has forgiven you, so you also must forgive. And above all these put on love, which binds everything together in perfect harmony. And let the peace of Christ rule in your hearts, to which indeed you were called in the one body. And be thankful. Let the word of Christ dwell in you richly, teach and admonish one another in all wisdom, and sing psalms and hymns and spiritual songs with thankfulness in your hearts to God. And whatever you do in word or deed, do everything in the name of the lord Jesus, giving thanks to God the Father through him."

—Colossians 3:12–17

Paul and Money

My grandmother always told me, "If you want to know what God thinks of money, just take a look at who he gives it to." I get some of that same attitude from Paul. Paul considered wealth and Christian faith to be incompatible. I know this is a sore subject for American Christians, but the fact is that Jesus, the Bible, the disciples, the early church, and Paul all stand squarely against the accumulation of stuff and worldly wealth. We can try to deny it and squirm our way out of it. But the truth is the truth.

Major Highways

"For I am already on the point of being sacrificed; the time of my departure has come. I have fought the good fight, I have finished the race, I have kept the faith. Henceforth there is laid up for me the crown of righteousness, which the Lord, the righteous judge, will award to me on that Day, and not only to me but also to all who have loved his appearing."

"Do your best to come to me soon. For Demas, in love with this present world, has deserted me and gone to Thessalonica; Crescens has gone to Galatia, Titus to Dalmatia."

—2 Timothy 4:6–10

I once asked the children of my confirmation class to make a list of their possessions. I then asked them to list whether these items were necessities or luxuries. The kids asked me to do the same. The results were spiritually sobering. The amount of stuff we own, and the money we spent to accumulate it is truly disgusting. We live in a nation where the recent political mantra has been, "It's the economy, stupid!" That is a sad, sad state of spiritual affairs.

Paul taught his followers that Jesus believed money …

➤ Should not rule our lives.

➤ Should be spent on helping others.

➤ Should not be seen as security.

➤ Should not be used for luxuries.

➤ Should not be the determiner of position or power.

➤ Should be thought of as in service to God.

➤ Can ruin our lives.

➤ Can destroy our faith.

➤ Does not help to build the kingdom of God.

Paul and Love

Paul's most famous words are 1 Corinthians 13. They are incredible and succinctly capture the essence of the spirit of Jesus Christ. They go right to the heart of faith. If faith is not about loving, it is about nothing at all. I give Paul full credit for recognizing that love is the core of the life and ministry of Jesus and must be the foundation of faith and the church.

Major Highways

"If I speak in the tongues of men and angels, but have not love, I am a noisy gong or a clanging cymbal. And if I have prophetic powers, and understand all mysteries and all knowledge, and if I have all faith, as to remove mountains, but have not love, I am nothing. If I give away all I have, and if I deliver my body to be burned, but have not love, I gain nothing."

"Love is patient and kind; love is not jealous or boastful; it is not arrogant or rude. Love does not insist on its own way; it is not irritable or resentful; it does not rejoice at wrong but rejoices in the right. Love bears all things, believes all things, hopes all things, endures all things."

"Love never ends; as for prophecies, they will pass away; as for tongues, they will cease; as for knowledge, it will pass away. For our knowledge is imperfect and our prophecy is imperfect; but when the perfect comes, the imperfect will pass away. When I was a child, I spoke like a child, I thought like a child, I reasoned like a child; when I became a man, I gave up childish ways. For now we see in a mirror dimly, but then face to face. Now I know in part; then I shall understand fully, even as I have been fully understood. So faith, hope, love abide, these three; but the greatest of these is love."

—1 Corinthians 13

Paul was extraordinarily human. He was also an extraordinarily effective church leader, possessed of a deep and passionate faith rooted in a dramatic conversion. His Damascus Road experience made his spiritual perspective unique:

➤ He felt a deep sense of urgency to his message.

➤ He wanted the Jews, his family and friends, to know what he now knew.

➤ He felt freedom in his new-found faith.

➤ He felt released from the perfectionistic trap of the law.

➤ He was aglow with the grace of God.

Paul was one of a kind. From Pharisee to Gentile evangelist, his life took quite a trip.

The Least You Need to Know

➤ Paul's letters sought to address practical and spiritual issues facing the early church.

➤ Paul expressed a strong opposition to legalism and legalists.

➤ Paul's faith was utterly dependent on the grace of God.

➤ Paul addressed the role of Jews, women, money, and love.

➤ Paul sought to build a church rooted in respect for diversity.

➤ Paul asked Christians to wear Christ like a cloak.

Chapter 24

Ministry as a Way of Life

In This Chapter

➤ The inspiring story of the life of Jesus Christ

➤ Preaching and teaching

➤ Blending the story of Christ with our life stories

➤ Pastors and prophets

➤ Christ, the community leader

Ministry begins and ends with the story of the life of Jesus Christ. Preaching, teaching, counseling, visiting homes, working with children, holding meetings, and running programs and work groups are all grounded in the story of the life of Jesus Christ. This chapter explains how ministers use this story in the different aspects of their work.

Ministry as Inspiration

I don't believe that ministry is about getting other people to believe in what you do. I think it is about living what you believe. Ministry is showing the love and mercy of God. Ministry is about embracing the lonely, the lost, and the outcast; feeding the hungry; clothing the naked; and visiting those in prison. The story of Christ inspires action and a living faith.

Major Highways

"... but he said to me, 'My grace is sufficient for you, for my power is made perfect in weakness.' I will all the more gladly boast of my weaknesses, that the power of Christ may rest upon me. For the sake of Christ, then, I am content with weaknesses, insults, hardships, persecutions, and calamities; for when I am weak, then I am strong."

—2 Corinthians 12:9–10

As a minister, I work on a daily basis with the story of the life of Christ. By keeping this story foremost in my thoughts, I can ...

➤ Find the purpose in my day.

➤ Give the day a dose of hope.

➤ Inspire acts of love and forgiveness.

➤ Inspire acts of kindness and mercy.

➤ Apply the will of God to my living of this day.

➤ Receive the day as the gift that it is.

➤ Bring folks to the story of Christ.

➤ Bring the story of Christ to life for others.

➤ Live as a witness to the story of Christ for others.

➤ Inspire new stories of ministry.

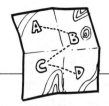

Map Key

The Passion is the story of Jesus' suffering from the Last Supper to his crucifixion.

Ministry as Storytelling

A good minister is first and foremost a storyteller, always ready with an open heart and mind to hear and tell a good story and always eager to receive a new piece of insight or wisdom. The story of the life of Jesus Christ is simple and pure. It has few embellishments other than the love and the faith of its writers. Its only elegance is in the dramatic movement of the story, the part of the story known as *the Passion* in particular.

Scenic Overlooks

"'A man can have no greater love than to lay down his life for his friends.' (John 15:13) For me these words summarize the meaning of all Christian ministry. If teaching, preaching, individual pastoral care, organizing, and celebrating are acts of service that go beyond the level of professional expertise, it is precisely because in these acts the minister is asked to lay down his own life for his friends .... But the minister, who takes off his clothes to wash the feet of his friends, is powerless, and his training and formation are meant to enable him to face his own weakness without fear and make it available to others. It is exactly this creative weakness that gives the ministry its momentum."

—Henri J. M. Nouwen (*Creative Ministry*)

If the story of the life of Jesus Christ is the greatest story ever told, it is because of all the storytelling it has inspired. Christ's life story has served as the starting point for so many other life stories: folks trying to be good neighbors, men and women trying to live according to their beliefs, and people inspiring goodness in others.

The story of the life of Jesus Christ invites you to …

> ➤ Listen closely to your life.
> ➤ Find meaning in your life.
> ➤ Find your self-worth in the stories you live.
> ➤ Love the characters in your life story.
> ➤ Make love and forgiveness the theme of your life story.
> ➤ Find your faith in the living of your own story.
> ➤ Fill your life with hope and joy.
> ➤ Share your story.

Scenic Overlooks

"Of course, it's the same old story. Truth usually is the same old story."

—Margaret Thatcher

"Listening to both sides of story will convince you that there is more to a story than both sides."

—Frank Tyger

"The reason we make a long story short is so that we can tell another."

—Sharon Shoemaker

Ministry as Preaching

Each week I struggle with writing a sermon. It is a struggle I often win and occasionally lose, sometimes badly. A sermon is the minister's attempt to apply a piece of the story of the life of Jesus Christ to the human story. A sermon is an effort to discern what this ancient story has to say about our modern lives.

Points of Interest

A good sermon makes a simple point, tells a simple story, is easy to understand, relates directly to your life, does not offer advise or answers, makes you feel better about life and live smarter, and gives you something to think about until the next sermon.

Most good sermons on the story of Christ contain the following:

➤ An analysis of the meaning of a biblical story.

➤ A description of what the story meant at the time in which it was written.

➤ An explanation of the meaning of the story for today's world.

➤ The minister's thoughts, feelings, and beliefs on the subject of the story.

➤ Personal stories that help illuminate the message.

➤ A message from the minister, which is his or her best effort to add some good points to the good news.

Scenic Overlooks

"Preaching should break a hard heart, and heal a broken heart."

—John Newton quoting Christopher Catherwood

"Preach not because you have to say something, but because you have something to say."

—Richard Whately

"It is no use walking anywhere to preach unless we preach as we walk."

—St. Francis of Assisi

"Only the sinner has the right to preach."

—Christopher Morley quoting Jonathon Green

Ministry as Teaching

Ministry is teaching—whether it's to children, adolescents, adults, people who know the Bible inside out, folks who have never opened the Bible, people who are living, and those who are dying. Ministry is teaching people about the story of Jesus Christ and about the lessons of their own lives.

Scenic Overlooks

"A master can tell you what he expects of you. A teacher, though, awakens your own expectations."

—Patricia Neal

"A great teacher never strives to explain his vision—he simply invites you to stand beside him and see for yourself."

—Rev. R. Inman

"If you would thoroughly know anything, teach it to others."

—Tyron Edwards

To teach the story of the life of Christ, you have to know the story. You do not have to have it memorized, nor do you have to have all the answers. The worst teachers are those who try to impress you with what they know. A lousy teacher is someone who sees you as the empty glass and him or herself as the full pitcher. Having someone pour knowledge down your throat is not learning. It is indoctrination. Ministry inspires rather than indoctrinates. You receive the ministry, and then you give it away. The story of Christ fills your spiritual tank, and then you deliver that "faith fuel" to others.

The story of the life of Jesus Christ can open you up to the following truths:

➤ Who you really are
➤ Who you are meant to become
➤ What matters
➤ Your longings

➤ What you are called to do and be

➤ Your own ministry

➤ Who and what you love

➤ What you believe

Detours

Feeling pity for a person is seldom pastoral. A good pastor is on intimate terms with those he or she serves, and intimacy requires equality. Pity suggests a superior to inferior relationship. Pity is often detached from actual caring for a person. Pity is writing the check for the cause while remaining aloof from any human contact. Pity is compassion without the passion.

Major Highways

"'... A prophet is not without honor except in his own country and in his own house.'"

—Matthew 13:57

Ministry as a Pastor

The ministry has many roles, and all of these roles are highlighted in the life of Christ. One of the primary roles of good ministry is to be a pastor, someone who looks after the needs of a group of people. The story of Christ is full of his tending to the wounds and needs of others. The life of Jesus was devoted to ministering in a spirit of compassion. To be a pastor is to radiate a spirit of genuine care and concern.

As you will see from the stories of scripture, a pastor's job is to ...

➤ Listen to those in crisis or need.

➤ Offer compassion to a person in pain, be it physical, emotional, or spiritual.

➤ Offer comfort and consolation during times of grief.

➤ Rebuild broken hearts.

➤ Mediate efforts at peacemaking.

➤ Be an example of a forgiving spirit.

➤ Offer affirmation and praise to those whose spirits are sagging.

➤ Offer encouragement to those who need it.

➤ Provide a safe place to vent anger and bitterness.

➤ Inspire a faith that expects the best and overcomes fear, which expects the worst.

The life of Jesus Christ bears witness to the importance of pastoral ministry. Jesus was a shepherd to his flock. He tended to their every need. He was responsible for their health and safety. He experienced his flock as family. As you survey Christ's life, you see the myriad ways he tenderly and graciously ministered.

Ministry as a Prophet

Jesus was often offensive. He poked, prodded, pushed, pulled, and probed. He was incessantly challenging his disciples and followers to become more than they believed possible—more loving and forgiving, more courageous and convincing, and more passionate about issues of justice and mercy. His message was frequently fierce and brutally honest. Crystal clear in his many mandates, he never minced words; he was never lukewarm. His words served as a boiling baptism for the initiates into the life of discipleship.

Jesus was a prophet. His story demonstrates the many times and places where Jesus chose not to tell his people what they wanted to hear, but what they needed to hear. He saw himself as a messenger of God, and he delivered a message that was blistering in its call to a life of service and sacrifice. Good ministry includes playing the prophet and fearlessly facing tough times, tough issues, and tough hearts.

Ministry as Community Building

The story of Jesus Christ is full of the stories of community—families, villages, synagogues and churches, and disciples. The context of most of the stories surrounding the life of Christ is community.

Jesus was always busy trying to create community. He worked tirelessly to bring people together:

➤ In celebration

➤ In diversity

➤ In worship

➤ In the pursuit of justice

➤ In the peace process

➤ In the building of the kingdom

➤ As families and congregations

➤ As friends and allies

➤ As disciples and followers

➤ As God's children

Scenic Overlooks

"Saints and prophets are terms used to describe those who most fully respond to God ... The false prophet speaks out of the self-centered conditioning of the world in which he lives."

—Gilbert Shaw

Detours

A critic is not a prophet. A critic sits in judgment. A prophet seeks only to jar someone, to challenge someone to be his or her very best. The critic speaks from a posture of being the best. The prophet includes him or herself in any call to change.

➤ As saved sinners

➤ As human beings

➤ As a force of forgiveness

➤ As the presence of faith, hope, and love

Ministry never builds walls. It never locks out people behind doors of dogma or doctrine. Ministry is not exclusive or elitist. Ministry is an equal opportunity employer. It opens windows and hearts and respects differences. It recognizes that God has created a world of difference and is wise enough to know that celebrating diversity will make a world of difference to the fate of the planet.

The Least You Need to Know

➤ The story of the life of Jesus Christ inspires ministry.

➤ Ministry tries to connect the story of Christ with the life stories of modern people.

➤ A good minister preaches and teaches by example.

➤ A good minister is a pastor, who nurtures his or her congregation.

➤ A good minister is a prophet, someone who takes the risk of challenging him or herself and those he or she loves to change, improve, better themselves, and to become more the people God created them to be.

➤ A good ministry seeks to strengthen communities.

Four Soloists Pretending to Be a Quartet

Four gospels, four versions of the same story, and four perspectives done by four writers/editors, each with a mission. These are four writers/editors we know little about, and we can't even be sure that they actually penned the gospels bearing their names. What we can be sure of is that these gospels bear the unique spiritual mark of the four men described briefly here. If they did not hold the pen in hand, it is still their hearts imprinted upon the gospel pages.

Matthew

About the only thing known about Matthew himself is that he was a tax collector. Jews hated tax collectors. Tax collectors were thought of as traitors because they were civil servants who worked for their own conquerors. Though Matthew was a Jew and his gospel was written for the Jews, he would also have known ample persecution from his own people and race.

Matthew was a man whose faith was in conflict. His Jewish roots went deep, but his resentment of those Jews who would have attacked him for gathering taxes went just as deep. He respected the past, but he clearly longed for a new age and a new faith. He saw Jesus as the creator of such a new world. In his gospel, Matthew goes to great lengths to show respect for Jewish custom and tradition. At the same time, Matthew often displays his struggles with the Jewish faith and with the Pharisees in particular. Chapter 23 of Matthew is a thorough denunciation of the Jewish religious establishment of that time.

Matthew was also a natural-born teacher. Like any good teacher, he was anxious to make his subject easier to read and follow. He was also a collector and an organizer. He had collected the sayings of Jesus in the Hebrew tongue and went to great lengths to assemble the material into a more meaningful format.

Matthew's gospel was aimed at convincing Jews that Jesus was the Messiah. In the Gospel of Matthew, Jesus is seen to fulfill the message of the Hebrew prophets on 16 occasions. While presenting this revolutionary message, Matthew retains a Jewish tone. Jesus is seen as one who comes not to abolish the law, but to fulfill it.

Mark

Mark was the son of Mary, a wealthy woman from Jerusalem. Mary often housed religious gatherings of the followers of Jesus. Mark was raised in the midst of a forming faith and church. He would have been spiritually fed on a steady diet of discussion about the message and meaning of the life of Jesus.

Mark was also the nephew of Barnabas, who was a companion of Paul. When Paul and Barnabas set out on their initial missionary journey, they took Mark along as a personal secretary. Mark ultimately chose to leave this missionary tour and departed at Pamphylia.

Nobody knows for sure why Mark left, but it most likely had to do with disagreements over the course this missionary journey was taking, as well as squabbles over leadership. Subsequently, Paul refused to have Mark along on a second journey, rejecting Barnabas' enthusiastic endorsement of his nephew's participation (Acts 15:37–40). This split over Mark's involvement lead to Paul and Barnabas parting company and never ministering together again.

Eventually, Mark reconciled with Paul and was with Paul while he was in prison. Near death, Paul described Mark as an extraordinary servant to the faith. Things came full circle: At first, Paul was furious with Mark for quitting the team; at the end, Paul counted Mark among his closest companions. Whatever happened, it must have been dynamic and powerful forgiving.

Mark's life was saturated with the stories of the life of Jesus. He was immersed in the lives and ministries of the early followers of Jesus and in the formation of the first churches. Mark would have known first-hand the power of Jesus to transform hearts and minds. He would have been a witness to the workings of the Holy Spirit.

Luke

Again, next to nothing is known about Luke. However, his gospel is so beautifully written and so focused on preaching good news to the poor and outcast that we can discern a few things about him:

➤ Luke was an historian.

➤ Although Luke clearly acknowledged the existence of other accounts of the same story, he wanted to write an orderly account of the events of the life of Jesus.

➤ Luke claimed to be aided by eyewitness accounts, but he himself was not an eyewitness.

➤ Theophilus was his patron, and supported his writing efforts.

➤ Luke may have accompanied Paul on a missionary journey.

➤ Luke may have written the bulk of Acts.

➤ Luke was educated and, therefore, most likely wealthy.

➤ Luke was passionately committed to the poor and oppressed.

Luke must have written some 10 to 20 years after the fall of Jerusalem. He clearly was writing to an increasingly Gentile audience. He sought to make sense out of a growing Christian movement that was moving farther and farther away from Judaism. He also tried to deal with the reality of being Roman citizens who claimed to believe in a Messiah crucified by a Roman procurator. The major issue he sought to address was how the rich must relate to the poor within the Christian movement.

Luke used his own position of privilege to help restore rights to those who had been left on the outside. Luke was a spiritual philanthropist and a political bleeding-heart liberal.

John

It is impossible to say who is the author of the Gospel of John. I can say that I regard him as part poet, part philosopher, and part theologian. As a theologian, he was a true genius. Although I doubt that this gospel was written by the beloved disciple John, I am confident that the author was most likely a devoted follower of his, someone who saw John as a worthy spiritual ideal. Such a devotee would have worked tirelessly to write as if he were in fact the disciple. Just as artists in the Rembrandt school tried to capture the style and substance of a beloved master, so it may have been with the author of the Gospel of John.

The central importance of the disciple John to this gospel is documented in its four references to him:

1. He leans on Jesus' breast at the Last Supper (13:23–25).

2. Jesus asks him to care for his mother following his death (19:25–27).

3. He and Peter are met by Mary Magdalene after she has discovered the empty tomb (20:2).

4. He is present at the last resurrection appearance at the lakeside (21:20).

Jesus' decision to entrust the care of his own mother to John speaks volumes about the spiritual stature of this disciple. John alone is seen to be that embodiment of tender mercy Jesus would have wanted for his mother.

These are the few facts we know about the Gospel of John:

➤ John was expelled from the synagogue for claiming Jesus as the Messiah.

➤ His gospel was aimed at a Greek audience and mind.

243

➤ The gospel was written some 70 years after the crucifixion from within a faith community in Ephesus. The religious establishment carefully scrutinized and frequently attacked this community.

➤ The style of this author was hauntingly poetic and did not pay homage to any historical quest.

➤ The author theologically stressed that Jesus was fully human, yet was pre-existent and omniscient.

➤ The author sought to explain the mind of God (logos).

➤ The author strived to combat the Gnostic heresy that held that all matter was evil and all that was spirit was good.

My main reason for believing that the author of this gospel was not the disciple John is that I doubt that a man reared on the wisdom of humility would have chosen to call himself "the beloved disciple." Nevertheless, the spirit and perspective of John is found on every page of this gospel.

The Motley Crew

The disciples were indeed a motley crew. There appears to be no rhyme or reason why Jesus chose them to serve. Although many were fishermen, the similarity ended there. Jesus chose twelve individuals of diverse backgrounds and perspectives. He selected men who, at least on the surface, could not have been more different. It is hard to imagine how this group came to agree on anything. Maybe Jesus saw something in each of them—a look, attitude, gesture, generosity, or graciousness. Whatever the reason, somehow Jesus knew that the chaos of these twelve would yield a dynamic and creative faith.

Simon Peter

➤ He was a fisherman.

➤ The name Peter means "rock."

➤ Jesus called him Satan for encouraging Jesus to avoid the cross.

➤ He denied knowing Jesus, as Jesus predicted he would, after Jesus was arrested.

➤ He preached a sermon at Pentecost that inspired thousands to convert to Christianity.

➤ He was a powerful spiritual leader to the church in Jerusalem.

James

➤ He was a fisherman and the son of Zebedee.

➤ He was short-tempered and called "Son of Thunder."

➤ He was one of the inner three.

➤ He was ambitious and wanted a place of honor in the kingdom.

➤ He was judgmental; he once wanted to set fire to a Samaritan village.

➤ He was the first disciple to be martyred.

John

➤ He was a fisherman, son of Zebedee, brother of James, and the other "Son of Thunder."

➤ He was the third member of the core group.

➤ He was ambitious and judgmental.

➤ Jesus asked him to care for Jesus' mother.

➤ He came to be known for his great love.

➤ He taught that grace is available to all.

Andrew

➤ He fished for a living.

➤ He heard the message of John the Baptist.

➤ He told his brother Peter about Jesus.

➤ He encouraged Jesus to meet with Greeks.

➤ He said discipleship is fishing for people.

➤ He was eager to evangelize.

Philip

➤ He fished.

➤ He questioned.

➤ He was a close friend of Andrew.

➤ He told Nathanael about Jesus.

➤ He wondered how Jesus could feed 5,000 people.

➤ He wanted to know God the Father.

Bartholomew

➤ He was also called Nathanael.

➤ We don't know what he did for a living, but knowing this group, he at least fished on the side.

➤ He initially rejected Jesus because he was from Nazareth.

➤ He became a believer when he met Jesus.

➤ He was boldly honest.

➤ Jesus called him "a true son of Israel."

Matthew (Levi)

➤ He was a tax collector.

➤ He was a despised outcast.

➤ He invited Jesus to a party with his notorious friends.

➤ He might have written the gospel that bears his name.

➤ He showed that faith is for those who know their sin.

➤ He abandoned his career to follow Jesus.

Thomas (The Twin)

➤ He risked going to Bethany to follow Jesus.

➤ He had strong faith and was willing to risk death for his beliefs.

➤ He struggled with accepting the resurrection. He would believe in the risen Christ only if he could touch his wounds.

➤ He had a mature faith that asked tough questions.

➤ He showed great courage in times of adversity.

James

➤ He was the son of Alphaeus.

➤ He was mentioned in Matthew 10:3, Mark 3:18, and Luke 6:15.

➤ This guy wasn't called James the Less for nothing. We know little to nothing about him.

Thaddeus

➤ Also called Judas, Thaddeus was the son of James.

➤ He wanted Jesus to be revealed to the world.

➤ He believed that Christians may not understand God's plan.

➤ He was mentioned in John 14:22.

➤ He believed that following Jesus was based solely on faith.

Simon the Zealot

➤ He was a fierce patriot.

➤ Like other zealots, he was a fanatic with a politically charged faith who sought to reform society.

➤ He was a kingdom builder. Like other kingdom builders, he did not cling to the ways of the world.

Judas Iscariot

➤ He was treasurer for the disciples.

➤ Angry with Jesus for squandering expensive perfume on himself, he led the authorities to Jesus in exchange for money. This betrayal led to Jesus' crucifixion.

➤ He failed to ask for forgiveness.

➤ He committed suicide.

The Cast of Characters

Abraham   The father of the Jews.

Apollos   A gifted and noted preacher and a significant apologist for the early church.

Aquila/Priscilla   The first clergy couple. He was a tentmaker, and they were close friends of Paul. They are thought to have told the story of Jesus to Apollos.

Barnabas   The "encourager," he was a popular spiritual leader in the early church and a companion of Paul.

Caiaphas   High priest in Jerusalem for 18 years. He planned Jesus' capture and encouraged his crucifixion.

Cornelius   A Roman officer and Gentile converted to faith in Jesus.

David   The greatest king of Israel and the slayer of Goliath.

Elijah   The best known of Israel's prophets. He represented God in a showdown with the priests of Baal. He appears with Moses and Jesus during the Transfiguration.

Elizabeth   Mother of John the Baptist. She was a bit taken aback by the news of being pregnant in her 90s.

Felix   Roman governor of Judea from A.D. 52 to 59. He imprisoned Paul for two years.

Festus   Replaced Felix and sent Paul to Rome for trial.

Herod   Was given the title king of the Jews by the Romans. He ruthlessly ruled Judea from 37 to 4 B.C.

Herod Agrippa   Roman-appointed king of the Jews. He imprisoned Peter and arranged the murder of James. He was the grandson of Herod the Great.

Herod Agrippa II   The last of the Herod dynasty. He was the ruler of most of Palestine. He rejected the gospel message.

Herod Antipas   A real power freak, he was ruler of the region of Galilee and Perea for the Romans and builder of the city of Tiberias.

Isaiah   A major prophet in Hebrew scripture, he is quoted more than 50 times in Christian scripture.

James   A disciple, and one of the inner three—the most prominently mentioned disciples. He was the first to be killed for his faith.

John   A disciple of John the Baptist who then became a disciple of Jesus. He was one of the inner circle of three with Peter and James.

John the Baptist   One wild and crazy guy. He prepared the way of the Lord and baptized him, too.

Joseph   A descendant of David, and Jesus' father.

Joseph of Arimathea   Helped by Nicodemus in burying Jesus.

Judas Iscariot   Not the betraying bum he was made out to be, but a devoted disciple who believed that Jesus had abandoned the cause of the poor. He committed suicide although he could have been forgiven.

Julius   Spared Paul when other soldiers want to kill him.

Luke   An historian, physician, and companion of Paul. He is credited with having written both the Gospel of Luke and the Book of Acts.

Lydia   Opened her home to Paul and helped establish a church in Phillipi.

Mark   A travelling companion to three great evangelists and the probable author of the Gospel of Mark. He unexpectedly left Paul and Barnabas during their first missionary journey. He eventually repaired his relationship with Paul.

Martha   The busy sister of Mary. She was a great host, but not much for taking devotional time.

Mary   Mother of Jesus, James, Joseph, Judas, Simon, and daughters.

Mary   Sister to Martha and Lazarus. She was probably the only person who realized that Jesus would soon be crucified. She took time to anoint his body and was a good listener.

Mary Magdalene   Present at the cross and the first to see the risen Christ.

Matthew   A tax collector and disciple who was credited with compiling the Gospel of Matthew.

Nicodemus   A member of the Jewish high council and a Pharisee. He came to Jesus by night and was born-again.

Paul   Was converted to faith in Jesus Christ on the road to Damascus. He became the evangelist to the Gentiles. He made three extensive missionary journeys and wrote important letters to several churches.

Peter   A leading disciple and one of the inner circle of three. He became the spiritual leader of the Jerusalem church after Pentecost.

Philip   A deacon and evangelist and one of the first to go on a missionary journey.

Pilate   The Roman governor of Judea, who was known to have zestfully clean hands. He knew Jesus was innocent but bowed to public pressure.

Rhoda   Her persistence brings Peter to safety inside Mary's home.

Saul   The first king of Israel and a great military champion.

Silas   A leader in the Jerusalem church and a career missionary.

Solomon   David's chosen heir and the third king of Israel. He was the author of Ecclesiates and The Song of Songs, as well as many proverbs and a few psalms. A wise and shrewd leader, he built the Temple in Jerusalem.

Stephen   One of seven deacons chosen to oversee the distribution of food to the poor, and the first martyr of the early church.

Thomas   The doubting disciple whose faith was every bit as great as his doubt.

Timothy   Converted during the first missionary journey of Paul, he became a close companion of Paul and received two letters from him.

Titus   A Greek believer groomed by Paul. He became another trusted travelling companion.

Zechariah   The father of John the Baptist. He was left dumbstruck by an encounter with an angel.

Further Reading

Barclay, William. *The Biblical Commentaries of William Barclay*. Philadelphia: The Westminister Press, 1975.

Bawer, Bruce. *Stealing Jesus: How Fundamentalism Betrays Christianity*. New York: Crown Publishers, Inc., 1997.

Buechner, Frederick. *Peculiar Treasures: A Biblical Who's Who*. San Francisco: Harper San Francisco, 1993.

——.*Whistling in the Dark: An ABC Theologized*. New York: Harper & Row, Publishers, Inc., 1988.

——.*Wishful Thinking: A Theological ABC*. San Francisco: Harper & Row, 1973.

Cahill, Thomas. *Desire of the Everlasting Hills: The World Before and After Jesus*. New York: Doubleday, 1999.

Fox, Matthew. *Wrestling with the Prophets: Essays on Creation Spirituality and Everyday Life*. San Francisco: Harper, 1995.

Gomes, Peter J. *The Good Book: Reading the Bible with Mind and Heart*. New York: William Morrow and Company, Inc., 1996.

Mitchell, Stephen. *The Gospel According to Jesus: A New Translation and Guide to His Essential Teachings for Believers and Unbelievers*. New York: Harper Collins, 1991.

Nouwen, Henri J.M. *Reaching Out: The Three Movements of the Spiritual Life*. New York: Image Books, 1975.

——.*The Return of the Prodigal Son: A Story of Homecoming*. New York: Image Books, 1992.

Parr, John, ed. *Sowers and Reapers: A Companion to the Four Gospels and Acts.* Nashville: Abingdon Press, 1997.

Sanford, John A. *The Kingdom Within: The Inner Meaning of Jesus' Sayings.* San Francisco: Harper San Francisco, 1987.

Spotto, Donald. *The Hidden Jesus.* New York: St. Martin's Press, 1998.

Tutu, Desmond. *No Future Without Forgiveness.* New York: Doubleday, 1999.

Wangerin, Walter. *The Simple Truth: A Bare Bones Bible.* Loveland, Colorado: Group Publishing Inc., 1996.

Wilson, A. N. *Jesus: A Life.* New York: W.W. Norton & Company, 1992.

Glossary

angels   Angels are emissaries from God who bring vital messages. When we hear these messages, we often get goosebumps, a lump in the throat, or a shiver up and down the spine, or we are moved to tears. Our bodies tell us when angel wings are touching us.

Ark of the Covenant   The Ark of the Covenant is a portable throne, upon which Yahweh was thought to sit.

Beelzebub   *See* Satan.

census   A Roman census was taken every 14 years to determine the population for military conscription and taxes. Jews were not allowed to serve in the Roman army, but they were required to pay taxes.

centurion   A centurion was a leader of a division of Roman forces.

covenant   A covenant is a spiritual relationship bound by faith. In this case is refers to the relationship between God and the Jews.

demon   A demon is a living lie; a lie lived.

Essenes   The Essenes were spiritually descended from the Hasidim. They practiced a radical withdrawal from normal religious and social associations. The Essenes established a community in Qumran, the site of the Dead Sea Scrolls. This community believed they were living in the end time. They read the prophets as if their words were speaking directly to their present life and saw themselves as the divine remnant. They took vows of poverty and lived in expectation of two messiahs. The Messiah of Aaron was to fulfill the priestly lines, and the Messiah of Israel was to fulfill the royal line. When these messiahs came, the Essenes believed that a new temple and a new Jerusalem would be established.

frankincense   Frankincense was the gift given to priests. This sweet perfume was used in temple services.

Gentile   A Gentile is anyone who is not a Jew.

gold   Gold is the gift given to kings.

grace　Grace is the unconditional and undeserved love of God. Jesus can be thought of as an instrument of this grace. For the believer, he is the very event of grace.

Greek Empire　The Greek Empire was dominated by worship of a great many gods. The Jewish belief in one God was threatening to the Greeks, and vice versa.

Holy Spirit　The Holy Spirit is the active presence of grace, the unconditional love and forgiveness of God in the world. This force cannot be controlled, but faith alone can open the door to its arrival in our lives.

kingdom　The kingdom is the dwelling place of God and the faithful. It is a sacred spot governed solely by the will of God.

myrrh　Myrrh was a gift given to someone who will die. Myrrh was used in embalming.

Passion　The Passion is the story of Jesus' suffering from the Last Supper to his crucifixion.

Persians　Persians were the people of the Persian Empire, which was dominated by the worship of idols. The Jewish faith was threatened by association with the many cultic practices of the Persian Empire.

Pharaoh　Pharaoh was the name given to the leader of Egypt.

Pharisees　Pharisees were members of a lay movement who were spiritually linked to the Hasidim. The Pharisees were separatists. They paid great attention to the writings of the prophets, and they also validated the oral Torah. The piety of the Sadducees was focused on the Temple of Jerusalem, but the piety of the Pharisees was focused on the Torah. The Pharisees were rigid in their absolute adherence to the law.

Prophets　Prophets were messengers of God, whose words sought to keep God's people in line.

Resurrection　Resurrection is the reuniting of the human spirit with the Holy Spirit following death. This reunion does not mean endless life or time. It means an entry into eternity, which has no such categories. To be resurrected is to be with God— whatever that reality may be.

Sadducees　The Sadducees' central guide to faith was the law of Moses, the first five books of the Old Testament. Their primary concern was the legitimate succession of the priestly office. They held dominant roles in the Temple of Jerusalem and the Sanhedrin. They were drawn from the wealthy, aristocratic, and priestly families and followed a path of peaceful coexistence with Rome. They did not want to rock the boat because they had very good seats on the boat.

Samaritans　The Assyrians had moved the Israelites out of Palestine and the surrounding foreigners in. While living outside of Palestine, the Israelites intermarried. This "mixed race" later resettled in Israel, and came to be known as the Samaritans, who were then despised by the Jews.

Satan (also known as **Beelzebub**)   Satan is the author of all lies and the advocate for living them.

Second Coming   The Second Coming is the belief that Jesus will return to Earth. Earlier Christians believed this to be imminent.

Seven Bowls   The scene is heaven, and the seven bowls are bowls of judgment. They are filled with the wrath of God and spell natural disaster for the peoples of the earth. The world is beset by plagues: ulcerous sores appear on the men, water turns to blood, the sun becomes scorchingly hot, darkness covers the kingdom of the dragon, and violent earthquakes and hailstorms occur.

Seven Seals   The Lamb, Jesus Christ, breaks open the seals to seven scrolls. These scrolls contain the gospel truth and are thought to reveal the will of God for our lives.

Seven Trumpets   The trumpet was often used in scripture to announce the intervention of God. The trumpet was used to sound the alarm as a warning, to announce the presence of royalty, or to call people to battle.

Seven Visions of the Coming of the Son of Man   The 144,000 followers of Jesus all bear the mark of Christ. This mark is a mark of ownership and protection. These followers of Jesus will face great pain and suffering, but they will remain safe. The Son of Man will come again and reign victorious, and those who bear his mark will share in the glory of that victory.

Seven Visions of the End   For the first time, God speaks. God can take a human being and re-create him, make him or her brand new. This same God will create a whole new universe for the saints who have been restored. The saints and Christ will reign for 1,000 years.

Seven Visions of the Fall of Babylon   Babylon is another name for Rome. Rome's wealth has come from taking advantage of other nations, the poor, and the needy. The fall of Rome is predicted here as the revenge of the angels and the followers of Jesus.

Seven Visions of the Kingdom of the Dragon   The dragon is the archenemy of God. The dragon has 7 heads and 10 horns, which signifies that it is a mighty power. It is thought to represent the antichrist. God is the creator of order, but the dragon creates chaos.

Synoptic Gospels   Synoptic Gospels are the Gospels of Matthew and Luke, which contain what is called the Marcan outline, which is Mark's synopsis of the life of Jesus Christ. Because these three books each share this synopsis, they are referred to as the synoptic Gospels. All but 31 verses of Mark are quoted in the other two Gospels.

Tent of Meeting   Moses would pitch this tent in order to hold his encounters with God. It marked a place of sacred sanctuary.

The Torah   The Torah is a work of Jewish law composed of Genesis, Exodus, Leviticus, Numbers, and Deuteronomy, which are the first five books of Jewish scripture and the Bible.

witness   To witness is to name and claim one's faith. Witnessing is traditionally thought of as verbally naming Jesus as Lord and Savior. I personally believe one can witness by thought, word, or deed.

Yahweh   Yahweh is the most commonly used Jewish name for God.

Zealots   The Zealots were those Jews fanatically opposed to Roman occupation and influence.

Index

father representations, 121

younger son represen-
tations, 120

Promised Land; Jewish
roots and history,
36-37

Ark of the Covenant,
37

Tent of Meeting, 37

pronouncement stories,
oral tradition of the
Gospels, 4-5

prophets, 38, 44

Amos, 45

Elijah, 45

Ezekiel, 47

Hosea, 45

Isaiah, 45-46

Jeremiah, 46-47

Micah, 46

Micaiah, 45

ministries, 239

second Isaiah, 48-49

Zephaniah, 46

R

raising Lazarus from the
dead, 148-150

*Reaching Out: The Three
Movements of the
Spiritual Life,* 253

reading resources,
253-254

Redemption of the First-
born (ancient cere-
monies), 61

rejection of Jesus, 68-70

religious establishments,
spiritual emptiness of,
106-107

resurrections

faith, 143

Jesus, appearances,
168

disciples, 170

two men, 169

two women, 169

*Return of the Prodigal Son:
A Story of Homecoming,*
253

Revelation

apocalyptic literature

apocalyptic Jesus,
190-191

attributes, 188-189

example of writ-
ings, 189-190

symbolic meanings,
188-189

beasts, 195-197

Bible verses, 191-194,
196-197, 199

letters to the
churches, 191

Ephesus, 191

Laodicea, 193-194

Pergamum, 192

Philadelphia, 193

Sardis, 192

Smyrna, 191

Thyatira, 192

new age, 199-200

Roman Empire, 198

seven visions, 194-195

Rhoda, 251

rich fool parable, 124

Roman centurion's ser-
vant story, 134-135

Roman Empire
(Revelation), 198

Romans, Bible verses,
222, 224

roots of the Jewish faith

Abraham and the
divine promise, 31

Babylonian captivity,
49

Israel and monarchy
governance

King David, 39

King Saul, 39

King Solomon,
40-41

Israel becomes like a
nation, 38

journey into the
wilderness of Sinai,
34

letters of Paul,
223-224

Moses and the
Exodus, 33-34

prophets, 44

  Amos, 45

  Elijah, 45

  Ezekiel, 47

  Hosea, 45

  Isaiah, 45-46

  Jeremiah, 46-47

  Micah, 46

  Micaiah, 45

  second Isaiah, 48-49

  Zephaniah, 46

the Promised Land, 36-37

  Ark of the Covenant, 37

  Tent of Meeting, 37

The Torah and the temple, 50-52

Tribal Confederacy, 38

S

sacrifices, accepted behaviors in building the kingdom of God, 83-84

Sadducees, 51

Samaritan parable, 125

Sardis church, letters to the churches, 192

Satan, 138

Saul, 251

sayings, oral traditions of the Gospels, 3-6

Second Coming, 206

second Isaiah (prophet), 48-49

second missionary journey of Paul, 213-214

self-righteousness, unaccepted behaviors for the kingdom of God, 105-106

seven visions (Revelation), 194-195

sheep, lost sheep parable, 118

shepherds, birth of Jesus, 59

Silas, 251

similes (clusters of), oral traditions of the Gospels, 6

Simon Peter (disciple), 245

Simon the Zealot (disciple), 248

Simple Truth: A Bare Bones Bible, 254

sins, Gospel of Paul, 22-23

Sinai, journey into the wilderness, 34

Smyrna church, letters to the churches, 191

Solomon, 251

Son of God, portrait of Jesus in the Gospel of John, 16

the sower and the good soil parable, 113-115

speechless man story, 138-139

spirituality

  death, 144-145

  emptiness, 106-107

  surrendering spirits, 82

  transformation, Gospel of Paul, 26

Stealing Jesus: How Fundamentalism Betrays Christianity, 253

Stephen (disciple and martyr), 251

storm, calming a storm miracle, 154-155

stories (miracle stories)

  boy with demons, 141

  calming a storm, 154-155

  faith versus fear, 129-130

  feeding of five thousand, 152-153

  Gospel of John, 15-16

  healing miracles

    Bartimaeus, 132

    bleeding woman, 133-134

    healing at the pool, 133

    paralyzed man, 130-131

    Roman centurion's servant, 134-135

    two blind men, 131

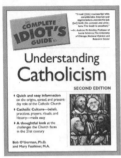

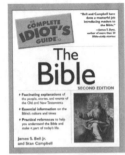

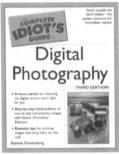
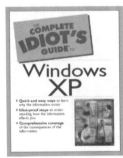